© Kadel & Herbert

John McGraw, Walter Johnson, George Sisler, Christy Walsh

BASEBALL
AS I HAVE KNOWN IT

Also by Fred Lieb

Sight Unseen: A Journalist Visits the Occult
The St. Louis Cardinals, the Story of a Great Baseball
  Team
Connie Mack, Grand Old Man of Baseball
The Detroit Tigers
The Boston Red Sox
The Pittsburgh Pirates
The Story of the World Series, an Informal History
Baseball Story
The Baltimore Orioles, The History of a Colorful Team in
  Baltimore and St. Louis
The Philadelphia Phillies (with Stan Baumgartner)
Comedians and Pranksters of Baseball

FRED LIEB

BASEBALL
AS I HAVE KNOWN IT

Coward, McCann & Geoghegan, Inc.
New York

SBN: 698–10815–9

Library of Congress Cataloging in Publication Data

Lieb, Frederick George, 1888–
    Baseball as I have known it.

    Includes index.
    1. Baseball—United States—History. 2. Lieb,
Frederick George, 1888– 3. Sportswriters—United
States—Biography. I. Title.
GV863.A1L5 1977 796.357′0973 77–5309

Printed in the United States of America

CONTENTS

Foreword   7

Preface   9

1   Boyhood Loves   13

2   On the Way to Being a Baseball Writer   19

3   1911: I Break In at the Polo Grounds   29

4   Honus Wagner: The Flying Dutchman   43

5   Ty Cobb: Mean and Magnificent   53

6   Hits Are My Bread and Butter   67

7   Heroics and Stupidities of the 1911 and 1912 World Series   77

8   Hal Chase: He Had a Corkscrew Brain   97

9   Baseball's Big Black Blotch: Dirty Business in the 1919 World Series   105

10   Judge Landis: Savior of Baseball   115

11   The Tragic Career of Carl Mays   127

12   A Gamble for Rain—for Matty   139

13   The Big Bambino   147

14   Lou Gehrig: The Iron Horse   169

15   Old Pete: Grover Cleveland Alexander   185

16 My Biggest Baseball Thrill   191

17 Expedition to Nippon   197

18 Granny and Damon and Heywood and Me   207

19 *The Sporting News* and the Spinks   219

20 At Our Home in St. Petersburg   225

21 The Old Perfesser   233

22 Baseball: Then, Now and Tomorrow   253

    My All-time All-star Teams   275

    Postscript   278

    Index   279

FOREWORD

Fred Lieb is a sorcerer. He weaves spells. When I first met him in St. Petersburg a dozen years ago, he hypnotized me for hours with stories about Walter Johnson, Babe Ruth, Casey Stengel, and countless other baseball immortals of yesteryear. He had known them all, known them well, and he possessed then—as he does now—the priceless gift of total recall.

At the time I was doing a book on the early days of baseball, *The Glory of Their Times,* and I knew immediately that I had stumbled on a gold mine. He gave me leads and insights that proved invaluable.

We have gotten together often since then, and every time the scene is the same: I sit open-mouthed and wide-eyed as Fred spins an endless stream of fascinating yarns—the strange World Series of 1911, Lou Gehrig's personality, Ty Cobb's prejudices. One tale leads into another and the hours disappear. Age has diminished neither his memory nor his ability to tell a story; if anything, the years have enriched his stockpile, and practice has perfected his art.

From Christy Mathewson to Tom Seaver, Fred Lieb has seen more baseball and known more baseball greats than any man alive. His recollections of Ed Delahanty in 1900 (when Fred was twelve) are as vivid as his memories of Willie Mays sixty years later, maybe more so. A conversation with him transports the listener to another world—one with horse-drawn carriages, where Teddy Roosevelt still charges up San Juan Hill and Honus Wagner still grabs half the infield as he scoops up a grounder and throws the runner out at first.

But I needn't tell you all this, because soon you'll find out for yourself. You are in for a marvelous treat—a conversation with Fred Lieb, who was there and, believe it or not, saw it all happen with his own eyes. But don't say you weren't warned. Remember: Fred Lieb is a sorcerer. He casts spells.

Turn the pages, and you'll see what I mean.

—LAWRENCE S. RITTER
April, 1977

To my beloved departed wife,
Mary Ann, who was the
inspiration for this book.

PREFACE
A Cooperstown Reverie

"Mister, will you please sign my ball?"
     Could that boyish voice be talking to me? I looked down
into the eager face of a twelve-year-old boy who was holding a baseball
in one hand and offering me a pen with the other. I could see that the
baseball already had some autographs on it. For a minute or two I felt
that we two were the only persons, surely the only two who mattered,
in the bustling, spacious lobby of the Otesaga Hotel in Cooperstown,
New York, home of the National Baseball Hall of Fame—an elderly
man and an eager boy-fan.

"Sonny, I'm not a Hall of Fame ballplayer," I replied. And thinking
how transported I had been at his age at the sight of a real live baseball
player, I added, "But you stick around here in the lobby and you'll spot
a lot of them."

"But I want *your* signature," the boy shot back at me.

"You don't even know who I am," I said to discourage him.

"Oh, yes, I do. You're Fred Lieb. You're one of the writers who elect
old-time baseball stars for the Hall of Fame. I heard you make a short
speech when they handed you a plaque."

I straightened up my eighty-seven-year-old spine a bit and stuck out
my chest in pleasure at the recognition. I took his ball and pen and
looked at the names on the ball: Bill Terry, Eddie Roush, Bob Feller,
Stan Musial, Burleigh Grimes. What company! I wrote "Fred Lieb"
with an extra flourish, thanked the boy, and wished him luck.

Tomorrow, I reflected, there would be five more inductees into the
National Baseball Hall of Fame, five more signatures to shoot for. They
would be Ralph Kiner, who in his day swung an ever-dangerous home-
run bat for Pittsburgh; Billy Herman, smooth-fielding second baseman
for the Cubs and Brooklyn Dodgers and a master at the art of the hit-
and-run play; Bucky Harris, another second baseman and onetime
boy-manager of the 1924 Washington Senators world champions; Earl
Averill, former Cleveland outfielder, remembered for his line-drive
hits, one of which spoiled and almost ended the pitching career of Dizzy Dean; and finally Judy Johnson, third baseman and once the speed
man of the old Negro leagues.

Always new Hall of Famers, I thought. Always new prospects for

9

that honor, playing on one of the twenty-four teams that then comprised the big leagues. Always more rookies coming up, hopeful of
making it big. What a marvelous succession! And always a new crop of
twelve-year-old boys, too, hero-worshipping. The faces change but the
scene is always the same.

But now, after autographing this one ball, I was suddenly surrounded by more than a score of men and boys, with a few girls mixed in. All
were armed with baseballs or autograph books, scorecards or Hall of
Fame brochures with pictures of all those honored at Cooperstown. Of
the signatures, Hall of Fame players ranked highest, naturally, but after Bowie Kuhn and league presidents, even members of the veterans'
selection committee like me were acceptable.

After I had finished my autographing, two middle-aged men approached me, and one of them said, "I have heard that you can answer
any baseball question. Is that so?"

"That's going a little far," I said, "but I can answer a lot of them." I
wondered if he was going to spring a trap question. "Go ahead, shoot,"
I said.

"I'm from New York. I'm a Giant fan, hated to see them go to San
Francisco. I knew all their records. I never understood this: How come
the Giants of 1916 won seventeen in a row in the spring and won
twenty-six in a row in September—forty-three games right there—and
couldn't do any better than finish fourth?"

"Not too hard," I answered, "though you're going back sixty years. It
was a freakish year and a freakish club. Only shortstop Art Fletcher,
among the infielders, started and finished the season at the same position. But the key to the two streaks was this: The four western clubs—
Chicago Cubs, Pittsburgh Pirates, Cincinnati Reds, and St. Louis Cardinals—were second-division patsies. All the strength was in the East:
the Brooklyn Dodgers, Philadelphia Phillies, Boston Braves, and New
York Giants, in that order of finish. The Giants ran up their streaks
against the four weak clubs almost entirely, but just couldn't handle
their eastern rivals. In those days a four-game series was normal, not
two or three games, as today. Much of that twenty-six game streak was
put together during a home stand in which all the western teams visited the Polo Grounds for a four-game set—maybe five games, if there
had been an earlier postponement of a game. And while the Giants
would be taking four out of four from the Cubs, say, the Dodgers
would be taking three out of four or perhaps all four from the Reds. So
the Giants made up very little ground on the league leaders. I think
you'll find that the Giants did get into third place for a day or two at the
end of the streak, but then the streak ended and they slipped back into
fourth. Have I answered your question?"

"You sure have, and thanks," the man said.

Now another man, older and white-haired, tackled me. "I'm probably ten years older than you," he started off, "and I saw Honus Wagner play. I saw Ty Cobb break in at Detroit!"

I asked him, "How old are you, Grandpop?"

"All of eighty-two years," he said proudly.

"You sure go back a long way, old-timer," I said. "It must have been wonderful to have seen Wagner." Not for the world would I have told him I was five years older and had often seen Wagner play.

Pretty soon a gang of us was discussing Cobb vs. Ruth, the Babe vs. Hank Aaron, the Yanks of 1927–28 vs. the Yanks of 1949–53, and other perennial topics of conversation worked over wherever baseball fans meet.

Then it came. It was the Giants fan who had asked me about their 1916 season. "Mr. Lieb, why don't you write a book? You've seen most of baseball's history, and you know all the history you haven't seen. Why don't you get to work and write it?"

A few minutes later I had a chance to slip off and be by myself. I strolled out of the hotel and wandered along the shore of beautiful Lake Otsego, long ago called Glimmer Glass by the Mohican Indians. I sat on the soft grass, watching the activity on the lake's surface.

Me write another book? I hadn't written one for twelve years and hadn't worked hard at book writing since Frank Graham and I between us had produced histories of most of the big league clubs for G.P. Putnam's back in the forties and early fifties. This stranger in the hotel had by no means been the first to suggest a book drawn from my memories. The most recent and vivid suggestion had come out of a long-distance telephone call from a total stranger who called me up out of the blue. "Know all about you," he said, "and just wanted to talk baseball." He was paying for the call, and we talked a long time. "You should write a book of memoirs," he said at the end. "No one else could write a book like it."

Now on the shore of Glimmer Glass, as the August sun brought a pleasant warmth to my body, I let my mind fall into a reverie. Somehow the lake scenery became shifted, and one panorama followed another. There were baseball fields, screaming masses of bleacherites, players running full tilt, press boxes and writers, newspapers and record books, and fans standing in line for tickets—all running together as if several slow-motion films were being played simultaneously across my mind.

Then the panorama dissolved into pictures of individual players. Here came Honus Wagner and Nap Lajoie, then New York's beloved Matty. Frank Baker hitting home runs against the Giants in 1911. Marquard and his nineteen straight wins. Fred Snodgrass dropping an easy fly in Boston in 1912 and costing the Giants the World Series. Ty

Cobb's slashing hits and flashing spikes, Connie Mack, Walter Johnson, Tris Speaker, Eddie Collins, Heinie Zimmerman chasing Eddie over home plate in 1917. The great Bambino, George Herman Ruth, famous for his prowess on and off the field. Lou Gehrig, the Iron Horse, brought down by a strange disease—such a close friend of mine.

On and on the scenes rolled and the players marched, each seeming now to flow into and through one another. I found myself trying to control the rush, to get things in sequence or some kind of meaningful order, to get a perspective on it all. I was enjoying the experience. When the parade had come down to the present, I rose and decided to take up the challenge of writing the book I had been asked to do.

And here it goes.

The Fred Lieb Nook in the National Baseball Hall of Fame, Cooperstown, New York.

1

BOYHOOD LOVES

My first acquaintance with big league baseball came through the medium of a scorecard boy in South Philadelphia in the mid-1890's. We kids in the neighborhood of South 21st Street, barely able to read, came to recognize this bearer of all-important news, riding on his bicycle. If you know what a scorecard boy is, you qualify as a genuine old-timer, or else you have read a book about baseball in its earliest years. A scorecard boy was a delivery boy who carried to paying clients large cards on which were printed the day's baseball scores and the resultant league standings. The boy who worked our neighborhood delivered a card to a neighborhood tobacco shop not far from my home and had another customer, a beer saloon, only a block away. It was a game among us kids to dash into the saloon, take a quick look at the scores of our Philadelphia teams, and dart back to the swinging doors before the barkeeper could swat us in the tail with his broom.

Occasionally I would catch more than a hurried glance and would focus on the standings. The first generalization I remember arriving at was that teams whose city name started with the letter *B*—Baltimore, Boston, and Brooklyn—were always at the top. As a loyal Philadelphian, this irked me. The scorecards all too often showed that our home-town favorites, the Phillies, would collect a lot of hits and score enough runs to win most games, but were always being topped by one of those annoying B teams. It was they who were always in first place, second place, and third place—or so it seemed to me at age seven and eight. Fifteen years later, when I was beginning to study baseball seriously and write about it, I checked record books to see how accurate my first recollections of B supremacy had been. Right as could be! The Baltimore Orioles (3), the Boston Beaneaters (2), and the Brooklyn Dodgers (2) had won all the pennants in the twelve-club National League in the period 1894–1900.

13

Mr. Mack—Connie Mack never left the dugout during a game. He used a score-card to motion his players into position.   International Newsreel Photo

The first players whose names I knew well and whose pictures I could recognize anywhere were Napoleon "Nap" Lajoie, Big Ed Dela-hanty, and Elmer Flick of our beloved Phillies, and Hans "Honus" Wagner of the old Louisville Colonels and later of the Pittsburgh Pi-

Nap Lajoie (left), Rube Waddell (top), and Chief Bender (bottom) of the Philadelphia Athletics of my boyhood. Lajoie credit: UPI; Bender credit: C.M. Conlan, New York *Telegram;* Waddell credit: St. Louis Globe-Democrat News Bureau

rates. Lajoie and Wagner were stars from their very arrival on the
scene, just as I began to be intrigued by baseball. We boys always pronounced Lajoie as "La-joy," as did most Philadelphia fans of the era,
but it was properly pronounced "La-jo-ay," with accents on the first
and third syllables. I can still recall an older boy, maybe nearly twenty,
tell us kids who had never seen King Larry (as he was also called) play:
"He glides around the infield with the grace of a tiger." I always suspected he got that phrase out of a Philadelphia newspaper.

The grace of a tiger was not a trait anyone ever attributed to Hans
Wagner. Honus looked more like the big clumsy Dutchman that he
was, but in the field at shortstop and on bases he moved with the speed
of an angry grizzly. So fabulous was his performance at the position requiring more skills than any other—if we forget pitching skills—that it
still seems unbelievable to me that he had to be conned into playing
shortstop. Sports writers of the day referred to him as the Flying
Dutchman in tribute to his speed, however clumsy he may have appeared on occasion. And of course his record eight National League
batting titles speak for themselves.

Older boys and men in our neighborhood used to argue by the hour:
Who is greater, Honus or King Larry? As I grew older and finally observed them consistently from the press box, I leaned toward Wagner.
With each finally playing about twenty years, Wagner led his only rival
in the period by small margins in hits, home runs, runs batted in, and
slugging average; and by a wide margin, 720 to 395, in stolen bases.
Lajoie excelled only in lifetime batting average, .339 to Wagner's .329.
Any way you look at them, they were true immortals among the baseball giants of their era and marvelous heroes for a bug-eyed boy in the
waning years of the nineteenth century. I would have thought anyone
out of his mind if he had told me in, say, 1900, that years later—1939 to
be precise—I would sit with my wife at a table right next to Napoleon
Lajoie and his wife. I would never have believed that we would be at
the dedication dinner celebrating the opening of the National Baseball
Hall of Fame in Cooperstown, New York, and that I would chat at lei-
sure afterwards with this man I considered only slightly less important
than God. Nor could I have even dreamed that one day—in a New York
Post column of mine in 1933—I would write of an impoverished Hans
Wagner, neglected by baseball's officialdom, and that he would thereafter begin a new life and enjoy nineteen more years in the game as a
coach for his old Pittsburgh Pirates.

Next to Wagner and Lajoie, in my boyish affections, came Ed Delahanty. While Honus and Nap were sluggers, they specialized mostly in
doubles and triples. Big Ed, on the other hand, was the home-run king
of the turn of the century. Ed was never in the class of Babe Ruth, Lou
Gehrig, Jimmy Foxx, Mel Ott, or Hank Aaron—but then, he wasn't
whacking the lively ball that appeared in the 1920s. Delahanty did

have one marvelous red-letter day, hitting four homers in a Philly game in July 1897—the second big leaguer ever to turn the trick. If he had never hit another, this feat made him a lasting hero and a recognized home-run specialist. A nineteen-year-old neighbor of mine was lucky enough to be in the ball park that day—Huntington Street Park, later renamed Baker Bowl. The biggest explosive from Delahanty's bat was a drive that reached a little bleacher on top of the center-field club-house there. My neighbor would tell us over and over again, "I never thought Del could reach that bleacher with a cannon, let alone a base-ball bat." Today two dozen hitters in each league could reach that bleacher as a routine part of a man's work at the ball park.

Ed Delahanty, who jumped to the new American League as an out-fielder and led it in batting in 1902, came to a tragic end in July 1903. On a New York Central train he became drunk, pugnacious, and gener-ally obstreperous as the train crossed Ontario on its way from Chicago to New York. The conductor put the belligerent batting king off the train at Fort Erie, on the Canadian side of the Peace Bridge to Buffalo. Ed bullheadedly started to walk across the bridge to the United States, but never got there. No one ever knew whether he jumped, or was pushed off the bridge, or if he passed out and collapsed into the fast-flowing Niagara River. His dead body was fished out a few days later.

As a kid, I was not particularly good as a ball player, though I liked to play. I was a left-handed thrower, and I still can hear my mother calling to me from an open window, "Freddy, throw with your right arm." It hadn't got through to her that Connie Mack's new 1901 pitch-ers, Rube Waddell and Eddie Plank, future Hall of Famers, were left-handers and in no way handicapped.

Strangely enough, since I was a left-hander, I mostly played second base. I was good enough to make my church team, the Prince of Peace, and I was proud of the big letters across my shirt front. Too often I was Mr. Strikeout at bat, but I remember one banner day in Betterton, Maryland, of all places, where we played the Monarchs, a camping club also from South Philadelphia. They had a left-handed pitcher, Teddy Mullaney, who was a professional boxer and later died from a blow in the ring. Everybody, including Mullaney himself, whom I knew slightly, thought Teddy was more than pretty good. I batted right-handed. I still don't know how I did it, but I hit three triples, all landing in a corn field behind right field. Whenever I met Mullaney af-ter that, back in our neighborhood, he would greet me with "Hello, slugger. Been hitting any more triples lately?"

In later years I invariably played for the newspapers I worked for, starting with the New York *Press.* The *Press* had a good team featuring Keats Speed, our managing editor. Keats had played two seasons for Louisville, an AAA American Association club. He was a hitter. I re-member a game we played against the *Globe* at the Dyckman Oval, then a well-known semipro field in upper Manhattan. Bob Ripley, of "Believe it or not" fame, pitched for the *Globe*. Speed hit Ripley for three three-baggers while "Lefty" Lieb struck out four times, each time on a called third strike. I blame Sid Mercer for that performance. Sid was then the *Globe* 's baseball writer, one of great talent, but he preferred playing tennis to playing baseball, so he sat on the sidelines advising anyone who would listen to him. "All you need to do is wait Ripley out," he told me. Alas, I looked sillier and sillier each time the umpire called "Strike three!"

There aren't many around today whose play has been criticized by John McGraw. Mine has been. The bawling out came in a game between New York writers and the San Antonio Newspaper Club in 1921, during the Giants' training period in San Antonio. Our sterling infield was made up of Warren Brown, a former minor leaguer, on first base; Lefty Lieb at second; Bugs Baer, ex-star of the Park Sparrows of Philadelphia, at shortstop; and Will Wedge of the evening *Sun* at third. My mistake was to try to take an extra base on a wide throw to first by the rival third baseman, running through a stop signal by our first-base coach, John McGraw. So "Mac" told me off. Later I muffed a line drive in the field. In one of his books Warren Brown wrote of the incident: "Lieb muffs a line drive, and McGraw leaves the park."

Compliments came in the course of two of the several annual games played on Sunday mornings at the Polo Grounds between the New York chapter of Baseball Writers and the old New York Press Club. In the first of these, with a man on first who set off to steal second, I tried hard not to strike out and slapped a pitch right through the spot vacated by the shortstop who ran over to cover second base. Babe Ruth, umpiring at first base, gave me a kindly slap on the rear and said, "That's as pretty a hit-and-run play as I ever saw." In another game I was playing rightfield at the Polo Grounds. The grass was wet and slippery from an early morning rain and I was playing in tennis sneakers. While I was coming in for a fly ball, my feet slipped out from under me and I sat ignominiously on the wet turf. But as I was falling I had my hands outstretched and the ball fell into my glove. Harry Heilmann, the first base umpire, came running out to congratulate me. "A helluva catch, Fred," he said. "Half the outfielders in our league wouldn't have caught it if they had lost their legs from under them."

Such bad moments and small triumphs on the diamond are part of the memories of millions of American boys and men. I was glad I played some baseball and just a bit sorry I wasn't better at it. But to watch it as paid work and to write about it, as I have done for sixty-seven years, has more than made up for any unrealized fantasies I may once have had.

2

ON THE WAY TO BEING A BASEBALL WRITER

From the time I was a kid and my parents gave me a small printing press for Christmas, I have always liked to write. The first thing I wrote for pay was a piece of fiction for a five-dollar gold-piece prize from the Red and Black, my school paper at Philadelphia's old Central Manual High. I was then aged fifteen and wrote about good guys and bad guys in Western Pennsylvania. Naturally, the good guys won.

My love of writing paralleled my love of baseball. Even though I had been an early Phillie fan, I hungrily followed the later team to come to Philadelphia, Connie Mack's Athletics, especially after they won the American League championship in 1902. The Athletics were an easy team to admire and follow closely, because the roster included very colorful players. For starters there were left-handed Rube Waddell, the ultimate in zany pitchers; right-handed pitcher Chief Albert Bender, the Chippewa Indian; Eddie Plank, the cross-fire left-handed pitcher from Gettysburg College; the colorful but erratic catcher, Ossie Schreck, whose full name was Schreckengost; the towhead blond and little guy in left field, Topsy Hartsel; the sluggish fat man in right, Socks Seybold; and an infield including the two Crosses, unrelated, Lave and Monte; second baseman Danny Murphy, my particular favorite; and first baseman-captain Harry Davis, a product of Philadelphia's own Girard College.

The boss man of this aggregation of talent and a well-publicized off-the-field character was a former catcher, the intriguing tall, lean New Englander Connie Mack, whose true name was printed on the rain checks—Cornelius McGillicuddy. Connie had caught for Washington,

Buffalo, and Pittsburgh, and had acquired managerial experience in Pittsburgh and Milwaukee. He already had won a reputation for baseball expertise and shrewdness. I had early admired the man and later came to know him very well. He owned a piece of the club and managed the team for fifty years. Connie lived to the ripe age of ninety-three and had a remarkable memory almost to the end of his life. In his latter years he wintered in St. Petersburg, where he and I chatted, on the Sunshine City's once-famous green benches, often for hours, of big moments in his long, distinguished, up-and-down career.

However much I followed baseball as a boy, I did not see my first professional game until 1904. By that time I had earned the twenty-five-cent admission charge for bleacher seats at Columbia Park, early home of the Athletics, and at the Huntington Park of the Phillies. In my first game, I saw Rube Waddell shut out the Detroit Tigers, 3–0. What joy! A few weeks later I saw the Phillies lose to the Pittsburgh Pirates by a score that escapes me. Hans Wagner, then in his prime, was all that I had expected. I can still see Honus's famed bowlegs roll down the baselines, as the Flying Dutchman twice stole bases on Red Dooin, the Phillies' peppery catcher.

My writing models in those days were Charley Dryden, Jimmy Isaminger of the old Philadelphia *North American,* and Ed Wolfe, who wrote and drew sports cartoons under the name of Jim Nasium of the Philadelphia *Inquirer.* Through later newspaper consolidations, Isaminger also wound up on the *Inquirer.* Dryden and Isaminger were prime writers of their time. They gave the reader all the facts of the game, the effectiveness of pitchers, the fielding gems, how the runs were scored, and usually the hero and culprit of the game. But these writers also injected a lot of fun and humor, such as Dryden's telling how Rube Waddell one night dove off a Camden, New Jersey, ferryboat to rescue a maiden in distress, only to come up with a floating log.

I never could understand how Dryden could write so well and so interestingly, for he had little education and had once worked in a foundry. For Dryden, writing baseball was a constant battle of wits between himself and the editors and proofreaders of his respective papers. He was constantly trying to work into his sentences double entendres, innocent-looking phrases that would shock Aunt Nellie if she understood them. Usually the copyreader won the battle, but ever so often Charley would slip through a good one. For example, in the 1920s, when Dryden worked in Chicago, the Cleveland club came up with a pitcher named Eugene Krapp. The name intrigued Dryden. He was proud of this one, which got by the editor: "Krapp squeezed his way out of a tight hole when, with the bases full, he induced Rollie Zeider to line to Bill Wambsganss for an inning-ending double play."

I began to pester Philadelphia sports editors with requests for a job or just an interview. Sometimes I enclosed an article as a sample of my work. Invariably I was told that their staffs were full and there was no chance of an immediate opening. One of them made his turndown a little less painful by adding a PS, "The piece you submitted was damn good, nevertheless." After my graduation from Central Manual High School in 1904, the youngest boy in a class of 120, I landed a job as junior clerk in the office of the secretary of the Norfolk & Western Railroad. In the meantime I had taken a night course in stenography and typewriting at the Central YMCA in Philadelphia. In 1904 many people worked from 7:00 A.M. to 5:00 or even 6:00 P.M. Office help worked from 8:00 to 5:00. My hours at the N & W were comparatively easy, 9:00 to 4:30. Such a schedule gave me a lot of time to fool with writing.

By 1909 I finally induced *Baseball Magazine,* then of Boston and later of New York, to buy from me a monthly biography of the top-ranking baseball stars. My first four stories were on the top stars and managers of the two championship clubs of that year, Hans Wagner and Fred Clarke of the Pittsburgh Pirates, and Ty Cobb and Hugh Jennings of the Detroit Tigers. These sketches took well with early fans, and my biographies continued into the 1920s.

Here is how I got my material. There were no public relations men then, either with the major leagues or with the sixteen major league teams that comprised the big leagues from 1903 to 1952. There were statistics available in *Spalding's Official Guide* and *Reach's Official Guide,* but nothing else. To get material for the Wagner story, I consulted George Moreland, an old-time baseball man who then ran a baseball statistical business out of Pittsburgh and was surprisingly accommodating, giving me a lot of good tips on Honus.

Though I had communicated with players for some years for my biographies, Eddie Collins was the first top name in baseball that I interviewed face-to-face, in 1910. I have interviewed several hundred ballplayers in my career—twenty-three years as a New York baseball writer and thirty-five more years as feature writer for *The Sporting News*—but that first chat with Columbia Eddie stands out as though it happened yesterday. Eddie boarded a few blocks from the ball park with the Harry Davises. He invited me to the Davis home for our talk. I didn't confess to Collins that he was the first player I had personally interviewed. I found him familiar with the earlier biographies I had written for *Baseball Magazine,* and he expressed surprise that I wasn't on a big newspaper. Eddie gave me all I wanted about his years at Columbia, where he was the 135-pound quarterback of the football team and the hard-hitting shortstop and captain of the baseball squad. The A's hadn't won a pennant since 1905, and Collins saw chances for the A's finishing on top in 1910. Beyond that, what I remember most vividly

Eddie Collins.

was that after chatting for an hour about baseball, we finished up on the subject of razors. The manufacturer of a new safety razor then on the market had sent Collins one of the new razors, and he was delighted with it. He became the interviewer. I told him I still used a straight razor, one my father had given me when I was old enough to shave. Eddie said, "Take it from me; get rid of it and buy one of the new safety razors. You'll never regret it. You never have to be afraid you'll cut yourself; it really makes shaving fun." I took Collins's advice and never regretted it.

As we left together for the ball park, Mrs. Davis called after us, "You fellows win today. Hit a home run, Eddie." Collins seemed a bit annoyed at the order and grumbled to me, "She should know by this time that I don't hit home runs." He hit only three in 1910.

By this time I had sold two baseball fiction stories to *Short Stories.* The first was called "Swatt, the Slugger"; I've forgotten the name of the second. I'd have to be paid to read them today.

People at the Norfolk & Western got to know of my outside writing activities. Eventually my boss, Secretary Ezra Hyde Alden, a lineal descendant of Priscilla and John Alden and one of the finest men I ever have known, called me into his office and said kindly, "Fred, I know you have ambitions to be a writer and have met with a little success. I am afraid that your office work here has become secondary in your mind to your writing. I have a friend from Boston, Clarence W. Barron, who is the big man in Dow Jones and the *Wall Street Journal.* He also owns the Philadelphia News Bureau and the Boston News Bureau. He'll be in New York tomorrow and I have made an appointment for you to meet him tomorrow morning in his room at the Waldorf-Astoria. He may have something of interest to you."

I had not the slightest idea that Barron was considered a tyrant, even an ogre, in his establishment. He knew to a penny what every employee was paid, had to okay every raise, and his hirelings were scared stiff when summoned to his private office. Nor did I know that he, like Ezra Alden, was a prominent lay member of the Swedenborgian faith. Their common religious background made my interview with Barron possible. When I knocked at his door, he called out, "Come in, young man." He apologized for still being in bed at 10:30 A.M. "I always stay in bed on rainy mornings," he explained. "Never on clear mornings, when I am up early."

The first assignment he gave me was to get him the opening stock market prices. "Only about the ten most active," he said. I didn't know one stock from another, so I said to a customer's man in a brokerage house on the ground floor of the hotel, "My friend Mr. Barron is in the hotel; he wants the opening quotations on about a dozen leading stocks." I got the information, wrote it down, and handed it to Barron.

He said, "General Motors and New York Central are strong. That is good."

He next asked me what religion I followed. I replied, "I don't exactly know. I was baptized German Reformed, but I was confirmed an Episcopalian largely because they had shuffleboard in the church basement and baseball and basketball teams. But I don't go for the long ritual in the Episcopal High Church."

"I agree with you on that," he said. "Do you know anything about the Swedenborgians?"

"No, sir," I said. "I know, of course, that Mr. Alden is an active member of that faith, but the crowd I go with generally classify them with what some call feet washers." There had been an amused twinkle in Barron's eyes, but it turned to a frown. "What do you mean by that, Lieb?" he asked. "What are feet washers?"

"I guess it means any sect or smaller denomination that isn't one of our standard Christian groups—Baptists, Methodists, Roman Catholics, Presbyterians, Lutherans, Congregationalists."

He looked me straight in the eye and said, "Lieb, you have much to learn. I am a Swedenborgian and a foot washer." I nearly turned to stone.

Suddenly Barron changed the topic. "So, you want to be a writer. What kind of writer?"

"I had hoped to land a job as a sports writer, but so far have been unsuccessful," I replied.

"Fie!" he said, almost in disgust. "Sports writers get little money. They get nickels and dimes. Aim to be a financial reporter. If you get to be a good one, you can get real dollars, more than the regular reporters."

Barron's next command was "Lieb, draw me a bath." I followed instructions, and he said I could stay and watch his ablutions. He was a short, stocky man, but until he got into the water I hadn't noticed the great pouch he carried in front of him. It extended above the waterline like a large turtle. "Lieb, what are you staring at?" he asked. "My stomach got that way because I love real good food, lots of it."

The talk ended with his putting me to work on the Philadelphia News Bureau, his outlet in Philadelphia, for fifteen dollars a week, starting the next Monday.

I was glad it wasn't immediately. My interview with Barron was on a Thursday, the day the players in the 1910 Cubs-Athletics World Series would travel from Philadelphia to Chicago. I had seen the first and second games of the series as a fifty-cent bleacherite in Philly's Shibe Park, my first of well over two hundred World Series games. By not having to report to the News Bureau immediately, I was in a position to "see" the third, fourth, and fifth games of the series being played in

Chicago by means of the Philadelphia *Record*'s fine electric scoreboard. It was forty-nine years, nearly a half century, before they would play another World Series without Fred Lieb in the press box.

My stint at the Philadelphia News Bureau was spot coverage of things of interest to banks, brokerage houses, and investors. I had some fun, and though it lasted less than a half a year, I made some lifelong friendships. It gave me a feel and smell for printer's ink, and the stationery of the Philadelphia News Bureau made a fine springboard from which to launch my campaign for a baseball writing job.

My big break came in the late winter of 1911, shortly after the big league teams had started their spring training. The way it happened sounds like something out of Horatio Alger. A part of my duties at the Philadelphia News Bureau was to scan the New York morning papers and alert people higher up to any news item I thought would be of interest. What I saw one morning was not something I was going to pass along to anyone else. This was for me alone. A short item in the New York *Press* reported that Ernest J. Lanigan was leaving his post as baseball writer for the *Press* to become secretary to Ed Barrow, the new president of the International League. I'm sure I read it several times, with wide-opened eyes and a scheming mind. Pretty soon I was at my typewriter, knocking out a letter to James R. Price, sports editor, New York *Press*, nominating myself for the vacancy. I played up my baseball biographies for *Baseball Magazine*, my two baseball fiction stories, and my writing experience with the News Bureau. I gave George Moreland, the Pittsburgh baseball statistician, as one of my references.

I suspect that I owe part of my success in crashing the Big Town to my later friends in St. Louis at *The Sporting News*. Alfred H. Spink, one of the two brothers who made a success of *The Sporting News* at the end of the nineteenth century, had just issued a baseball book which had a closing chapter on interesting, worthy, or significant people in and around the national game. Lo and behold, my name appeared as "baseball's foremost biographer." Furthermore, Albert and Charles Spink were uncles of Ernie Lanigan, whose shoes I wanted to fill. How much conversation about me took place between Price and the Spinks I never discovered.

In reply to my letter Price sent me a telegram (so easy and cheap in those days!) asking me to come to New York for an interview. I climbed on the first train I could get and hustled to Price's office in the *Press* building, 7 Spruce Street, in the heart of New York's old Newspaper Row. The German language daily, *Volks Zeitung*, then with a circulation bigger than most of the city's American dailies, was across the street. The *Tribune* established by Horace ("Go West, Young Man") Greeley was around the corner on Park Row. The *Morning* and *Evening Sun* were neighbors of the *Tribune*, and the *Morning* and *Evening*

World were another half block away, near the Brooklyn Bridge. You could really smell printer's ink in that locality. Do young men coming to New York today for the first time in their lives or looking for a job there at age twenty-three have such a burning sense of excitement as I did?

At that time Jim Price was perhaps the most baseball-minded sports editor in the country. He too had come from a smaller eastern city— Baltimore—and he had been a baseball writer. Summer and winter, even on the Fourth of July and on Christmas Day, he opened the sports pages of the *Press* with a column on baseball either by one of his staff, or from another paper.

When I entered Price's section of the *Press*'s newsroom—it was partitioned from the rest of the City Room—he peered appraisingly at me through glasses. "So you want to become a New York baseball writer," he said.

"Yes, sir."

"Lanigan's shoes won't be easy to fill. He's a damn good reporter. He knows how to write. We're a little different here from the other papers. We have a reputation of being number one among baseball fans. That's a reputation we want to keep. Our fans know baseball. They won't stand for sloppy writing."

How many times during this little speech I mumbled "Yes, sir," or "That's right, sir," I don't recall. But at the end I said, "I don't like sloppy writing myself, and I would hate to disappoint you or your readers."

"Well," he said, "I'll give you a shot at the job. Get yourself a room for the night—the Astor is nearby—and come back this time tomorrow."

When I returned the next day, Price had on his desk two 200-word skeleton reports of the activities of the two New York teams that evening—the Giants in Marlin, Texas, and the Yankees (Price always called them the Highlanders; the name petered out for good in 1913, when the team moved into the Polo Grounds) in Athens, Georgia. Sid Mercer had wired in the brief on McGraw's team, and Bill Hanna, then of the *Morning Sun,* had contributed the few lines on Hal Chase's Yankees. The Dodgers—this will shock Dodger fans of a later era—were routinely handled by a Western Union operator. Price let me read the two pieces of telegraphed copy and said, "There's your material. Write me a column on the Giants and one on the Highlanders. And make it sound as though you are today in Marlin and Athens—both of them!"

There were my orders. On this rested my future in New York. But I had no doubts at all. My years as a baseball nut placed me in good shape for the test, for I knew the Giants and Yankee players as thoroughly as I did those of our Philadelphia Athletics and Phillies, though I may have loved them less. Since both New York teams had finished second in their leagues in 1910, I started off with pretty good clubs, and I took the line that both were now, in 1911, pennant-bound. (That one of them—the Giants—made it, made me a respectable prophet.) Anyway, Price read my copy on both attentively, blue-penciled it here and there, rewrote a couple of paragraphs, and seemed satisfied.

"Come in tomorrow, same time. You have the job," he said matter-offactly. "It pays thirty-five dollars a week. Most of the men who have held your job previously have come in on Sunday for a few hours for another day's pay. That brings it to around forty dollars plus." I probably beamed. "Oh, there's something else," he added. "The writer from the *Press* automatically becomes the New York official scorer for

New York Highlanders' Park at Amsterdam Avenue near 165th Street. Brown Bros.

American League games here. You'll inherit the job. You'll get an extra three hundred dollars a year from them for that. Besides," Price went on, "Ernie Lanigan has always sent out the daily box score and lead for the Associated Press and done other baseball writing news for them. Also he's been New York correspondent for certain out-of-town city newspapers. I guess you'll inherit this, too."

The proverbial feather would have knocked me over. Wow! It added up to about sixty dollars a week, a lot of money for a kid of twenty-three in 1911, one with no college degree and little newspaper experience. After I computed it several times, I acted predictably and asked my Philadelphia sweetheart, Mary Ann Peck, to marry me and come join me in New York. We were married on April 24, 1911, and there never was any other love in my life. She did much to enhance my career and even more to enrich my life in every way.

I was totally happy to be in New York. My sudden prosperity was a new experience and most enjoyable for me. I loved my job. Every day I grabbed the briefs sent in by Mercer and Hanna, let my imagination have full play over their bare bones, and blew them up to almost epic length and drama as the clubs worked their way through the so-called Dixie exhibition circuit to New York. After the season opened and my stories appeared nearly every day, I could see only one small drawback. Except for Hearst's morning *American,* which featured its new man, Damon Runyon, none of the morning papers had by-lines over any of their sports stories. Oddly enough, all the New York evening papers did carry by-lines. I was now just cocky enough to let it bother me a little. But before I blew it up into an issue, Frank Munsey, the magazine tycoon, bought the *Press* in 1912 so that Theodore Roosevelt would have a newspaper voice in New York, and Munsey a means of supporting Teddy in his Bull Moose campaign against Wilson and Taft. Munsey liked by-lines over sports stories. Presto! Less than a year and a half and I had a by-line!

3

1911: I BREAK IN AT THE POLO GROUNDS

My excitement grew and grew as opening day drew closer. I paid my first visit to the Polo Grounds when the Giants played their then customary Saturday afternoon preseason game with Yale. Then came an exhibition game with the Newark team of the International League, managed by McGraw's former pitching ace, Iron Man Joe McGinnity. All I remember about the game was that Sid Mercer pointed to the Newark second baseman, Johnny Nee, and told me he was a grandfather. I thought Sid was kidding me. Johnny never made the big leagues, but he later became one of the Yankees' best scouts, digging up Bill Dickey, Johnny Allen, and many others.

A Giants opening day game in that era may not have equalled the frenzy of opening day now in Cincinnati, where the entire city gets into the act, but you could feel an electric pulsation in the air. I'm sure I was running a fever. The Polo Grounds was dressed in all its finery. The great wooden horseshoe of a grandstand was festooned with bunting of the nation's colors wherever it could be hung, from the high roof to the outside of the field boxes. And Irish John Murphy, the grounds keeper, had stuck into the ground old Irish flags with the gold harp on a field of green at the positions played by captain and second baseman, Larry Doyle, and the redheaded rightfielder, Red Jack Murray.

Opening day was a holiday outing for the New York theatrical clubs then in their heyday, the Friars and the Lambs (the latter included John McGraw among its members). George M. Cohan, Richard Mansfield, Digby Bell, DeWolfe Hopper, and Eddie Foy were among the

The Polo Grounds, 1905, during the World Series game between the New York Giants and the Philadelphia Athletics.

stage greats who were on hand, enhancing their visibility by stopping to greet friends as they made their way along the aisles towards their seats. Every El train brought hundreds of Wall Street brokers, their assistants and their customers. The breadwinners of the upper middle class, not yet addicted to golf, still looked to the Polo Grounds for their sports recreation.

With the band playing "East side, west side, all around the town," Manager McGraw was presented a ten-foot-high floral horseshoe. Joe

Humphries, the raucous announcer of the Madison Square Garden
(then located on Madison Avenue at Twenty-Third Street), made the
presentation, expressing the hope that the good-luck horseshoe would
bring McGraw a third National League pennant in 1911.

Before these brief ceremonies began, Ernie Lanigan introduced me
to those New York writers I hadn't met at the Yale game. They were all
there for opening day, the cream of the crop. I met Damon Runyon for
the first time. "I'm a new boy around here myself," were the friendly
first words he spoke to me as Ernie told him I was the new man for the
Press. There was a big handclasp with gracious Grantland Rice of the

Evening Mail, no rookie at sports writing, as were Runyon and I, but new to the New York scene. Then came an affable, pudgy, slouchy giant named Heywood Broun, from Brooklyn and Harvard. Heywood's paper was the *Morning Telegraph,* a Broadway racing and theatrical newspaper. The 1911 freshman class of Runyon, Rice, Broun, and Lieb now have their places in the writers' section of the Cooperstown Hall of Fame.

I suppose I am prejudiced, but it seems to me that New York's newspaper world was then at its zenith. In 1911 the Big City had seven morning papers and six more in the afternoon. Of course each had its writer covering the Giants, the number one team in town. I remember my first view of the tall and wide three-hundred pounder, ponderous George Tidden of the *Morning World.* "Jim Price will make a writer out of you if you are smart enough to take his advice" was his greeting. Sitting with Tidden was his counterpart on the *Evening World,* Bozeman Bulger, who would later become my very good friend.

The other New York writers included that hypochondriacal, irascible bachelor, Bill Hanna, of the *Morning Sun,* who took a bit of knowing but who had a warm heart and a good share of humanity. Once when we were in Shreveport a few years later he walked to the middle of the bridge across the Red River. I asked him why. "I wanted to drop my razor blades into the river," he said. "I am always afraid they will cut the maid who takes care of my room."

The oldest man in the press box was Sam Crane of the *Journal,* Hearst's afternoon paper. Sam had been a ball player; in fact he had played second base for the Giants in 1890. While all New York writers pulled for the Giants, Sam Crane lived and died with them. With Sam, neither McGraw nor his men could do anything wrong. Another loyalist, first-class, was John Foster, sports editor and number one baseball writer of the *Evening Telegram.* John used to work a lot of fruit words into his stories. A Giants win over the Reds was "peachy." "Fred Merkle earned a bowl of cherries" for a catch. "Raspberries for that Cubs scoundrel, Heinie Zimmerman." Joe Vila of the *Morning Sun*—a sturdy, individualistic Bostonian of Spanish ancestry and as ardent an American League man as Foster was pro-Giants and National League—collected a dozen of Foster's "fruity" stories and mailed them to him with a note reading, "Eat all of this fine fruit and have a good bowel movement. You need it." Later, when Joe became sports editor and columnist of the *Evening Sun,* and Foster secretary of the Giants, they became good friends.

One man Lanigan failed to introduce me to was sitting wrapped up in a shaggy bearskin overcoat. It turned out to be John (Jack) Wheeler, a recent Columbia graduate who was a baseball writer for the New York *Herald.* He later became one of the most successful and wealthi-

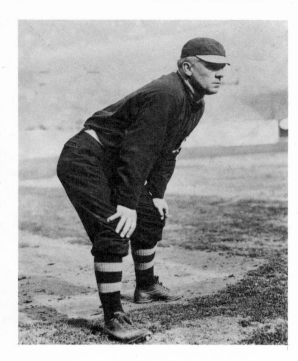

John McGraw wearing the black uniform of the New York Giants, 1911.

est newspaper syndicate men in the country. Jack was my senior by two years, and when he died in 1975, I was left the dean of the Baseball Writers Association of America. Another early friend in the press box was Harry Cross of the New York *Times.* I thought Harry a very good writer whose natural Naugatuck, Connecticut, sense of humor, sharppened at Harvard, made his prose sparkle. When asked what he majored in at Harvard, Harry would say, "Beer-drinking," and reach for another bottle. He later became sports editor with the New York *Evening Post.*

Despite all the Harvard men in the press box (Vila was one also), the indubitable aristocrat among us was Walter Trumbull. He was a direct descendant of Jonathan Trumbull, governor of Connecticut from 1769 to 1784 and an ardent Revolutionary patriot. Walter Trumbull was the only sports writer then to drive his own car. Furthermore, he had a personal manservant, a likable black man from North Carolina who loved his job. For some reason Walter took an early fancy to me. As a young man, I was a pipe and cigar smoker. I would start every game with a five-cent cigar, a Cinco. Perhaps Trumbull didn't like the smell of it, or maybe he thought I deserved something better. Anyway, after the first few games in 1911 he would drop by before each game got underway and hand me a twenty-five-cent Havana cigar.

Perhaps the handsomest man in the press box was Sid Mercer, then of the New York *Globe.* He had black hair, shining brown eyes, and a patrician face. Sid came from an Illinois town across the river from St. Louis, where he had done some writing and then for a while had been secretary of the old St. Louis Browns. He came to New York in 1907 as a sports writer with the *Globe* and was promptly assigned to cover the Giants. Reputedly one time an enthusiastic Sunday School teacher in his pre-New York days, the Sid I came to know was a sophisticated, worldly New Yorker.

How Freddy Lieb looked to the veteran New York baseball writers in April 1911 was brought home to me a decade later. Harry Cross brought a younger brother into the press box, sat him on a seat in the rear row, and then took his accustomed chair and table in the front row. Sid Mercer, not noticing I was within earshot, pointed to young Cross and said to Harry, "Who is that young guy? He looks just like Freddy Lieb when Freddy first came here from Philadelphia."

The Giants-Phillies ball game that followed the opening-day ceremonies was an anticlimax to me and a disappointment to the many thousands of fans present. The Phillies had been strengthened during the winter by a multiplayer deal with Cincinnati that brought them third baseman Hans Lobert, centerfielder Dode Paskert, and pitchers Jack Rowan and Fred Beebe for third baseman Eddie Grant, outfielder Johnny Bates, and pitchers George McQuillan and Lew Moren. Lobert and Paskert did some hitting, and Earl Moore spun a two-hitter for Philadelphia, and that was that—Phillies 2, Giants 0.

Giants fans were certain that tomorrow things would be different: Matty would pitch. McGraw through the years consistently held his superstar, Christopher Mathewson, out of the opener in favor of someone like Leon K. "Red" Ames. Ames unfortunately was a hard-luck pitcher, losing, for example, an opening game to Brooklyn, 3–0, in twelve innings after pitching a no-hitter for nine. Ames had taken the loss in my first league game in New York, to Moore. Now Matty was expected, as usual, to even things up. But not this time. Pat Moran, manager of the Phillies, pitched Rowan, one of his new men from Cincinnati, and the Giants could manage only three hits off him. The great Mathewson went down to a 6–1 defeat. This second game provided me with the thrill of one of the greatest catches I have seen in seven decades of watching big league baseball. The Giants had something going in the eighth inning. With two on and two out, that unlucky Giants first baseman, Fred Merkle, hit a tremendous drive toward the deepest part of the Polo Grounds field in right center. It was ticketed triple, at least, and maybe an inside-the-park home run. Dode Paskert, the Philly centerfielder, started off with the crack of the bat. When it looked as if the ball was up the gap in right center, Paskert made a tremendous last moment dive parallel to the ground, speared the ball, rolled over and came up with it. His wondrous catch ended the Giants' hopes for the day.

Shortly after midnight the next day (there was no game that day), the great wooden horseshoe of a grandstand at the Polo Grounds went up in flames—one of New York's biggest and most spectacular fires up to that time. Almost totally out of control, it lit up the night sky in upper Manhattan, the Bronx, and eastern Queens. Frightened citizens swamped newspaper offices with worried questions about the ominous red-orange light in the sky. The fire started under the right-center-field bleachers and before the first horse-drawn fire apparatus reached the scene it had leaped to the wooden grandstand proper, the horseshoe. Within minutes the grandstand, from ground level to the high roof, was wrapped in flame. Firemen, called from all over the city, could save only the left-field bleachers and part of the sun seats in dead center. The official cause of the fire was a lighted cigarette dropped by a careless fan in the right-center-field bleachers. It ignited some discarded newspapers that had not been removed after the opening day game and probably smoldered for some thirty hours. However, reporters who were there liked to call the official account of the fire's origin nonsense: it was Paskert's electrifying and sizzling catch, they said, that sparked the Polo Grounds holocaust.

Fans immediately wondered where the Giants would play their 1911 schedule, for there was no love existing between the Giants and the Highlanders. But Frank Farrell, owner-president of the Highlanders, surprised everybody by offering the Giants use of the Highlander park at 165th Street and Broadway (with its western boundary Fort Washington Avenue, where Presbyterian Hospital is today) until such time as John T. Brush of the Giants could rebuild his Polo Grounds again. Though the New York American League park seated 12,000 fewer than the Polo Grounds, Brush accepted Farrell's generous offer with gratitude. This offer by Farrell ended a period of bitterness and antagonism between the clubs that had begun when the American League invaded New York in 1903. In fact, the management of the Giants, their immediate circle, and hangers-on invariably spoke of their rivals disparagingly as the Invaders. But now an era of goodwill began, one that would see the Highlanders move into the new Polo Grounds with the Giants in 1913, under the name of Yankees. A decade later this era would end when the rivalry of the two teams on the field and in the hearts of New York fans—abetted by the egos of John McGraw and Col. Jake Ruppert—caused the Yankees to pull out and build their own ball park across the Harlem River.

From my very first day in the press box I did not have any trouble writing up the home games of the Giants and the Highlanders for the *Press*, though I did benefit by having my work put through the editorial hands of Jim Price.

One of my strengths, I think, was that I knew what I could and couldn't do. I couldn't, for example, attempt flights of literary fancy. I did try to inject humor into my stories but I was never an iconoclast. By temperament I belong to neither what has been called the Gee Whiz school of writers nor the Aw Nuts variety. I took baseball seriously as a profession, despite its being a game, and I took baseball writing seriously as a profession. I think I wrote first of all to satisfy Fred Lieb the reader of sports pages. As a reader I wanted honest reporting, and I wanted to know not just who won, but how and why. If I could be made to feel by the writer that I had missed something exciting by not being present, so much the better. It was perhaps natural that as a writer without talents of a creative literary sort—such as the talents of Runyon and Broun—I modeled myself on my own preferences as a sports-page reader.

Nor did I have any real trouble when thrust into the official scorer's role at the Highlanders' Park (also called Hilltop Park) on their opening day in 1911, soon after the fire at the Polo Grounds. I once heard Curt Gowdy, now one of our top TV sportscasters, tell a nationwide audience that the first time he televised from Yankee Stadium was the first time he had seen the great Yankees play. In my case for the first Yankee game I covered as a reporter, I was also the official scorer. Today a man has to write baseball for ten years before he is eligible to serve as official scorer. The status of the official scorer in 1911—and for years after that—was quite different from what it is today. In some cities the identity of the official scorer was kept secret, and the players never knew who called their hits and errors. Not until the official averages were computed and published during the winter following the season did a batter learn his final and official batting average or a pitcher find out exactly how many games he had won.

In the meantime the baseball writers were going their own merry individualistic ways. They did their own scoring and made out their own box scores for the use of their papers. Sometimes the *Press, Tribune,* and *Morning Sun* would have different hit totals for the Giants, for example, and one paper might have credited Fred Snodgrass with two hits in yesterday's game, another one hit, and another, none at all. In those days the Associated Press box scores for New York games, which I always made up, were not sent to the New York dailies. Every baseball writer was supposed to know how to make his own box score. But there were some who didn't. Damon Runyon would say to me, "Freddy, will you let me copy your box score? I never did learn to get up one of those damned things." After he had asked me this a few times I just handed it to him automatically and would get it back a few moments later.

Underneath the box scores the *Press* writers added two items not found in other newspapers, items instituted by my predecessor, Ernie Lanigan. The first was a summary of runs batted in, which might read like this: "Runs batted in: Doyle 2, Murray, Fletcher." Here, where a numeral did not follow a player's name, *one* run was batted in. So a fan could tell whose hits scored runs for the Giants. The second item credited catchers with men thrown out stealing. It might read: "Thrown out by catcher: Meyers, 3; Schulte, Sheckard, Evers." Here, the last three names are those of the opponents' men thrown out, each one once.

Today, in the condensed box scores made necessary by the greater number of clubs, AP has omitted the old defensive columns of putouts (p), assists (a), and errors (e), but they have included the RBI column, and RBIs are now regarded as a most important statistic in gauging a hitter's worth.

For compensation official scorers in 1911 received pennies in comparison to the fat checks paid them in 1976. I received $300 a season for the seventy-seven games of the Highlanders' home schedule. This modest sum was $50 more than was collected by John Foster, who scored for the Giants, and by Abe Yaeger in Brooklyn. "The pay means little," Foster used to say. "It's the honor, the distinction of being the official scorer that really matters." And I believed him with all my heart.

By May of 1911 the Giants were ready to announce plans for their new steel-and-concrete stands that would replace the old wooden horseshoe. All of the sports editors of New York were invited to a gala luncheon at the Claremont Inn, a swank restaurant facing Grant's Tomb in the area between the separated lanes of Riverside Drive, next to today's Riverside Church. Jim Price said he still would be sleeping that day and asked me to attend in his stead. We gathered at a downtown hotel and were taken by automobiles to the Claremont. It was the first time this twenty-three-year-old kid from Philadelphia had ever ridden in an automobile, and the day brought me my first taste of caviar and champagne.

John T. Brush, owner-president of the Giants, was host at the luncheon, but he was a sick man, a victim of locomotor ataxia, which took his life the following year. After a few brief remarks, Brush let the New York club's treasurer John Whalen, the secretary William Gray, and the architect of the new ball park do the talking. The trio envisaged a new super-structure, a grandstand that would put all other baseball parks to shame, a veritable baseball Colosseum. Retaining what was usable of the old wooden bleachers, the new grandstand and bleacher, it was estimated, would hold between 40,000 and 50,000 fans. "A veritable Eighth Wonder of the World!" Bat Masterson, sports editor of the *Morning Telegraph,* whispered to Bob Edgren.

Gray reported that the lower stands would be ready by August, and if the Giants loomed up as a World Series contender, the entire grandstand would be ready by late September. The new edifice was to be named Brush Stadium; the new name promptly appeared on the club's stationery, but it never took with the team's fans. Until the field eventually was abandoned by the Mets in 1965, New Yorkers invariably spoke of it as the Polo Grounds, though polo was never played at that site.

The Giants took a commanding lead in late August and September, and the fans came out to the new park in droves. No Sunday professional baseball was permitted in the East in those years, so Saturday was the big baseball day of the week. Crowds jammed the new park to capacity on several occasions. When we writers would ask Secretary Gray to tell us the size of the crowd, he would offer estimates of 40,000, 45,000, even 50,000—figures that were to plague the Giants' management a few months later.

On the field the Giants had quickly rebounded from their two early pre-fire defeats at the hands of the Phillies, and most of the way they were in a close race with the Chicago Cubs, 1910 champions. Frank Chance's once smooth-working machine faltered badly after Labor Day, and McGraw's men pulled away from them to win by seven and one half games. The 1911 Giants stole 373 bases, still a team record, with five men stealing from 38 to 61 times. Captain-second baseman Larry Doyle had a great year, both with his bat and glove, and was voted the Chalmers car for being the most valuable National League player of 1911. Christy Mathewson was as good as ever, the beloved Matty carding a 26–13 season. But the pennant was made possible by the blossoming of left-handed pitcher Rube Marquard.

Brush purchased Marquard late in the 1908 season from Indianapolis for $11,000, the biggest sum paid up to that date for a minor league player. Rube was then eighteen years old. However, Rube was mediocre in 1909 and 1910, and many of his fellow players and most of the New York fans had given up on the big fellow the spring of 1911. Writers called him the $11,000 lemon. But in May a terrific first-inning volley made it possible for Rube to spring suddenly to stardom. With Mathewson the starting pitcher against the Cardinals, the Giants set off a thirteen-run barrage. McGraw said to Matty, "You can take the rest of the day off. I'm putting in Marquard. With that thirteen-run lead perhaps Rube can get somebody out." Marquard did get fourteen men on strikeouts in the last eight innings. He gave up a few runs, but his fast ball was exploding. Experienced St. Louis batsmen like Roger Bresnahan and Ed Konetchy looked foolish trying to connect with Rube's chained lightning. That game gave Marquard the confidence he had lacked. From then he was off to 24 wins against only 7 defeats, with 237 strikeouts, tops for the National League that year.

As a special concession to Charley Ebbets, the Brooklyn club owner who was crying poor, the National League dragged out its regular season schedule until Columbus Day to give Ebbets a final large "gate" with a Giants-Brooklyn doubleheader. This delayed the opening of the 1911 World Series until Saturday, October 14. The site of the first game then was decided by the toss of a coin. Tom Lynch, the National League president, called it correctly "Heads" and that gave the Giants the first game in their new Polo Grounds.

At the time my wife and I were living in an apartment house on West 145th Street in Manhattan, the second door in from Broadway. When I woke up the morning of the fourteenth I saw an endless queue lined up across the street. Most of the people were reading newspapers and some had packages—packed lunches, I later discovered. I said to Mary, "I wonder what those men are lined up for across the street? It looks as though they have been out there for some time." After breakfast I asked a police officer across the street what was going on. The cop looked at me with surprise and said to this young baseball writer, "Don't you know what is going on in this city today? They're lined up to see the first game of the World Series at the Polo Grounds."

"Good God," I said. "The Polo Grounds is a mile from here!"

"Yea," answered the cop. "For those at the end of the line, more than that. And half of this crowd never will get in."

For the World Series the Giants management sold reserve tickets by mail only for the upper grandstand. These seats went for $3 a ticket. However, the big lower stands at $2 and the bleachers at $1 were put on sale on the morning of the game, first come, first served. They also put on sale some 5,000 standing-room ducats, but by noon everything was filled up except for reserved box and upper grandstand seats. As the policeman had rightly predicted, half of the people in that long queue never got to the ticket windows.

When ticket sales had been counted by the National Commission (baseball's governing body and ultimate authority before Judge Landis), the attendance at the game was announced as 38,291, by far the biggest World Series crowd up to that time, and a high which would last five years. However, the ball players were suspicious and displeased with the official figures. They thought they were being rooked by the National Commission. The calculations of the players were warped by Bill Gray's blithe figures of 40,000 to 50,000 for regular-season Saturday attendances. "How could the crowd have been only 38,000 when we had 45,000 and 50,000 for league games in Septem-

Baseball writers at Lake Oscawana, New York, August, 1927. From left to right: Lieb—*Post*, Bozeman Bulger—*Evening World*, Jim Harrison—*Times*, Bob Ripley—*Globe*, and George Daley—*Morning World*.

Fred Lieb, 1913.

ber?" argued Chief Meyers, the Giants' catcher, speaking for the players.

Meyers and Harry Davis, captain–first baseman of the Athletics,
were named as player-representatives. The National Commission was
composed of chairman Garry Herrmann and league presidents Ban
Johnson and Tom Lynch. The players were met by three angry, ag-
grieved commissioners. Ban Johnson, the American League president,
frequently spoken of as the Czar of Baseball, was vehement. "Do you
men think the Commission is trying to steal money from the players?"
he asked sourly. "Do you think Mr. Herrmann, Mr. Lynch and I are
crooks? For myself, I resent your insinuations, and take it as a personal
insult." Meyers and Davis, glad to get away from the tongue-lashing,
said meekly, "We had given too much attention to Bill Gray's late-sea-
son attendance figures," which was true. Paid attendances of the other
two 1911 games in New York when the police stopped fans from sitting
in the aisles were 37,216 and 33,228. These figures showed clearly that
the players had no basis for a gripe and that the commissioners had a
degree of justification for their indignation.

There was a ticket scandal after the series, but this stemmed from the
handling of tickets for the reserved upper stands. Speculators had been
allowed to acquire big blocks of reserved seats, which were then sold
to actors, Broadway habitues, and some part of the citizenry that operated outside the law and was willing to pay fancy prices. These tickets
were traced to Gray's office, and John Brush fired Bill after an investigation.

4

HONUS WAGNER: THE
FLYING DUTCHMAN

I have already mentioned my love and admiration as a small boy for John Peter (Honus) Wagner. I did not get to see him play until 1904; he was the subject of my first "baseball biography" in 1909, and I covered him only in the last seven years of his National League career, which ended in 1917. Yet from boyhood to this moment I have always had an abiding affection for the player they called the Flying Dutchman.

Wagner won eight National League batting championships, one more than either of the stars of later generations of National Leaguers, Rogers Hornsby and Stan Musial. Even though he played four seasons after reaching his fortieth birthday, seasons in which his average fell below .300 for the first time, he ended with a lifetime batting average of .329. He was one of the original five to be elected to the Hall of Fame: Honus Wagner, Ty Cobb, Babe Ruth, Christy Mathewson, and Walter Johnson.

The current baseball commissioner, Bowie K. Kuhn, once gave a talk in Pittsburgh shortly after his election in 1969. To show he knew his Pirates history, Kuhn mentioned some of the Pirate greats: the two Waner brothers, Pie Traynor, Kiki Cuyler—all Hall of Famers—and such later Pirate standouts as Vernon Law and Bill Mazeroski. When he was finished Kuhn felt something was wrong, that he hadn't "gone over." Later, back in his hotel, it suddenly dawned on the new commissioner that in talking of Pittsburgh's all-time greats, he had made no mention of the greatest of them all, Honus Wagner. Kuhn's youth-

Honus Wagner.   Paul Thompson, New York *World*

fulness in terms of baseball's long history was his best excuse: he was born in 1926, nine years after Wagner had played his last of 2,785 National League games.

Two smart, efficient baseball men, John McGraw and Ed Barrow, were better positioned than Kuhn and they didn't forget it. Both McGraw and Barrow rated Wagner as baseball's number one player of all time, putting the Dutchman ahead of even Babe Ruth and Ty Cobb. McGraw had played against Wagner when Mac was a Baltimore (National League) Oriole in the years just before the turn of the century and then managed teams against Honus and his Pirate teammates in the first seventeen years of this century. McGraw said, "I consider Wagner not only as the number one shortstop, but had he played in any position other than pitcher, he would have been equally great at the other seven positions. He was the nearest thing to a perfect player no matter where his manager chose to play him."

Barrow's views also must be respected, for he managed Babe Ruth when he was a superb pitcher with the Red Sox, turned him into an outfielder in 1919, and then was Babe's general manager on the Yankees from 1921 to 1934. Barrow managed Detroit just before Ty came there in 1905, but knew of Cobb back in his minor league days and saw him play hundreds of times. He had great respect for both Ruth and Cobb, but said, "If I had a choice of all players who have played baseball, the first man I would select would be Honus Wagner." Incidentally, Barrow was Honus's minor league manager in Paterson, New Jersey, and it was he who sold the wonder player to the old Louisville National League club in 1897. Barrow blamed Wagner's failure to hit more home runs (he hit 101), on the dead ball used during Wagner's entire twenty-one-year career. "If Wagner had batted against a lively ball he would have fifty homeruns almost every year."

Interestingly, Wagner had to be tricked into playing shortstop. When he came into the National League with the Louisville club in 1897, he was an outfielder. In his first five years with Louisville and Pittsburgh, he played all three outfield positions as well as third base and first base.

The Pirates of 1901 had a satisfactory shortstop named Fred Ely. During the National–American League war which was raging then, Ely jumped to Washington in the American League. Fred Clarke, Pittsburgh manager, wanted Wagner to take over shortstop, but Wagner would have none of it. "I'm an outfielder who can play third base and first base, but I really prefer center field." Clarke then moved his third baseman, little Tommy Leach, over to shortstop, with Wagner covering third base. Quietly Clarke told Leach, "Work gradually on the Dutchman. Tell him that as a little man you haven't got near the range of a big fellow like Wagner. Butter him up and belittle yourself. Try to shame him into playing the position." After about a week of this, with Leach nagging at him continually, Wagner said one day, "All right, little man, you win, I'll play shortstop today." Once he played a few games at shortstop he liked the position and realized its possibilities for being where the action is.

Wagner never played a better shortstop than in the 1909 World Series between the Pirates and the Detroit Tigers. He really loved to play ball, and by this time he loved to play shortstop. The 1909 series was not only a confrontation between the champion clubs of the two leagues, but also a confrontation between the two batting champions, Wagner and Ty Cobb. And Wagner, twelve years older than Cobb, wel-

The Flying Dutchman heads for home.   International News

comed the duel. When it was over, Wagner had outbatted Cobb .333 to .231 and had stolen six bases to Ty's two—but one of Cobb's steals was a magnificent clean steal of home.

In the game after he stole home, Ty reached base on a single, and from first base he yelled down to Wagner, "I'm coming down on the first pitch, Krauthead."

"I'll be ready for you, Rebel," Honus answered.

Getting a pretty good lead on George Mullin, the Detroit pitcher, Cobb went down on the first pitch, as he had said he would, and he came into the bag, sliding high. Wagner took catcher Gibson's throw, and with the ball in his gloved hand, vigorously tagged Cobb in the face, loosening three of Ty's teeth. "We also play a little rough in this league, Mr. Cobb," Honus said as the deflated Cobb collected his wits.

Of the many columns I have written through the years, I am particularly proud of one I wrote early in 1933. It rescued aging and retired Honus Wagner from poverty and obscurity and gave him nineteen additional years in Pittsburgh baseball as a useful coach, goodwill man, and inspiration to goodness knows how many young ball players. A lady from Pittsburgh wrote me of Wagner's plight in the Depression year of 1933. I still don't know why she wrote to me rather than a Pittsburgh sports writer. Anyway, her letter said that the Wagner family was in dire straits. Honus had married late in life and had two daughters whom he called "his boys." The lady said they hardly had enough to eat. Because of the high rate of unemployment and scarcity of dollars to spend on anything beyond necessities, his sporting goods business in Pittsburgh had failed. He had other debts and couldn't get a job. The lady wrote, "He is too proud to ask for charity from the Pittsburgh club, but surely the National League should do something now for this greatest of players, now that Honus is sorely in need." So I wrote a piece in the *Post* on the woes of Honus and his family. After telling of the Wagner family's being just a step away from the bread line, I pitched into the National League and the Pittsburgh club for letting such a thing happen. I also wrote of other former players in want in those Depression times, with nobody doing anything about them.

I told of Wagner's loyalty to the National League during the National-American war, 1901–1902, when practically all of the big stars of the National League jumped to the new American. While Wagner remained loyal, Nap Lajoie, Willie Keeler, John McGraw, Cy Young, Ed Delahanty, Elmer Flick, Bill Dineen, Sam Crawford, and Bill Donovan sought greener pastures in the American League. Christy Mathewson jumped twice, first to the Philadelphia Athletics, and later to the St. Louis Browns, but he jumped back to New York in 1901 and was awarded to the Giants by the Peace Commissioners in 1903.

Soon after my column appeared, I received a gracious letter from

Wagner himself, thanking me for what I had done. He wrote me on February 13, 1933, as follows:

DEAR FRED:

Your article in the *Post* sure was a great one for us old-timers. If only the club owners could see it in the same light as you write it. Some of us old-timers could use a job of that kind, myself included.

I have been in the sporting goods business for thirteen years, but owing to the Depression and lack of funds for working capital, I have been unable to weather the storm. I am out now but I am still full of fight and I never quit.

I wish to thank you personally for your interest in the old-timers. Maybe something will yet develop. I have a letter from Clark Griffith telling me he brought up the subject before the club owners, but the time is not quite ripe. They, too, have been hit and unwilling to take on any more obligations at this time. However, "Griff" tells me he is strongly in favor of the idea.

Again assuring you of my appreciation of your efforts in our behalf, I remain,

Sincerely,
J. HONUS WAGNER

Reaction to the column was quick and all to the good. John Heydler, president of the National League, was one of my readers. He felt the sting of the column and sent it to Bill Benswanger, then the new young president of the Pittsburgh club. Benswanger, Barney Dreyfuss's son-in-law, had just recently taken over the presidency; the elder Dreyfuss had died in 1932, following a prostate operation, and his son Sammy, raised to be president of the Pirates, had died the same year. Both Heydler and Benswanger were by nature kind and warm-hearted men. The elder Dreyfuss had been much more hard-boiled. Neither Heydler nor Benswanger had known anything about Wagner's difficulties. Times were hard for most people, and many were too worried about their own affairs to think of people who were less flush than themselves. Benswanger, however, immediately paid off Wagner's debts, paid his rent six months in advance, and offered him a job to return to the Pirates as a coach and goodwill ambassador for a nice salary.

When Honus joined the Pirates at their 1933 training camp it was his first appearance in a Pirate uniform since the war year of 1917. In 1918 he had had some differences with Barney Dreyfuss. The war had riddled the big league teams on account of the military draft and players volunteering for service. It was the year of the 4-Fs (army rejects) and players who were too old or too young. In 1915 at the age of forty-one, Wagner had had a truly remarkable year. He played every inning of Pittsburgh's 156 games, nearly all at shortstop, and hit a satisfactory .274. The next year, by now aged forty-two, he had a falling off to 123 games but raised his batting average to .287. In 1917 he was down to 74 games and hit only .265. The old legs had slowed up; his once fine arm had lost its strength and zip. He no longer was a shortstop but played an easier position, first base. Dreyfuss felt the old gent could go one more season, 1918, but cut Wagner's pay "because of war conditions." Honus probably could have waddled through 1918, but he felt deeply hurt over the pay cut. He did not sign a contract and did not report. It left hard feelings on both sides, and Dreyfuss regarded him as just another former player who was no longer of any use. Probably few other owners of that era would have regarded their overaged players at all differently. Anyway, after his departure from the Pirates, relations between Dreyfuss and his former greatest star were strained. In the years between 1917 and 1933 there had been practically no contact between the player and his former club.

Benswanger's signing of Wagner was humane, and it also was good business. Industrial Pittsburgh had been hard hit by the Depression, but when Wagner stepped to the coach's box in the 1933 opening game, he got a hero's reception. Even though he no longer played, he still could pull them in at the gate. It was the same all over the circuit. Cities outdid themselves in welcoming Honus back to National League baseball. In New York he was honored at City Hall by the mayor, who gave him the key to the city. In Brooklyn the old Dodger and National League fans were even more demonstrative as they paraded him through the streets of downtown Brooklyn and gave him a big reception at Borough Hall.

On that visit he did not forget me. He appeared at my desk in the New York *Evening Post* office. Waving his hand in the direction of Brooklyn, he said, "You were responsible for all that."

I said, "Oh, no, Honus, they always loved you in Brooklyn."

He replied, "I know that, but your column in the winter started it all, and I am here to thank you again."

Later, whenever I visited the Pirates or stopped at their bench during pregame practice or encountered Honus in hotels and on trains, he almost embarrassed me with the profusion of his thanks. After having been out of big league ball for seventeen years, he closed with nineteen more years as a coach and goodwill ambassador. Finally, at the age of seventy-nine he called it quits with the game he loved second only to his wife and "two boys."

I find that few people today, even true fans, understand the nickname "Honus." It comes from the German name "Johannes," another form of which is "Johann"—both equivalent to our "John." ("Hans" is still another form, German and Dutch, of this name.) "Honus" is German vernacular for the last two syllables of "Jo-han-nes." A "big Honus" is a clumsy, awkward fellow, but "Honus" can also be a term of endearment as is our "Sonny" and our "Babe."

For an outstanding player, Wagner was shy. He usually dodged newspapermen, and except on the ball field, he kept out of the limelight. For example, on a hot, rainy summer day in New York the sports editor of the New York *Times* told Harry Cross, his ranking baseball writer, "Why not go up to the Ansonia Hotel where the Pirates are stopping and see whether you can get a story from the Big Dutchman?" When Harry knocked at his door, Wagner, dressed only in his shorts (it was long before any hotel had air conditioning), greeted him in a friendly spirit. "I'm from the New York *Times* and would like to do a story on you," said Harry. Wagner showed him into his bathroom. The tub was filled with cracked ice and bottles of beer. "Drink all the beer you want, but no story," said Honus.

After Wagner won his fourth straight batting championship in 1909, his sixth in seven years, the National League decided to invite their number one star to the dinner that concluded their winter meetings at New York's old Waldorf Astoria. "No, thanks" Wagner wired back to Tom Lynch, the newly elected president of the league. To an intimate, Wagner confided, "What would I do up there with all those swells? Besides, I ain't got a monkey suit and I ain't going to hire one. I don't make speeches—I let my bat speak for me in the summertime."

After his 1933 return to the Pirates, he learned to make amusing speeches at baseball dinners in Pittsburgh and in surrounding Pennsylvania, Ohio, and West Virginia. Honus was witty and interesting as the Pirates' goodwill man. In his later years he was as loquacious as he had been mute in his playing days.

Wagner also had a splendid influence on young players, especially kids who were homesick. Most of the stories he told them were pure imagination—and he did tell tall tales! Exposition Park, an early home of the Pirates, was often flooded by the Monongahela River. One day Wagner told a group of young players how he once rode his horse across the river to get to the ball park. "I rode my horse right down to the river and I told him, 'Chief, you've just got to get me to that ball park.' He swam across the river, right into our outfield, and he let me off at second base." One of the boys spoke up and said, "Mr. Wagner, I think you've telling us a lot of lies." Wagner replied, "Son, maybe I did exaggerate a bit, but I never told you or any of the other players anything that you couldn't repeat to your mother."

Wagner as a player was unbelievable. He was 5 feet 11 inches and weighed 200 pounds, but he looked taller and heavier. He was very bowlegged, and when he sped from first base to second on one of his 720 stolen bases, he looked like a hoop rolling down the base lines. Compared to the great Nap Lajoie, his nearest rival at the turn of the century, he looked clumsy and awkward. But Wagner's appearance

Honus Wagner coaching Cookie Lavagetto, 1934.   AP

was deceiving, and he was much faster than Lajoie. In the field he could move to his right or left with equal dexterity, his big hands reaching for ground balls like a lobster reaching for tidbits with its claws.

When I first met Wagner, he was, I believe, the healthiest man I knew. He said, "I never have been sick. I don't even know what it means to be sick. I hear other players say they have a cold. I just don't know what it would feel like to have a cold—I never had one." He wasn't bragging. Other players attested to that. I think he was so well put together and his system so well adjusted that his bodily functions were near to perfection. This is especially remarkable because for several years, starting at age twelve, he worked in a mine near his hometown of Mansfield, Pennsylvania, now renamed Carnegie. In the mines and later the steel mill he breathed smoke-filled air—and when he played in Pittsburgh from 1900 to 1917, Pittsburgh was truly the smoky city of the nation. Housewives would have to brush the soot off their dressers and tables every day; the stuff clung to mirrors and windows. Yet Wagner thrived and played the greatest ball in the country.

Honus wasn't married until he was forty. He rarely touched hard liquor but drank oceans of beer. "Why not? I'm the Flying Dutchman," he once said. However, disease eventually caught up with the man who didn't know what it meant to be sick. There was a deterioration of his nervous system, which lead to a weakening of his sturdy constitution, and he suffered in the last three years of his life. Death came in Carnegie, the town of his birth, on December 6, 1955.

When I am asked to pick an All-Star team of all times, there is only one position for which one player stands in a class by himself: While at first base, there is Lou Gehrig, Bill Terry, Frank Chance, the brilliant George Sisler, and the outcast Hal Chase; at second base Lajoie, Eddie Collins, Rogers Hornsby, Charlie Gehringer, and Frank Frisch; and at third Pie Traynor, Jimmy Collins, and Brooks Robinson; at shortstop only one truly great player comes to mind—Honus Wagner.

5

TY COBB: MEAN AND MAGNIFICENT

The second of my "baseball biographies" was on Tyrus Raymond Cobb. I chuckle every time I think of the naive way I acquired the material for my piece on Ty.

Since there were no public information services at the time, I sat down and wrote a letter to the postmaster of Ty's hometown, Royston, Georgia. I asked him what kind of boy Ty was, how and where he learned his baseball, and what his family background was. Fairly promptly I received a lengthy, friendly reply! I still recall one sentence of it: "Tyrus Cobb was a good boy and always attended Sunday School." (Later I found there was an explanation for Cobb's attendance record.) His father had been a state senator and later was superintendent of schools for Banks County, in which lay the small town of Royston. My postmaster-correspondent said Tyrus had played well as a teenager for the red-suited Royston Rompers. The father had objected strongly to his son's determination to become a professional ballplayer, but Tyrus persisted.

That was a starter. Soon I obtained more information from the Reverend John Yarborough, better known locally as Brother John. Brother John was Ty's former Sunday School teacher, assistant pastor of the Cobb family's Methodist Church, and catcher-manager of the Royston Rompers. He was a red-haired evangelist, and one of the requisites for playing on the Rompers was to be a member of Brother John's class; and if a boy missed a class, he spent the next ball game on the bench. Young Cobb easily met that requirement and Brother John was the first to recognize that Ty had baseball skills surpassing those of the other

Ty Cobb in a Detroit uniform in 1905. Ty wrote in 1947 that this picture was probably taken in Detroit at old Bennett Park, and only because he was a rookie playing his first game.

Royston boys. Dad Cobb wanted his son to go to college and become a doctor. That sounded good to Ty, but the feel of a bat meeting a baseball, the fun of stealing bases, and the challenge of combat with other young men won out. He was soon, at age seventeen, writing all the clubs in the South Atlantic (Sally) League advertising his talents and asking for a tryout. Not a single club replied.

Cobb recognized his need for help, so he told Brother John of his ambition to become a big leaguer—one of the best, he insisted—and asked Brother John's assistance. The Reverend Mr. Yarborough said he would pray about it. As he told me, "I did pray about it. And I weighed all the sins ball players are prone to encounter—wine, women, song, and gambling—with Cobb's unquestionable skills, his ambition to star in the game, his great desire." After thinking and praying, Brother John told Ty, "I have prayed, and the answer I get seems to be that you should forget baseball and follow your father's plan for you to get an education and become a doctor. But if the baseball in your blood won't let you do that, then I will give you a letter of introduction to the owner of the Augusta club. But I warn you, you will not last out the season."

"Why not?" the hurt Cobb snapped.

"You are too butt-headed, quarrelsome, and resentful over being given orders," Brother John snapped back. "You will be fined and fired before the season is over!"

How right Brother John was quickly proven! Tyrus Raymond Cobb was signed by the Augusta club, but after playing two games he was fired by a hard-boiled manager, Con Strouthers, who told him, "I only want players who follow orders."

Cobb promptly hooked up with another club in Anniston, Alabama. When he wrote his father of his move, the senior Cobb, though still disapproving of his son's choice of careers, wired back: "NOTE NEW ADDRESS. DO NOT COME HOME A FAILURE."

"That wire," Ty told me years later, "spurred me on. I carried it with me for years. And I never did go back to Royston a failure."

Cobb played twenty-two games for Anniston, hitting .370, and he got another chance with Augusta and fared better under his new manager, Bill Leidy, a grizzled old first baseman from Phillipsburg, New York. Leidy seemed to recognize the boy's inherent capabilities and worked with Cobb for hours on the things he had learned in many years in the minor leagues. When the 1904 season was over, Cobb was down to .237 and had stolen only one base, but he knew he was on his way. Grantland Rice, then writing for the Atlanta *Journal*, began to print notes in that paper and in *The Sporting Life* to the effect that one Ty Cobb was attracting attention and showing promise in Augusta and Anniston: "This Cobb has great talent and may be one of the coming stars of baseball," and "Cobb hits well and has speed on the bases."

Actually, Granny was being conned by Cobb, who composed notes to Rice saying how good he was and signing the names of Augusta and Anniston fans who wanted to tip Rice off. Later in life these two great friends had many a laugh over Ty's boyhood publicity stunt.

In the spring of 1905 Cobb was hot with the Augusta team. Soon he had his first opportunity to look at a big league team, for the Detroit Tigers, under manager Bill Armour, trained in Augusta and played exhibition games with the Augusta teams. In these games Cobb ran and ranted. He got his share of base hits, and once on first base he was always looking to steal another. At first the big leaguers took the kid as a joke and spoke of him as "that crazy kid who is always running." When they joshed him he always talked back and frequently called them damn Yankees. The Tigers naturally retaliated by calling him a damn Rebel, adding, "Hasn't anyone down here told you the Civil War is over?"

When the Detroit club broke camp at Augusta they left behind for "ground rent," a young right-handed pitcher named Eddie Cicotte, who would become one of the White Sox players to be disbarred from baseball in 1920 as a result of charges of throwing the 1919 World Series. Cicotte and Cobb were just two of the remarkable group of players on that Augusta minor league team. There was also Nap Rucker, to become Brooklyn's top left-hander before Sandy Koufax, and infielder-outfielder Clyde Engle, who later played with the Yankees and Red Sox and who hit the outfield fly in the 1912 World Series on which Fred Snodgrass made his ignoble muff. Despite this core of superb talent, Augusta finished only fourth in an eight-club league in 1905.

This finish was through no fault of young Ty Cobb, not yet nineteen years old. Ty hit .326 and stole forty bases and had no need of further self-promoting notes to Granny Rice, who incidentally was now the Sally League's secretary. In fact, before the season ended Cobb was plucked off the Augusta roster to help fill gaps in the Detroit outfield caused by injuries.

Will today's readers believe that Cobb was acquired by Detroit for a mere $700? He was, and it happened like this. Before Armour left Augusta in late March 1905, he made an agreement with the Augusta club whereby Detroit acquired the right to buy the pick of the club's players for $500 for delivery in 1906. Armour sent his scout Heinie Youngman to look over Augusta's personnel and to pick the player he regarded most highly. Youngman quickly decided there was no contest—Cobb stood out. To persuade the Augusta owner to part with Cobb before the season was over—in view of the pressing need in the Detroit outfield—the Detroit club threw in another $200. This immortal Ty Cobb was acquired by Detroit for $700—surely the baseball bargain of all time.

At Detroit, Cobb was stuck quickly in the middle of an outfield between Matty McIntyre in left field and Sam Crawford in right. In forty-one games he met with indifferent success—a batting average of .240 and one stolen base. But baseball men pronounced him a good prospect and they became true prophets the very next season. Though he didn't open the 1906 season—Armour played an outfield of Davey Jones, McIntyre, and Crawford—injuries again gave him his chance. Once in the lineup he started to hit with the regularity of Sam Crawford, and no manager after that would think of returning him to the bench. He hit .320 in ninety-seven games, his first of a string of twenty-three consecutive seasons batting over .300—only one of this man's many records.

How Ty fared with his "butt-headed and quarrelsome" nature that Brother John worried about is another subject entirely. It was almost a fight a day. He fought with nearly every member of the Detroit team and licked most of them. The outstanding exception was his fight with catcher Charlie Schmidt, a two-hundred-pound husky from Arkansas. Schmidt gave him a bad beating as the other Tigers howled with delight. Schmidt was a remarkably strong man; later as a Dodger coach he drove nails into the clubhouse floor at Ebbets Field, using his fists as a hammer.

Cobb was, of course, hazed unmercifully by the older Detroit players. Hazing rookies was then practiced much more than it is today. If the young player took it in stride, the hazing soon quieted down. If the rookie was fresh and talked back, as Cobb did, they gave him the full treatment. They sawed young Ty's bats in half, tried to push him away from the batting cage when it was his turn to bat, put crazy things in his locker, mocked his Georgia accent.

Tyrus was born in the Deep South only twenty-one years after General Lee's surrender at Appomattox. Hatred of the North and bitterness over Sherman's march through Georgia were ingrained in most every Georgia boy born in that period. Cobb also came from an area predominantly Protestant. He knew few Catholics until he got into baseball—and had foolish ideas about them. Most of Cobb's new companions were northerners, and perhaps half of them were Catholics. This new social environment was bound to arouse forces within Cobb's makeup of which he had no understanding. The situation was made worse by Cobb's combative nature.

Ty had a contempt for black people and in his own language, "he never would take their lip." In his early Detroit years he had to keep out of the state of Ohio for a year and a half to avoid arrest for knifing a Negro waiter in Cleveland. The Detroit club eventually settled the case out of court by paying off the waiter. "Gabby" Street, Rogers Hornsby, and Tris Speaker, fellow stars from the old Confederate states, told me they were members of the Ku Klux Klan. I do not know whether Cobb was a Klansman, but I suspect he was. His general attitude toward black fellow citizens and his unreasoning dislike for the Church of Rome and its hierarchy clearly made him eligible for Klan membership.

Despite troubles in the clubhouse and off the field, the 1907 season saw a star of first magnitude ascend, following the naming of Hugh Jennings, ironically a Knight of Columbus, to the post of manager on the Detroit club. Jennings (now in the Hall of Fame) had been a marvelous shortstop for the legendary Baltimore Oriole National League champions in 1894–6. He was an intimate friend of John McGraw, Giants manager, who played beside him at third base for Baltimore. McGraw, Willie Keeler, and Jennings were the fastest base runners on the old Baltimore team. Hughie liked fast runners and running teams, and had early decided to make full use of "the crazy kid who was always running," Ty Cobb.

It was a great year for Jennings and Cobb. Jennings won Detroit's first American League championship by two and one half games in a close battle with Mack's Philadelphia Athletics. Cobb won his first of twelve American League batting titles with .350, and under Jennings's new speed plan, stole forty-nine bases. Ty had won his first batting championship before he was twenty-one years old.

Jennings's quick pennant was not a new man's lucky flag, for the Tigers repeated in close races in 1908 and 1909, while Cobb stretched his string of batting titles to three.

Neither Jennings nor Cobb did well in their three World Series appearances. In 1907 after a first-game tie with Chicago the Tigers lost four straight and scored only three runs. In 1908, again playing the Cubs, the Tigers won only the third game and were shut out in the last two. In 1909, against the Pittsburgh Pirates, the Tigers did much better, winning games two, four, six, but losing the wind-up seventh game by a humiliating 8–0 shutout to Babe Adams, who won three for the Pirates.

Except for 1908, when Ty hit .368, his World Series hitting was mediocre. He batted only .219 in 1907 and .231 in 1909. During his long American League career he never had another chance to face National League World Series pitching.

"I didn't do much in my three World Series, I know," Ty once admitted to me. "I was very young, and in 1907 and 1908 I was batting against the best three-man staff in the game: Mordecai Brown, Orville Overall, and Ed Ruelbach. (In these two years, Brown's won-lost record was 49–15; Overall's 38–19; Ruelbach's 42–15.) In 1909, against Pittsburgh, that youngster Babe Adams was very tough on all of us. I have often wished that when I was at the peak of my playing skill in my late twenties or early thirties, I had had another crack at a World Series. I'm sure I would have done better. But that chance never came to me."

Jennings stopped winning pennants in 1909, but Cobb didn't stop being the leading American League batsman and often the leader in stolen bases. He won annual batting titles up through 1915, yielded for one year to his friend Tris Speaker, and then won three more in a row, 1917, 1918, and 1919—twelve batting championships out of thirteen. What a magnificent record! He also stole a total of 892 bases for an American League record. In 1915 he stole 96 bases for the longtime major league high. For years this mark was believed to be unbeatable, but Maury Wills of the Los Angeles Dodgers erased it in 1962 with 104 steals, and Lou Brock of the Cardinals advanced it to 118 in 1974. (In my opinion TV cameras and slow-motion photography give modern base runners a significant advantage over players of more than twenty years ago. It is now possible for Lou Brock or Pete Rose to scrutinize in close-up photography Luis Tiant's motion, for example, and learn from it—a huge advantage for them over Cobb.)

In late years Hank Aaron of Atlanta and Milwaukee has closed down a number of Cobb's most cherished records, but Ty's total of 4,191 hits remains untouchable. He still holds the top major league lifetime batting average of .367 and shares with Rogers Hornsby and Jesse Burkett (an old-timer of 1890–1905) the honor of three .400 batting averages—.420 in 1911, .410 in 1912, and .401 in 1922.

Even as Cobb established these great records, his bullheadedness and love of combat made space in the newspapers along with the hits that helped Detroit win ball games. Cobb usually could be depended on for at least one newsworthy fight a season. One was with a delivery boy who left the family groceries at his home in Detroit; another was with Umpire Bill Evans under the Cleveland stands; a third was with Charlie Herzog in the latter's hotel room in Dallas. He cowed infielders and catchers by filing his spikes to a razor's edge while sitting on the Detroit bench. It was a trick he learned from Jennings, the old Oriole. Cobb's most notable spiking incident came in Philadelphia late in the 1909 season when he cut a sixteen-inch tear in Baker's knickers and the cut on Baker's leg needed ten stitches. For the rest of the series Cobb needed a Philadelphia police motorcycle escort to take him to and from Shibe Park, and there was a wall of uniformed and plainclothes police between right fielder Cobb and the Philadelphia overflow crowd in front of the right field bleachers. Enraged fans wrote letters to Philadelphia newspapers, threatening violence to Cobb.

In New York in 1912 he climbed into the grandstand to get at a pestering, noisy New York fan who was shouting insults at him. Cobb was hardly guiltless in prolonging the incident. All of us writers in the old wooden press box could hear every word of the exchange between Cobb and the insulting fan. I recall Ty shouting at his tormenter, "I was out with your sister last night." The fan yelled an epithet back at him, one that any southerner would well resent, and Cobb really blew

Ty Cobb's sliding skill is depicted vividly here. The third baseman is Frank Baker of the A's.

This famous picture of Cobb making third base in 1909 may be the earliest baseball action photo to survive. The third baseman is Jimmy Austin of the New York Highlanders.   C. M. Conlon, New York *Evening Telegram*

up. He leaped over a rail that separated the playing field from the grandstand, climbed up twelve rows, and took a swing at his tormenter. He stopped swinging only when he noticed that the little man was a cripple. His name was Lucker and he worked in the pressroom of one of the New York newspapers. (Lucker also was a minor Tammany politician.) Umpire Silk O'Loughlin put Cobb out of the game, and that night Ty received a telegram from the league president, Ban Johnson: "YOU ARE SUSPENDED UNTIL FURTHER ORDERS."

Even though Cobb wasn't a popular player, not even on his own team, in this incident he was well supported by his fellow Tigers. A telegram was sent to Johnson, signed by all the players, to the effect that if the suspension was not lifted, the players would not play the next scheduled game in Philadelphia. A team of semipros was hastily assembled by Jennings and his coaches Jim McGuire and Joe Sugden, aided also by Connie Mack. It was necessary for the Detroit club to put a team on the field to avoid a league fine of $5,000.

The pitcher on this hodgepodge Detroit team was a Jesuit priest, Albert Joseph Travers, who later became dean of Philadelphia's St. Joseph's College. He was offered $25 by Jennings and was paid an extra $25 for completing the game. The other Tigers-for-a-day were reward-

Hugh Jennings, longtime Detroit manager and coach, going into his unforgettable Indian war dance, complete with war whoops, in his third base coaching box. *The Sporting News*

ed with a $10 bill. One of them was Joe Maharg—a name which, read backwards, gives his real name, Graham—a gambler and preliminary fighter who later was a go-between in the Black Sox Scandal of 1919–20. The Athletics won the farcical game, 24–2, with Travers going the full nine innings. Eddie Collins, Amos Strunk, and Stuffy McInnis each fattened their batting averages with four hits. Collins also stole five bases.

League president Johnson, roaring in from Chicago, was indignant at the burlesque and threatened vengeance on the striking players. Sunday, May 21, was an off-day, and Johnson assembled all the Detroit players who had signed the telegram in his hotel room. He threatened to throw out of baseball any player who refused to play in the next scheduled game in Washington. Ban was all-powerful then, and when the lion roared, everyone stood at attention. Meekly the strikers went back to work the next day. Johnson fined each player who struck $100. Cobb got off with a $50 fine and a ten-day suspension. An offshoot of this rumpus was the start of the Players Fraternity, with Cobb and Mathewson serving as vice-presidents.

In the last six years of Cobb's long stay in Detroit he served as player-manager. His performance as a manager was not regarded as one of his successes, but Ty, of course, would argue that he was a good one. About his wealth there was little or no argument. The only question about it was its size. Cobb was probably the wealthiest of all ball players, certainly of his era. He got into Coca-Cola early, and his original batch of stock was split and split and split as sales zoomed nationally. He was also an early investor in Detroit automobile stocks, which grew in value almost as fast as his Coca-Cola stock. Some of the more financially knowledgeable baseball officials, discussing the subject in my presence one evening about the time of Ty's retirement, estimated his wealth at about $7 million. That would be $20 million today.

In 1926 Cobb and Tris Speaker were beset with the gravest problems of their respective careers. Indeed, both were close to expulsion from baseball. About a month after the close of the 1926 season, word came out of Cleveland that Speaker, who had a fine second-place finish that season as playing manager, had decided to get out of baseball and give full time to a Cleveland trucking business. Equally perplexing was a statement from the Detroit club that Ty Cobb would be retired. All over the country baseball fans and sports writers were asking why.

Later it came out that both superstars had been "dropped" from the American League on the recommendation of league president Johnson at a special meeting of the American League club presidents. Ban had somehow got possession of two letters written back in 1919, one signed by Ty Cobb and the other by Joe Wood, onetime Red Sox pitcher and in 1919 a Cleveland outfielder and buddy of Speaker's. The letters were addressed to Hub Leonard, in 1919 a pitcher for Detroit, and the subject was a suspicious game played between Detroit and Cleveland late in that very bad year of baseball "fixing." The letters suggested strongly that the Indians allowed the Tigers to win. Furthermore, some of the players who were "in" on the fix bet as much money as they could put down on Detroit's winning that afternoon. Speaker was not mentioned in the letters that were printed in 1926, but since Wood, Speaker's pal, wrote one of the letters, Tris was regarded as having to know what was going on.

At the time of the 1919 game in question, the Chicago White Sox had clinched the American League pennant and Cleveland had clinched second place. All that was in doubt was third place and third-place money, which were being contested by Detroit and New York.

When the American League presidents decided to drop the two superstars, nothing was said of the suspected "fix" in the public announcement because Ban Johnson did not wish to hurt their families. The clamor of the American press, however, made it necessary to reveal the evidence Johnson had. Speaker made no attempt to reinstate himself and seemed willing to move silently into the trucking business. Cobb, however, backed by U.S. Senator Hoke Smith of Georgia, put up stiff resistance to his ouster. The fans on the whole were on the players' side.

Commissioner Landis, then feuding with Johnson, took over the case and summoned Cobb, Speaker, Wood, and Hub Leonard to his Chicago office for a hearing. Cobb, Speaker, and Wood attended, as did several employees of the Detroit club who were supposedly there when the fix was arranged and bets were placed with a bookmaker. However, Leonard, who apparently brought the case to Johnson's attention, refused to come east. Landis wired him and telephoned him, but Leonard, who was doing well out of baseball in California, stubbornly refused to attend the confrontation with Cobb. Ball players who knew of Cobb's terrible temper told me that Leonard was afraid to come to the hearing for fear that Cobb would tear him apart physically. Landis's eventual decision, acquitting Cobb, Speaker, and Wood, who was by then baseball coach at Yale, was centered on the failure of Leonard to come to the Chicago hearing. "I cannot hold these men guilty if the accuser fails to confront the accused despite all the pressure I have brought upon him," said Landis in his finding. Knowing full well that Ban Johnson had said, "Neither Cobb nor Speaker will play again for the American League," Landis gave an outright order that the American League must find employment for these two superstars. Several National League clubs had made offers to the players, but Landis knew that if they went into the National League, Johnson would have won a nominal victory. There was no love lost between Johnson and Landis.

I understood and accepted Landis's finding. Even though the letters written to Leonard were incriminating, the affair concerned a matter which had happened seven years before and in the fag end of a bad season for baseball in which gambling had penetrated the game, but had now in 1926 been pretty well sealed out. I felt, as I think Landis did, that to expel these superstars of baseball on less than conclusive evidence might have given professional baseball a blow from which it could not recover.

So Cobb was signed by the Philadelphia Athletics and Speaker by the Washington Senators. In 1928 "Spoke" joined Ty on the Athletics, and both went out together on a team which finished only two games behind the great New York Yankees of that year. Cobb played his last game a few months from his forty-second birthday. His joints were creaky, and he was battered from nearly a quarter of a century of base running, but still he closed with a remarkable batting average of .323.

Ty Cobb was so complex it is difficult to sort out his many aspects. He certainly had his good qualities, which were perhaps shown only to friends of his own choosing. When you were his guest he was a magnanimous host and entertaining conversationalist. He did not hold his enmities—though he and Sam Crawford feuded most of the years they were top stars on the Tigers, Ty for years championed Sam for election into the Hall of Fame and saw it happen in 1957.

After Cobb became a citizen of California in his retirement, he returned to his native Georgia to build a memorial center in Royston for his parents. Their tragedy had left a deep scar in Cobb's psyche. In 1907, the year he won his first batting championship, his mother shot and killed his father. The county school superintendent supposedly was on a visit to a school at the other end of the county and was not expected back that night. When a man entered the house, Mrs. Cobb thought he was an intruder. In the semidarkness she called to him to stop, not recognizing the man was her husband. Then she shot and killed him. That was the story told to the county sheriff and he accepted it. Another version was that there was a love triangle and Senator Cobb, as he was called, did not go out of town, but upon returning home, found a male visitor in his house. Supposedly there was an argument, a shot was fired, and Mr. Cobb fell dead. This version was printed in an issue of *Baseball Magazine* in the 1960s.

Ed Barrow, a man who knew Cobb from his days as a rookie player with Augusta, said that tragedy helped make Cobb the mean and successful player he was. The trouble with this theory is that Cobb was like that before the tragedy occurred. All I can add is that from conversations I had with Cobb I know he loved and venerated his father. I never heard him mention his mother.

Cobb certainly wasn't loved by players with the affection they felt for Hans Wagner in an earlier era and later for Babe Ruth. Fans recog-

Ty Cobb in his later years as a player.   Paul Thompson

nized him as a great player, a dynamo, a fighter; but he lacked warmth as a human being and anything approaching love for—even understanding of—other people.

I believe that Cobb had a cruel streak in his nature. Newspaper friends who were at the hunting lodge called Dover Hall when Cobb was also a guest told of an incident with a dog. A number of hunting dogs were stabled around the lodge, and everyone had been told never to pet one of them. While Cobb sat on the porch, one of the hunting dogs started up the porch, perhaps expecting a few pats from some of the uninitiated northern guests. Cobb sprang from his chair, cursed the dog, and kicked him so hard the squealing hound landed some fifteen feet away. "That damned dog knows he doesn't belong here," Cobb explained to my newspaper friends. "He is a working dog, and down here we never pet a working dog."

Cobb was undeniably and notoriously a difficult person to live with. He always was on the go, wanted to go somewhere, wanted to do things. His first wife, a charming Augusta girl, the mother of his five children, started divorce proceedings against Ty three times and then dropped action because of the children. She finally went through with it on the fourth attempt, saying, "I simply can't live with that man any longer." After half a dozen years Tyrus tried it again, wedding a lady from Canada, but their meeting wound up in a divorce court two years later.

Joe E. Brown, the deceased movie comic and father of Joe L. Brown, former general manager of the Pirates, told me he spent about a week with Cobb in the last four months of Ty's life. "I've had a lot of time to think things over and meditate on things of the past, what I did and what I didn't do," Cobb told Brown. "I think if I had my life to live over again, I would do things a little different. I was aggressive, perhaps too aggressive, maybe I went too far. I always had to be right in any argument I was in, and wanted to be first in everything."

Joe Brown said, "No, Ty, you wouldn't have done anything different, you just had to be yourself—Ty Cobb."

A few days later Cobb returned to the same subject with Brown, saying with a tinge of regret, "Joe, I do indeed think I would have done some things different. And if I had, I would have had more friends."

6

HITS ARE MY BREAD AND BUTTER

In my first year in the press box and my first year at official scoring, Frank Farrell, president of the Highlanders, called me up and said, "What does a player have to do to get an error in our park?" I said, "Make an error." And he said, "Then why don't you put some errors in our box scores? Yesterday Jack Knight made two errors that you scored as hits for Ty Cobb."

"Well," I said, "about those hits, I thought one of them was too hot to handle. The other one was hit to deep short, Knight had a long throw, and maybe the throw pulled Chase a little off the bag, but I thought Cobb had it beaten anyway. So I marked them both hits."

"Listen," Farrell retorted, "when my players make errors, I want you to give errors. I pay Jack Knight forty-five hundred dollars a year (supposedly a lot of money in 1911) for playing shortstop, and when he makes errors I want you to give 'em to him."

That telephone conversation I will let stand as a fair measure of this not untypical franchise owner of the period. I knew enough about the relations between Farrell and Knight to know that Farrell was looking for statistical support to help him knock down Knight's salary when contract time came around. The more errors made, the lower the offer to him would be. The statistical game can be played by owners as well as by players.

Criticism for a scoring decision can also come from parties with no financial interest in it. I once drew about my head the unleashed sarcasm of Bill Hanna, then of the New York *Sun-Herald*. It was in 1919 and I was substituting as official scorer for Bill Farnsworth. It involved a no-hit game pitched by a Cleveland pitcher, Ray Caldwell, a former Yankee. It happened that my wife and Mrs. Caldwell were very friendly, and the Caldwells and Liebs frequently visited each other's houses. But this had nothing to do with my judgment on the play that gave Ray his no-hitter. In the middle of the game Frank Baker, Yankee third baseman, hit a smash towards right field. Bill Wambsganss, the Cleveland second baseman, who would make an unassisted triple play in the World Series in 1920, was playing Baker deep in the hole, on the grass. As I saw the play, Wamby made a good play to knock it down, but then cuffed it around enough to let the slow Baker beat his throw. I thought this added up to an error, I so scored it, and didn't give any further thought to it. The next morning Hanna started his story of the game in this manner: "A no-hit game was credited to Slim Caldwell at the Polo Grounds yesterday. It was so scored by the official scorer, but I will insist till my dying day that it was not an error but a hit for Frank Baker."

Bob Shawkey, who pitched thirteen years for the Yankees, also reproved me for that scoring decision. "I think you took a hit away from Bake yesterday," he told me through the screen before the next day's game. I laughed. "Bob, I think it's funny for a pitcher to be grousing at my scoring another pitcher with a no-hitter. And Caldwell was your pitching teammate here until last year." Then I closed the door on him by telling him what is the essential truth about any "score" a scorer makes: "It was my judgment that it was an error, that's the way I scored it, and that's the way it goes into the official records."

Most controversies over a scoring decision burn themselves out quickly, but a decision I made in August 1922 had repercussions for several months and kept popping up years later. It is the story behind Cobb's .401 batting average in 1922. In brief, a hit I scored for Cobb—and I wasn't even the official scorer—made it possible for Cobb to hit .400 for the third time. Without that hit he would have finished at .399.

A bit of background is necessary to understand the tangle. First, a man named Irwin Howe, who was the American League statistician, also ran a baseball statistics bureau and sold unofficial hitting, pitching, and fielding records to a lot of newspapers. Now, Howe took his figures day by day from the AP box scores, and I was scorer for the AP, but not the official scorer.

On the day of this particular play it had started to rain, and I moved back into the stands from the uncovered press box. But Jack Kieran, then of the *Tribune* and that year the official scorer, stayed at his post despite the rain. When Cobb came to the plate on the disputed play, it was raining fairly hard and the infield was getting gooey. Cobb hit a grounder toward Everett Scott, the Yankee shortstop. It rolled close to the ground, and in going over a soggy field a ball picks up a lot of wet soil. Scott had just a little trouble handling the muddy ball, and he

Official scorers, World Series of 1923. Left to right: Frank (Buck) O'Neill, George W. Daley, Fred Lieb (chief scorer).　C. W. Conlon, *Evening Telegram*

didn't get Cobb by a full step. Considering the condition of the field and Cobb's speed, I gave it a hit. I wasn't near Kieran and gave no further thought about it. Neither did Kieran, who sent in an official score for the game, showing Scott had made an error.

Meanwhile Howe, using my AP score, fed "hit" into his computations, and at the end of the season Howe's unofficial statistics showed Cobb at .401 (his third season batting over .400) and the official figures in due course showed him at .3995. Now if the difference had been between Cobb's hitting .348 and .346, Howe would have thought no more about it. It was very common for unofficial and official averages to vary a point or two. But here the question was whether this immortal had or had not again hit the magic .400 figure. If Howe had just given out his 1922 official American League averages—with Cobb hitting .401—without comment, I feel no one would have challenged. Neither the public, nor the baseball writers knew anything about the August incident. However, perhaps from a sense of guilt, Howe sent out a brief explanation along with the figures to explain Cobb's .401 average. It went: "I noted that the averages reached from my official scoring sheets had Cobb hitting .3995. With the unofficial averages giving him .401, I felt how can we deprive this great player of a third .400 average over a fraction of a point?

"It was then that I compared Cobb's official sheets with the unofficial figures we had in the office, game for game, until we reached the August game in the New York Polo Grounds in which Kieran had scored as an error for Scott, and Fred Lieb's Associated Press showed a hit for Cobb. I took into consideration Lieb's long experience as a scorer. Since Kieran was scoring officially for the first year, I felt I was justified in using Fred Lieb's score."

In the meantime Ban Johnson, American League president, got into the act. Ban was a stickler for supporting his umpires, and now he stood behind his designated statistician, Howe, one hundred percent. Johnson and I exchanged some vitriolic telegrams, which appeared in the national press. He said he always had regarded me as a competent scorer, and he was dismayed that in the Cobb case I did not have the guts to stand up for my score. My reply was that my scoring was not an issue. I was standing up for a principle, that the official scorer is official. The fat was now in the fire. In no time at all the situation was splashed across the sports pages, and the fans for the most part were on Cobb's side. The New York writers, I'm happy to say, argued that the official scorer should have the final decision, and there wasn't any point in having official scorers if they'd throw out one of his decisions just to give a man a .400 batting average.

So the case came up at our Baseball Writers Association meeting the following winter. I was in an awkward position, as I was both national president and chairman of the New York chapter. Speaking as chairman in behalf of John Kieran, who felt concerned that his score had been tossed out and mine accepted, I told the members that I felt the same way: Kieran was the official scorer, and if the situation had been reversed and my official score had been tossed out, I'd have been incensed.

Some of the chapters, particularly Detroit and Philadelphia, were strongly in favor of Cobb. After I had made my statement several writers asked, "Don't you like Cobb? Are you penalizing him for something he may have done in New York or to you? Why would you deprive Cobb of a .400 average for a fraction?" There were other chapters that stood behind Kieran loyally. They were basically defending the official scoring system and trying to make other writers see that their turn at official scoring could come to them some time, and also that to change something for Cobb opened the door to protests by some Joe Blow backed by a few friends.

When it came time to vote, two of the chapters, Brooklyn and Washington, decided to abstain. Then by a narrow 5–4 vote, the Association upheld Kieran's official score. Furthermore it added a statement to the resolution to the effect that the 1923 *Baseball Guides* should be instructed to carry an asterisk after the .401 figure, the footnote reading, "Not recognized by the Baseball Writers Association."

John Kieran was not at all satisfied with the decision and I fully understand why. He had been supported at the end, when the vote was taken, by only five of the eleven chapters—a minority—counting the abstainers as nonsupporters. They had let an "unofficial" hit carry the day. They had undercut the official scoring system. It took some years before the kettle stopped simmering in the Association over this one. And as an aftermath of the controversy, the Baseball Writers Association changed its bylaws so that no one could hold the positions of national president and chapter chairman at the same time.

The next year, in 1923, I became more personally involved in a different kind of controversy with Cobb. It happened this way: The managers of the teams playing each day always gave the evening papers the starting lineups about ten minutes before game time, which then was 3:30. This enabled the writers to telegraph them downtown and catch one of the early editions. We were consistently having trouble getting the lineup of the Detroit Tigers when they came to town. Cobb by this time was player-manager. Somebody complained to Jack Lenz, the announcer. Jack blamed Cobb: "Cobb doesn't give us his lineup until just the minute the game starts." (In those days before public address systems, an announcer with a big cheerleader's megaphone would read off the lineups, facing the stands from behind the home plate.) We persuaded Lenz to complain to Cobb, whose response was, "Why should I give a damn about those twenty-five- and thirty-dollar-a-week sons of bitches?"

The next day in the *Evening Telegram* I took a whack at Cobb for his high-handedness towards the press and wrote that he had done pretty well over the years and that a lot of us "twenty-five- and thirty-dollar-a-week" boys had probably given him a lot of doubtful hits. I had in mind the two I had given him in 1911 that Frank Farrell had complained to me about.

The next day Cobb sent the Tigers' trainer up to the press stand with a message: "Mr. Cobb wants to see you after the game." So when I saw Cobb, he began, "I don't like what you wrote about me yesterday, that wasn't very nice." I said, "Well, I don't like the way you acted when Lenz asked you to send the lineups a little earlier." We got to jawing at each other and he said, "Do you believe that stupid SOB over me?" I said, "I have no reason to think that Jack would lie." Cobb said, "Well, we may have to have this out man to man." I well knew Cobb's reliance on fisticuffs to settle arguments, so grinning weakly, I said, "You probably weigh one hundred eighty-five and I weigh one hundred sixty-five, and you're in shape and I'm not, so I guess I'm not in your class."

Oddly enough, my lack of interest in a fight didn't rouse him further, and he soon calmed down. Out of this came a good friendship between us. I remember especially an all-day conversation with him in 1931, as I stopped over in San Francisco after my arrival from Japan at the end of a tour with an all-star team. Cobb, then in retirement, was living in the suburb of Atherton. Ty was on a talking jag that day—he had an old acquaintance to talk baseball with and wouldn't let me go. During the evening he pumped me about his chances of getting the general manager's position with the Philadelphia Phillies; he thought he could put some guts into the team and get it out of its rut in the second division. I remember recommending that he buy the Phillies, a franchise he could have picked up for perhaps $300,000 at the time. But Ty, perhaps the prudent investor, wasn't interested in financial control or ownership. Nor did he want another job as field manager. He wanted front-office managerial control, a salary commensurate with his baseball name, and a return to baseball. As it turned out, he never did get back inside.

Equal in importance, in the realm of baseball statistics, to my scoring the hit that ultimately gave Ty Cobb his .401 batting average in 1922 was the decision I made against Howard Ehmke of the Red Sox the next year. This was, in retrospect, perhaps the saddest decision I ever made, for it prevented Ehmke from becoming the first pitcher ever to throw two successive no-hitters. (Johnny Vander Meer of Cincinnati would do it for the first and only time in 1938.) Ehmke was then with the last-place Red Sox of 1923, and the Yankees were winning an easy pennant, their third in a row. Ehmke had had a great season: he would wind up winning twenty games with a bad ball club. It was in September, on what I believe was the last swing around the East for the eastern teams. The first batter for the Yankees was Whitey Witt, a fast little leadoff man who got a good jump from the plate and was quick getting down the line. So he hit a chopper down the third-base line to Howard Shanks, a former outfielder who was playing third. The ball took an odd hop, and Shanks muffled it against his chest. By the time he was ready to throw, he saw there was no chance to get Witt, and so he didn't throw. Considering all these things—the ball took a strange hop and Witt was the fastest man, I think, in the American League at that time in getting down to first base—I decided it was a hit, however scratchy. There was no murmuring over my "score" in the press box at the time.

Strange as it may seem, that was not only the only Yankee hit that day, but Witt was the only Yankee to reach first base. After that, Ehmke retired twenty-seven men in order. As early as the sixth inning some of the Boston writers said, "Don't you think you ought to change that, Fred? This man has a chance to be the first two-no-hit man." "No," I said, "I scored it a hit then, and it's a hit in the early edition of my paper, and it's a hit in my scorebook."

As the innings progressed and Ehmke went one-two-three, one-two-three, the pressure on me became heavier, and even the New York writers, Boyd of the *Evening World* especially, said, "Oh, Fred, you *must* change that!"

I said, "No, it's a one-hit game in my book and it's going to stay that way." So it went in as a one-hitter. Of course, it *was* a doubtful call on my part, and if it had happened later in the game I just might have scored it as an error for Shanks. My obstinacy about not changing my score stemmed from a talk I had in 1912 with Tom Lynch, president of the National League, best known as "king of the umpires." The day before our talk, Jeff Tesreau of the New York Giants had been given a no-hitter by the official scorer in Philadelphia under pressure after the game from Sid Mercer. Mercer was backed up by the Giants first base-man, Fred Merkle, who told the scorer that the one hit charged against Tesreau was really his (Merkle's) error. The scorer let himself be swayed and between games of a double header reversed himself. Lynch was angry at such scoring and told me never, never change a scoring decision once I had made it. "Be like an umpire," he said. "He can't be influenced by anyone to change a decision he made in the sec-ond inning. Whether right or wrong, it was his honest judgment. As a

Howard Ehmke, 1923.

scorer, hold your ground the same way. I don't like no-hitters that are scored in the clubhouse."

My ruling against Ehmke caused quite a rumpus, for the game was taken to the American League headquarters, and the editor of *Baseball Magazine* had four hundred signatures on a petition sent to Ban Johnson, American League president, protesting this scoring decision. The umpire, Tom Connally, was asked about the play and he said, "If that wasn't an error, I never saw one." That made me feel even worse. So there was quite an aftermath to it.

In the year after I had been Yankee official scorer, Ossie Vitt, then second baseman for the Detroit Tigers, came to the chicken screen in front of the press box and said, "How many hits did I get yesterday?" I looked in my score book and said, "Two." And he said, "Well, I made three." And I said, "Well, my score book says that you had two, and the other time you got on base by an error by Ward, our second baseman." Vitt said, "I got *three!*" Then I said, "What I say doesn't count anyway, because I'm not the official scorer." Vitt said, "Sam Crawford says you are." I said, "Well, I'm not."

So Vitt went back to the bench and his teammate Sam Crawford repeated I was the official scorer. "You are the official scorer." Vitt then shouted, "And I want you to know that when I make hits I want you to give them to me. *Hits are my bread and butter!*" Vitt's phrase made a good title for a *Saturday Evening Post* article I wrote a few years later. But it took a while for the players to understand I was no longer robbing them of hits as official scorer.

In 1920, as a nonvoting member of the Rules Committee of organized baseball (serving on behalf of the Baseball Writers Association) I introduced a rule whereby a batter knocking the ball out of the park in the bottom of the ninth inning or in a succeeding extra inning, would receive credit for a home run, even after the winning run was scored. The batter would also be credited with all the runs that crossed the plate on the hit, exactly as he would be if he had hit the home run in the first or eighth inning.

Up to that time if the score was, say, 1–1 in the bottom of the ninth (or tenth or eleventh) inning and a batter hit a ball into the bleachers with a man on third, the batter received credit for only a single on the theory that the game ended when the man on third scored and it took only a single to bring him in. Furthermore, the home-run hitter in this case received credit for only one run batted in.

My suggestion was hotly criticized by Hank O'Day, a veteran umpire who was one of three representatives of the National League on the committee. Hank insisted vociferously to the last that no run could be scored after the winning run had crossed the plate. This particular rule he regarded as sacred and untouchable. Hank also charged me with trying to get more home runs for Babe Ruth, whom the Yankees had bought from Boston a few weeks earlier.

In the final vote, however, my measure won, 5–1, with Hank still beating his fist on the table and shouting, "I'm telling you, it is illegal. You can't score runs after a game is over!" By now my amendment has been in the rules for over half a century, and hundreds of players have me to thank for additional home runs and RBIs credited to them under such last-inning circumstances.

Sam Crawford.

7

HEROICS AND STUPIDITIES OF THE 1911 AND 1912 WORLD SERIES

Perhaps the first World Series you ever see as a reporter is the one you remember best. Although I still get an electric charge through my body when a Tom Seaver or Catfish Hunter stares at the first opposing batter, it's not like the one I got when Christy Mathewson faced outfielder Bris Lord of the Athletics in the opening game of the 1911 series. As I look back across sixty-six years of watching the October play-offs, I find the 1911 and 1912 match-ups were unusually chock-full of sensational plays, tense pitching duels, timely extra-base hits, egregious errors of omission and commission, front-office stupidities, internal bickering and baseball oddities—the kinds of things that make for baseball legends and fuel arguments among fans. These series also provided marvelous contrasts with the way the game is played today, on the field and in the front office.

The 1911 World Series did not begin until October 14 so that Charley Ebbets might rake in a Columbus Day gate for his impoverished Dodgers. The college football season was in full swing, but that really didn't matter, for baseball still was king in the minds of most sports followers.

What I was about to watch and write about at age twenty-three came to be known as the Home Run Baker Series. In it John Franklin Baker, the Athletics third baseman, would hit two dramatic homers and become the nation's idol, foreshadowing the popular affection that began a decade later for another home-run hero, Babe Ruth.

Christy Mathewson.

The first game at New York's Polo Grounds saw Christy Mathewson, a Bucknell graduate, and Chief Albert Bender, a part-Chippewa Indian dropout from Dickinson College, facing each other. They had met once before, in the final game of the 1905 Series, with Mathewson winning, 2–0. This time New York's beloved Matty prevailed again in another pitching duel, 2–1, New York's winning run scoring on a fumble by the top star of the A's, Eddie Collins.

The second game shifted to Shibe Park, Philadelphia, and was a battle of left-handers. Connie Mack called on his veteran left-hander Eddie Plank. John McGraw, the Giants skipper, selected Rube Marquard, the transformed "$11,000 lemon." For five innings both men pitched exceedingly well. Then in the sixth inning, with the score tied 1–1, Baker delivered a blast that carried him into fame.

Eddie Collins had started the A's rally with a double to right. Then Baker swung, and swung big. "Bake" was unusually strong in the wrists, arms, and shoulders. He connected solidly with a Marquard fast ball and sent a liner over the right-field wall, which made the score 3–1 and ended the scoring.

The next morning Matty, aided by his ghostwriter (*Herald* baseball man Jack Wheeler), gave Rube quite a dressing down in his syndicated New York *Herald* column: "Marquard made a poor pitch to Frank Baker on the latter's sixth-inning home run. There was no excuse for it. In a clubhouse talk with his players, Manager McGraw went over the entire Athletics' batting order, paying special attention to the left-handed hitter, Frank Baker. We had scouted Baker, knew what pitches were difficult for him to hit, and those he could hit for extra bases. Well, Rube threw him the kind of ball that Baker likes."

The two teams were back at the Polo Grounds the next day. Pitchers then knew no such luxury as a four-day rest between games. Mathewson, winner of the first game, was back on the mound. His Philadelphia opponent was Colby Jack Coombs, winner of three games over the Cubs in the 1910 World Series. Coombs was so effective that he gave up only three hits, but he yielded one run in the third inning. After that the two pitching aces were superb, and as the game reached the late innings, the run scored by the Giants catcher Meyers looked bigger and bigger.

Big Six, another nickname for the New York pitching star, retired the dangerous Eddie Collins to start the ninth inning. Matty needed only two outs for a 1–0 shutout. Then, crash! The sound was so ominous that it seemed the whole new Polo Grounds grandstand would come

Rube Marquard   Indianapolis *Star*   Frank (Home Run) Baker.

down. Baker had again connected for a home run into the lower right-field grandstand, tying the score. Giants fans were aghast; a Baker home run off Marquard could happen, but not off Matty! I still can remember the awesome silence that followed the crash of Baker's bat. It was so quiet that those with especially good hearing could pick up the patter of Baker's feet as he romped joyfully around the bases.

While Mathewson retired the side without further scoring, there was a premonition of doom in the great crowd—a feeling that the A's would win in extra innings and eventually take the series. The depression permeated the press box, affecting even writers most loyal to the Giants.

As was feared, the game's end came in the eleventh, when errors by Herzog and Fletcher, resounding singles by Collins, Baker, and Harry Davis, were good for two runs. But the home crowd had one more near thrill. With Herzog on base, Chief Meyers drove a ball deep into the left-field bleachers that again could have tied the score. It was very near the foul line, and the American League umpire, Connolly, rightly ruled it a foul. Herzog eventually scored on an error by the usually steady Collins, but that was it. Final score: Athletics 3, Giants 2.

In the eighth inning of this third game, Fred Snodgrass, Giants center fielder, tried to go to third on a short passed ball. In sliding into the bag, Snow, as fellow players called Snodgrass, ripped a foot-long tear in Baker's knickers and dented Frank's thigh with his spikes. The play was compared to one late in the 1909 American season when Ty Cobb also spiked Baker. The newspapers and fans raised quite a storm after the game. Many of the Athletics and most Philadelphia fans felt Snodgrass had made a deliberate attempt to put Baker out of the series. Manager McGraw, a former third baseman, defended Snodgrass, saying he agreed with Ty Cobb that Baker had an awkward way of taking a throw at third base. Connie Mack got into the argument, saying Baker was one of the best fielding third basemen in both leagues, and that Snodgrass had come into the bag with a needlessly high slide. Philadelphia fans, egged on by the Philly sports writers, were prepared to give Snodgrass an overly warm welcome when he returned to Philly for the fourth game. There even were threats that Snodgrass would be shot if he appeared at Shibe Park.

Fortunately, the elements intervened to cool off the fans. For five successive days it rained hard and steadily. It took old Ben Shibe, Athletics' president-owner, a sixth day to partly dry his field by burning gasoline over its soaked sod.

The six-day interval between games three and four gave this young writer a chance to see baseball writers at play. Some had looked so serious and dedicated as they wrote or dictated their stories, especially when they put on extra steam to make an edition about to go to press. At play they were different fellows. Bill Phelon from Cincinnati was perhaps the zaniest of these writers. He and Hugh Fullerton rented a hotel room as an office and put an ad in a Philadelphia newspaper for female models.

This was an era when a young male thought he was seeing something if he beheld two or three inches of a lady's shapely ankle. It was decades before a modeling agency attendant would say "Take 'em off" to a girl under inspection for a modeling job. Bill and Hughie had lesser requests. "You young ladies will have to take off your petticoats so we can make proper measurements," Phelon told the applicants. Armed with tape measures and note pads, the crazy pair went to work, measuring busts, waists, buttocks, knees, and ankles. Fullerton would go, "Um-m-m," approvingly, and Bill would offer compliments like "What pretty knees you have! You should be in the chorus of the Follies." When baseball's high commissioner, Garry Herrmann, announced the fourth game of the Series definitely would be played on October 24, the modeling agency of Phelon and Fullerton suddenly went out of business.

Among the men I met during this playful interlude was John George Taylor Spink from St. Louis, one of the official scorers. Taylor Spink was a short and stocky man of my age, whose father was Charles C. Spink, owner of *The Sporting News*, which then was regarded as a strongly pro–American League baseball weekly. He wore a porkpie hat and a bright bow tie, and he had a hearty, boisterous laugh.

"Fred Lieb," he said when we were introduced. "Though I have never met you, I've been reading you since you succeeded my cousin Ernie Lanigan on the New York *Press*." Little did I then suspect that Taylor Spink and I would be closely associated in the later years of my life and writing career.

In addition to reverberations from the Snodgrass-Baker spiking incident, we had a Mathewson-Marquard pitching feud to help fill our World Series void. After Baker's home run off Matty had made possible the second Athletic victory, Marquard and his ghost, Frank Menke, had a merry time blistering the Giants' ace in print, in retaliation for the Mathewson-Wheeler column. The pair were at it for several days, and there were tales that the feud was genuine. "I guess I had a lot to do with it," Menke told me years later. "Marquard was interested mostly in the money he was to get out of it. He was satisfied to have me do the writing. He was pretty mad at Mathewson's blast at him after Baker's first home run. So, when Baker smacked Matty, I told Rube, 'Now is our chance to get even.' He agreed, saying 'Don't make it too easy.' So I didn't."

Eventually, on October 24, the Series was resumed at Shibe Park on a soggy field. Again it was Mathewson vs. Chief Bender. It was their third meeting in World Series competition. Mathewson had a full week's rest, but maybe it was too much. He needed to work every fourth day to be sharp, and on this occasion the Athletics had a batting picnic at his expense. In the eight World Series games that I saw Matty pitch, I never saw him used so roughly. He gave up ten hits in seven innings, seven of them doubles. None of these was a scratch infield hit or a puny fly that fell in safely. These hits crashed by the infielders, and many whistled by the outfielders for extra bases. The result was a 4–2 defeat for New York. On the A's side, Bender never was better, yielding only five hits. Josh Devore, New York's little leadoff man, who was the first I ever heard speak of the World Series as the "World Serious," said of Bender, "The Chief makes the baseball look like a pea. Who can hit a pea when it goes by with the speed of lightning?"

The Giants now had their backs to the wall. For eight innings of the fifth game at the Polo Grounds it looked like another easy victory for the A's and the end of the series. Rube Marquard again was victim of a homer, this time a three-run shot by Rube Oldring, and for five innings Jack Coombs pitched as well as in his earlier effort. Only two Giants had reached base before Coombs suffered a torn ligament in his groin while pitching to Art Fletcher in the sixth. Jack caught the sole of his left shoe and his spikes between the pitching rubber and some loose earth, and when he let go his delivery, something snapped in his lower abdomen.

Across the last three innings it was apparent to both benches and the fans that Coombs was pitching with considerable pain. Several times Connie Mack had catcher Ira Thomas or Bender go to the pitcher's box to ask Coombs about his condition and whether he wanted a relief man. Jack repeatedly shook his head and said to Thomas, "Tell Connie it's nothing serious. I'm still fast, have control of my pitches, and I think I can sew it up."

That is the way it was when, with the Giants trailing, 3–1, they came up for their ninth time at bat. Coombs got rid of the first man up, Charley Herzog, in a jiffy, and Giants fans moaned. There was a flicker of hope when Art Fletcher dropped a Texas League double in short left. But fans' hopes sagged again when the hard-hitting Indian, Chief Meyers, grounded to shortstop Jack Barry for the second out. Now the Giants were only one out away from a humiliating four straight losses after Matty's opening victory. Many of the fans already were in the aisles to get a quick start for the El train platform outside.

But there was one last lingering hope for the Giants: Otey Crandall, a former Indiana plow boy, who was the first pitcher hired solely for relief pitching. Crandall could hit as well as pitch and now batted for Red Ames, who had succeeded Marquard on the mound. Crandall was equal to the need, driving a two-bagger over Oldring's head in left field. The hit scored Fletcher, and Otey was on second base.

There were more conferences on the mound, but Coombs begged permission to finish the job. He argued that he could retire Josh Devore, who had made just three hits for the series. Thomas, Bender and Mack made the wrong decision, leaving Coombs in. Little Josh came through magnificently, rifling a single through the infield that scored Crandall with the tying run.

Josh's hit created the greatest explosion of sound I had heard in a ball park up to that time. It was also one of the most spontaneous demonstrations of unadulterated joy I have observed in my career. True, it only tied the score, but after innings of frustration it released all the pro-Giants feeling that had been bottled up. The noise could be heard all over upper Harlem and the lower Bronx, and it lasted ten minutes. Except for the outburst that followed Bobby Thomson's historic home run that won the 1951 pennant for the Giants I can think of no comparable crowd-roar. George Herbert Daley, sports editor of the New York *Tribune* who sat near me in the press box, came panting back. He had left the game when Meyers had grounded out. "I already had paid my fare on the El when I heard that roar of sound," said Daley, who had one hundred dollars riding with me on the series on the Giants. "I knew something good had happened."

In the tenth inning, Coombs, a good hitting pitcher, stayed in long enough to beat out a high chopper to first. Mack then had Amos Strunk run for Coombs, but Amos was left when Crandall, now pitching, worked a strong scoreless inning.

Eddie Plank was the Athletics reliever. Eddie couldn't stop the victory-hungry Giants, and they quickly scored the winning run on Larry Doyle's opening double, a bunt sacrifice by Snodgrass and a sacrifice fly by Merkle, a ball which Danny Murphy caught with his back against the right-field wall. Danny made a good throw to the plate. Catcher Lapp seemed to take it for granted that Doyle had legally scored, for he joined the players of both clubs in a dash across the field to the center field clubhouses, in order to beat the crowd. That night Bill Klem, the plate umpire, dropped a bomb by saying that Doyle never touched home plate. Klem had stood for about ten seconds after Doyle came sliding toward the plate. "I stood there, awaiting an Athletics protest, but none came. If Lapp or any other Philadelphia player had tagged Doyle with the ball before Larry left the park, I would have called Doyle 'Out,' and ordered the eleventh inning to begin."

Connie Mack wasn't immediately available for comment, for he was on the train back to Philadelphia when Klem made his statement. Years later Connie told me how he felt at the time. "Our players, especially Jack Lapp, erred in leaving the field so quickly. They all wanted to get to their clubhouse before the crowd charged on the field, which was the custom at the Polo Grounds. Lapp should have noticed that Doyle did not touch the plate, also that Klem made no 'safe' sign. Lapp should have gone after Doyle and tagged him. But it required an immediate action on his part, before the victory-crazed crowd poured onto the field.

"While I knew no legal run had scored, Lapp was running away. I had to consider the moment. I knew that within three minutes there would be 20,000 shouting fans on the field. Just three years earlier, the Giants had lost a National League pennant on a technicality, the failure of Fred Merkle to run from first and touch second base while the winning run was scoring on a single. The New York fans were very angry at that earlier decision.

"In 1911 we were in a tight situation after that fifth game. The Giants had snatched a victory from us. Had someone then tried to tell the Giants that they had not won that fifth game, I believe they would have torn down the place. That's why I didn't send someone after Lapp or lodge an immediate protest. Also, I was confident we would get them next day."

Though the Giants had won a spine-tingling fifth game, it was only a respite. After five nip-and-tuck ball games, the sixth in Shibe Park was an Athletics runaway, 13–2. It was disaster for McGraw and the Giants. The Giants were wearing their special black World Series uniforms with white trimmings, designed by club president Brush. He had introduced them in 1905, when his team won from the Athletics, four shutouts by Giants pitchers to one shutout by Chief Bender. This time the uniforms brought them no luck, for after the last game the black-suited Giants looked like a team of mourners.

Cartoonist McManus of Hearst's *American* drew little white Joys (the Athletics) and black Glooms (the Giants), which were spotted throughout Damon Runyon's running accounts of the games. In the last game, McManus, who must have been an American League fan, had the Joys beat up the prostrate Giants with their clubs.

All told, the A's hammered out thirteen hits which, with seven bases on balls by Ames, Wiltse, and Marquard and two Giant errors, put thirteen runs on the scoreboard. While all this was going on, Chief Bender toyed with the Giants hitters, giving up only four hits.

So ended the 1911 series, henceforth known as the Home Run Baker Series. I ask you to believe this (if you don't, look it up in the record, as Stengel would say): In 1909, his first full season, Baker hit *four* home runs. In 1910, when the A's won their first World Series from the Cubs, Baker was down to *two*. In 1911 he won the American League home-run title with a figure that must look ludicrous to the present-day fan, *eleven*. He tied Speaker in 1912 with *ten*. In his entire American League career with the Athletics and Yankees (1909–1922), the Hall of Famer known as Home Run hit only ninety-six home runs.

How good was Home Run Baker? An important fact to remember is that Bake twice interrupted his career, by holding out the entire 1915 season, and by a voluntary one-year retirement in 1920 after four good seasons with the Yankees. The Yankees persuaded him to return in 1921, when he was thirty-five, and he played two years, but only part-time, hitting nine and seven home runs. Excluding these two Indian-summer years, Bake played only ten-plus years.

Home Run Baker hit 96 career home runs. Among his contemporaries, some with much longer time spans, Wildfire Schulte of the Cubs hit 93, Fred Luderus 84, Sherry Magee 83, Larry Doyle 74. From 1908 to 1919, excluding Baker's holdout year of 1915, Cobb hit 58 homers, Speaker 45, Baker 80. Only Gavvy (Cactus) Cravath of the Phillies, who succeeded Bake to the home-run crown, did better, with 119 over thirteen seasons.

Home Run Baker has to be rated a strong hitter. If playing today, he would, in my opinion, hit forty home runs a year and be one of the most feared left-handed hitters in the game.

I was given an expert lesson on the art of handling the World Series press from Joe McCready, a former Philadelphia sports writer who was in charge at the Philadelphia end. One of the things Joe did after the game was arrange transportation, in open automobiles with police escorts, to take writers to either Broad Street station in downtown Philly or to the Pennsy's North Philadelphia Station, nearer to the ball park. Joe unwittingly provided me with my biggest non-baseball thrill of the series.

My paper, the *Press*, wanted me back in New York directly after the games in Philadelphia. Immediately after the second game I hustled downstairs from the press box to a place where I was told I could get an automobile for North Philadelphia. There was only one other passenger in the car that was ready to go, but the moment I jumped in we were off, with an officer on each of the running boards, part of the equipment on 1911 cars. It was hilarious fun at cross streets to see our two escorting officers waving their hands and yelling "Stop! Stop!" at horse-drawn carriages, teamsters on wagons, bicyclists, and drivers of other early automobiles as we whizzed by. Here I was, a kid of twenty-three, on my second automobile ride, getting treatment that might have been accorded the President, the Pope or the Prince of Wales. At the station a New York Express was waiting. As soon as the other man and I got aboard, the conductor pulled the "Go ahead" cord, and we were off to New York while the crowd was still leaving Shibe Park.

How did a deep-seated Athletics fan adjust his psyche so he could write from the viewpoint of a New York fan? From the first story I wrote for the New York *Press* under Jim Price's eye in March 1911, I realized that I was writing above all else for New Yorkers. So in my accounts of the games I suffered in print over Matty's two defeats, the havoc done by Baker and Eddie Collins, the ignominy of the 13–2 defeat, and the failure of Jack Murray, McGraw's clean-up hitter, to get a single hit in the series. But deep in my heart the Athletics victory was mighty pleasant.

One of my weirdest experiences at a World Series happened to me after the third game of the 1912 series in Boston. I hustled back from Fenway Park to the Copley Plaza Hotel, the official headquarters of the Series. Going into the men's room, I encountered a Boston fan who yelled, "Boston wins! What a great game for the Sox to pull out! What a ninth inning!"

I was surprised, having just seen the Giants vanquish the pride of all New England. Eventually I said, "But the Red Sox lost. The Giants won, 2–1."

The man's face flushed angrily, "What do you mean, the Red Sox lost? I've just come from the game. I was there, and the Red Sox beat Marquard in the ninth, 3–2."

I said, "Well, there must be a mistake somewhere. From where I saw it in the press box, the Giants won, 2–1."

This time the man exploded: "What are you doing, trying to make a damn fool out of me? I should take a punch at your nose!"

I decided to try to cool things. "Well," I said, "before we start punching noses, let us see just what happened. The sports extras of the evening papers should be out by now and we can see just who did win the game."

We went into the main lobby and saw a big-shouldered bruiser carrying a heaping armful of evening newspapers, the Boston *American.* There was the banner headline on the front page: GIANTS WIN THIRD GAME; TIE SERIES.

"Well, I'll be damned," said the man. "What happened anyway?" I said, "Well, what happened is that Devore caught that last line drive. You didn't see the catch in the light fog and gathering darkness, so you thought Boston won. And you left the park in a hurry, without checking."

World Series games started then at 3:00 P.M. It was a dusky day and as the game moved along, a light fog drifted in from Massachusetts Bay. For eight innings Rube Marquard, opposing the Sox right-hander Bucky O'Brien, had all the better of it. The Giants led, 2–0, and Rube had given up only five scattered hits. But in the bottom half of the ninth inning the Red Sox made their move. As a result of a single by Duffy Lewis, a double by Larry Gardner, and a two-base wild throw by Art Fletcher, the Red Sox had one run in and runners on third and second with two out. The crowd was on its feet and everyone was yelling like mad.

Forrest Cady, Boston's tall catcher, now slashed a long line drive into right center. Most of the crowd could see only Jake Stahl and Heinie Wagner, the runners on base, cross the plate; they thought they were bringing in the tying and winning runs. Meanwhile, out in right center field, little Josh Devore ran full speed with the crash of the bat, snatched the ball on the fly, and, without losing a step, kept on running to the center-field clubhouse. Because of the gathering darkness and the fog, only a part of the crowd could see what happened. Most thought the Sox had won and were cheering a Red Sox victory. Among these was my pugilistic friend.

It was to be like that all through the Series. Everything could and did happen. The third-game victory by the Giants was the only one the New Yorkers won out of the first five, including a tie, but the Giants wound up only a half-inning from being the Series victor and drawing the big checks, which in 1912 amounted to something over four thousand dollars—more than a lot of the players received for their entire season's work, and a sum regarded by ordinary working men as a king's ransom.

It was the year in which Joe Wood, stocky right-handed speed-ball pitcher of the Red Sox, who had come up in 1908 at the tender age of eighteen, now twenty-two, won an incredible 34 games, lost only 5, and had one winning streak of 16 straight. Boston appropriately called him Smokey Joe. We have had such fast ball pitchers as Amos Rusie, Rube Waddell, Walter Johnson, Lefty Grove, and Bob Feller, but I doubt if any of them threw any harder or faster than did Wood in 1912. Naturally Jake Stahl, the Boston manager, started Wood in the first game against twenty-three-year-old Big Jeff Tesreau, a 225-pound spitball pitcher from the Ozarks and 1912 "freshman phenom" with a 17–7 record. Wood struck out eleven Giants with his fast ball, but he wasn't invincible. The Giants got to him with some rousing hits, but Joe won, 4–3.

In a cruel schedule that required travel after each game to the other city—for most of us by the midnight sleeper, the Owl—the second game was billed for Boston, October 9. McGraw had deliberately held back his ace, Christy Mathewson, to go against a lesser opponent than Wood. In this second game, Stahl pitched left-hander Ray Collins and later called in Sea Lion Charlie Hall and Hugh Bedient. With any kind of support Mathewson could have won, but the Giants made five errors, three by Art Fletcher, their shortstop. Boston would have won in regulation innings but for a muff by Duffy Lewis on the hill in left field.

At Fenway Park in 1912 the wall known today as the Green Monster had not yet been erected. Instead, there was a much lower wall carrying billboard ads for products such as Bull Durham tobacco. But the striking feature of this left-field region was an embankment which rose up in front of the wall, perhaps eight feet high, starting its rise about twenty-five feet from the fence. So the left fielder going back for a ball over his head had to run up this embankment while keeping his eye on the ball. The great trick was not to run up to the top of the embankment for a ball that was hit too high up the wall to catch, or for a ball hit short of the wall.

Duffy Lewis ordinarily played this hazardous terrain so well that the embankment became known as Duffy's Cliff. But this time he didn't. This game was called because of darkness after eleven innings, a 6–6 tie.

The rules then provided an immediate replay of tie games on the same field where the tie occurred. The third game was the Marquard 2–1 victory where the fans didn't know who won until they saw their evening papers.

The so-called "Hundred Thousand Dollar Infield" of Connie Mack's A's. Left to right: Stuffy McInnis, 1B; Dan Murphy, utility (later RF); Frank Baker, 3B; Jack Barry, SS; Eddie Collins, 2B. C.M. Conlon, *Evening Telegram*

Smokey Joe Wood.

For the fourth game it was Joe Wood to take a second crack at the Giants at their home Polo Grounds. After a two-day rest, Joe was even better than the first time. He struck out eight, walked none, and again beat Tesreau, this time, 3–1.

Most of us writers felt that the fifth game played in Boston on Columbus Day, October 12, would be the deciding game of the Series. Mathewson, who had been unlucky in World Series pitching since he lost two games to the Athletics in 1911, was McGraw's starter, and he was in for another painful defeat. Matty's opponent was a young right-hander from Falconer, New York, Hugh Bedient, who in his boyhood days had been a Mathewson hero-worshiper. It now was his job to down the mighty Matty.

Matty gave it everything, but it wasn't enough. Young Bedient, who had a good 20–9 season in his freshman year, gave up only three hits to the National League champions. Christy yielded five, but two of them were back-to-back triples by Harry Hooper and Steve Yerkes in the third inning. Steve scored the second run of the inning on Doyle's fumble of Speaker's grounder. New York's lone run came on a Red Sox error. The Red Sox took it, 2–1.

Leading by three games to one, the Red Sox were in prime position to put on the crusher at the Polo Grounds. And with no game the next day, Sunday, Wood would be ready again.

There was jubilation in the two Pullman cars occupied by Red Sox personnel on the leisurely Sunday daytime trip to New York. They could smell the sweet scent of victory and those fat World Series checks. In the midst of the laughter in the first Boston car, Jim McAleer, president and part-owner of the club, stepped into the stateroom occupied by player-manager Jake Stahl.

"Who are you going to pitch tomorrow, Jake?" asked McAleer.

Stahl looked at his boss in surprise and said, "Who else but Joe Wood?"

"Well, let's talk that over a bit," said McAleer. "Remember that Bucky O'Brien pitched real well in the third game. If he holds them to two runs again, I think we can win; and should he lose, it would give Joe another day's rest and he could finish it for us in Boston."

Stahl demurred, "Why, all the boys are expecting Wood to pitch. Joe had told me he's ready and wants to pitch." They discussed it some more. When McAleer finally left the stateroom he said, "Think it over, but I think O'Brien deserves another chance. And remember, we always would have Wood available if we have to return to Boston."

There was a lot of bitterness and recrimination on the train when word spread around that Bucky O'Brien, not Wood, would pitch the Monday game in New York.

Possibly McAleer was half hoping to have another game in Boston and therefore another big gate. Only the winter before, Bob McRoy (Ban Johnson's former secretary), Stahl, and he had bought the club from J. Irving Taylor, son of the previous owner. McAleer, McRoy, and Stahl were not men of wealth and were pressed to meet time payments.

Perhaps the feelings of his teammates upset O'Brien when he walked out to start the sixth game at New York's Polo Grounds. He showed none of the stuff that he had in Boston and was knocked out in the first inning when the Giants rushed five runs over the plate. After that, left-hander Ray Collins held the Giants scoreless, but Rube Marquard, pitching another strong game, won handily by a score of 5–2.

There was more bickering and name-calling in the Boston cars of the Owl train sleeper to Boston. I heard that Paul Wood, Joe's brother, had a fist fight with O'Brien on the train and blackened one of O'Brien's eyes. Paul, expecting his brother Joe would pitch, had bet and lost one hundred dollars on the day's game.

The seventh game proved one of the "Days of Infamy" in Boston's baseball history. With Boston still ahead, three games to two, Wood was supposed to wrap it up. He didn't . The fault was in Boston's business office. By an incomprehensible blunder, they sold out the pavil-

On the basis of fielding ability alone, this is surely the greatest outfield of all time (1912). Left to right: Harry Hooper, RF; Tris Speaker, CF; Duffy Lewis, LF.

lion seats assigned for the earlier games to the Boston Royal Rooters, whose leader was the top-hatted Boston politician John "Honey" Fitzgerald, father of Rose Fitzgerald Kennedy and grandfather of President John Fitzgerald Kennedy. The Royal Rooters were an institution in Boston. In 1897–98, marching and parading, they sang to victory the old Boston Nationals who nosed out Baltimore in those years. They early adopted the Red Sox when the American League invaded Boston in 1901; in 1903, when Jimmy Collins's team won Boston's first American League pennant, they sang and marched through a two-week-long, eight-game victory over the Pittsburgh Pirates, National League champs of that year.

In games two, three, and five of this 1912 Series the Royal Rooters had backed Stahl's Red Sox with every ounce of energy in them. Now, when they went out for the seventh game, they found total strangers in their accustomed pavillion seats. The business office, not expecting a tie game (the second), had sold to the Royal Rooters seats for the three games expected to be played at Fenway Park. The Rooters, believing their seats were sacrosanct, did not go to the trouble of buying new tickets for the pavillion seats for the fourth game at Fenway, the seventh game overall. Somebody in the business office had stupidly sold these seats on a first-come, first-served basis. It later was said that a minor clerk in the office had made this tragic mistake, but Treasurer Bob McRoy was made the goat and caught most of the criticism.

Just as Joe Wood walked to the pitching mound to start the game, the Royal Rooters, who had blocked the aisles and passageways in the stands, opened the gate to the playing field and marched through it, their band trumpeting their fight song and the men swearing and displaying their anger. They were some five hundred strong, with Honey Fitz at their head, parading around and around the field. Wood and the other Red Sox players retreated to the dugout. An attempt by foot police to drive back the Rooters failed. Then the captain of the foot police called in about a dozen mounted police trained to handle unruly crowds. Skillfully using the shoulders of their horses as rams, they cleared the field while the Royal Rooters cursed them and shouted their bitterness and anger at the Red Sox's high command.

After a half hour's delay Wood walked out to the pitcher's mound for the second time. While Joe had stood around during the early part of the demonstration without a windbreaker, his arm had deadened. There was no smoke on his delivery, and the Giants hit him as though he were a batting practice pitcher. Whereas the New Yorkers had walloped Bucky O'Brien for five runs in the first inning of the sixth game, they now pounded the Pitcher of the Year for six runs in the first inning of the seventh game. As New York triumphed, 11–4, there was mighty little solace for the Boston fans other than the unassisted double play of Tris Speaker, the center fielder.

The one-sided New York win, evening the Series at three victories apiece, plus the Boston police's riding down the Royal Rooters, left Boston in an ugly mood the morning of the eighth and deciding game in Fenway, October 16.

Prior to the seventh game, the National Commission had held a meeting to determine where a deciding eighth game would be played in the event that New York should win the seventh game. Ban Johnson, the American League president, had called "Heads" and heads it was;

so the eighth game was scheduled for Fenway Park. Had there been any collusion, it certainly would have called for the game to be played in New York, where the park capacity was greater.

In Boston on the Wednesday morning of October 16 not only were the fans rabid, but many of Greater Boston's citizens were in a nasty mood. They were especially incensed at the treatment of the Royal Rooters by their own police. One newspaper compared the Boston police to Russian cossacks working over Moscow citizenry. McAleer and McRoy and the entire executive department of the Red Sox were under attack for selling the Rooters' pavillion seats. On the streets were heard shouts of "The hell with the Red Sox" and "Who cares a damn whether they win or lose!"

That feeling was reflected in the size of the crowd—only 17,034 came to see the greatest, most talked-of World Series game ever played up to that point. The previous four Boston games had averaged crowds of 33,000. Not a single member of the Royal Rooters attended.

McGraw naturally called on his number one man, Christy Mathewson, to go after this all-important eighth game. Stahl pitched young Hugh Bedient, the 2–1 winner over Matty in the fifth game. Both men, the veteran and the youngster, pitched beautiful baseball. Matty went ahead, 1–0, in the third inning, when little Josh Devore was walked by Bedient and later scored on Red Murray's double to center. The Red Sox tied it in the seventh when Stahl hit a pop fly double to short left. With two out Olaf Henricksen, a pinch hitter, tied the game with a hard line drive which smacked the first-base bag and was deflected into foul territory for a two-base hit.

Wood took over for Boston in the eighth and the game remained tied, after nine innings. New York would have won, 2–1, but for a spectacular catch by Harry Hooper in the sixth inning which robbed Larry Doyle of a home run. Hooper threw himself back into an open-field box and with some of the spectators holding him up, he caught the ball in a prostrate position and held it tightly.

The McGraw men broke the tie in the first half of the tenth when Murray cracked out his second two-base hit and scored on Merkle's single. The skilled Mathewson then needed to retire only three batsmen to give the Giants a great uphill victory. But those three outs never came.

Big Six felt sure of the first out when he induced pinch hitter Clyde Engle to lift an easy fly to center. I since have heard it described as a screeching drive and no cinch to catch. I recall it quite distinctly. Any high school center fielder could have caught it with ease. The only possible excuse for Snodgrass's finally dropping it for a two-base error was that he'd had too much time to think while the ball was in the air.

On the very next play Snodgrass made a running catch of Hooper's

Fred Snodgrass, unfortunate to be best known for his disastrous muff in the 1912 World Series.   C. M. Conlon, *Evening Telegram*

long line drive, one of the very best defensive plays of the Series. After that, Mathewson walked Steve Yerkes, not a strong hitter. This was a mistake. Next came another bad break for Matty. Tris Speaker, Boston's best hitter, raised a fairly high foul about five feet from the first-base coach's box. It was clearly first baseman Merkle's ball, but it was a windy day and the wind had been playing tricks with foul flies. Catcher Chief Meyers also came down from the plate to take it.

Mathewson moved over just into foul territory, and I thought it was he who called out, "Take it, take it, Chief, you take it." I later heard it was Speaker, the base runner, who offered this "advice." Anyway, confusion reigned and the ball fell in foul territory in the middle of the triangle formed by Merkle, Meyers, and Mathewson. In returning to the batter's box, Speaker passed Mathewson and whispered, "Matty, that play will cost you the game and the Series."

Tris was as good as his word. His batting life saved, he rammed a long single to right, easily scoring Engle with the tying run and sending Yerkes to third. In desperation McGraw ordered Mathewson to walk Duffy Lewis, a dangerous hitter, making a double play possible at any base. But Larry Gardner, Boston's third baseman, refused to be the fall guy and rifled a long fly to Devore in deep right, on which Yerkes scored the winning run after the catch.

In my many years of following World Series, I never saw such dejection as that of the New York contingent, following Gardner's sacrifice fly. Coming from far behind in the Series, the Giants just missed winning it by an eyelash—really two eyelashes—an outfield muff and a failure to agree who should take an easy foul fly. I was working next to Sid Mercer of the *Globe* in the press stand; tears rolled down Sid's cheeks as he dictated the details of the bitter defeat to his New York paper's telegrapher. Fat Wilbert Robinson, who worked on and off with the Giants as coach, sat deflated on the bench; Harry Sparrow, another fat man, who was McGraw's close friend and bodyguard, collapsed in a field box like Humpty Dumpty falling off the wall. Broadway actors, McGraw's pals from the Lambs Club, sat stunned in their box seats. Some did not leave the park until a half hour afterwards—they just stared into space.

On the Boston side the victory was accepted without any of the fervor that would have been generated if the Royal Rooters had not been humiliated the day before. In the Boston papers, besides stories of the Red Sox victory, were columns asking for an investigation as to why the Rooters' seats had been sold out for the seventh game and why the mounted police had been called to ride them down. On all sides there were calls for McRoy's dismissal. Both McAleer and McRoy were out of the management of the club by the end of the 1913 season. With the blessing of Ban Johnson, the pair who botched the later games of the 1912 Series sold their interests to Joe Lannin, a Garden City, New York, hotel man.

My first two World Series gave me more thrills and excitements and strange doings off the field and behind the scenes than any other pair of back-to-back Series to the present date.

8

HAL CHASE: HE HAD A CORKSCREW BRAIN

When I arrived on the New York scene in 1911 there was talk of crookedness in baseball but no effort was being made to pin anything down on anyone.

As I came to learn my way around, it seemed that Hal Chase, the spectacular, beautiful fielding first baseman then playing and managing for the Highlanders/Yanks, was in a great measure responsible for the suspicions and talk. George Stallings, Chase's predecessor as Yankee manager, accused Hal of throwing games on him. The American League president, instead of investigating Chase, sharply criticized Stallings and accused George of saying nasty things about the league's second-best drawing card. But my second thoughts on the subject were that the league officials were responsible for Prince Hal's continuing career in big league baseball despite some strikingly peculiar happenings wherever he played—New York (Highlanders), Chicago (White Sox), Buffalo in the Federal League, Cincinnati (Reds), and New York again (Giants). Hal was a superstar of the first and second decades of this century, and baseball's moguls allowed him to play under curcumstances that Judge Landis would later not tolerate. Hal was too big to bounce without proof positive and too slick to nail down.

Jim Price, my sports editor at the *Press*, gave me this summary of Chase soon after I reported for duty. "He is a remarkable fielder. I don't think anyone ever played first base as well as Hal Chase can play it—if he wants to play it. But he has a corkscrew brain."

I was a little surprised and asked, "What do you mean, 'a corkscrew brain'?"

"Well," Price said, "I don't want to tell you all I know. I'll just say he can be the greatest player in the world if he wishes. Some days he doesn't want to be. He isn't a man I would trust."

Price's comment made an impression on me. I looked up Chase's fielding averages and discovered that for about six years in succession, Chase, supposedly the peerless first baseman, wound up with something like nineteen to twenty-one errors. Now that, I knew, was pretty unusual for a first baseman, who normally has far fewer errors than the other infielders. In fact Stuffy McInnis, while with the Red Sox, once went through a season with only *one* error. I made a mental note of Chase's suspicious error totals.

In 1913, when Frank Chance was managing the Yankees, I was fixing up my Associated Press box score after a game. Heywood Broun was sitting with me, waiting for me to join him on our usual ride downtown together on the Sixth Avenue El. Frank Chance came over to us and said, "I want to tell you fellows what's going on. Did you notice some of the balls that got away from Chase today? They weren't wild throws; they were only made to look that way. He's been doing that right along. He's throwing games on me!"

So I asked my sports editor—by that time Price was no longer my boss—whether I should use the conversation in print. He thought it over and said, "I guess you'd better pass it up." Broun, too, made nothing of it except a short note to the effect that Manager Chance had told some of the press that Chase wasn't playing up to his ability and was letting games get away with his loose play at first base.

Despite the innocuous nature of Broun's remark, Frank Farrell, Yankee owner, came to the press box the next day and bawled out Broun. He said, "That was a terrible thing you wrote about Chase."

Heywood replied, "I only said something that Chance told Fred Lieb and me, and he told us a lot more than I wrote in the paper."

Two days after that, Chase was traded to the White Sox for a lesser first baseman, Babe Borton, and a third baseman-shortstop, Rollie Zeider. Mark Roth, later road secretary of the Yankees, but then a baseball writer for the *Globe*, assigned to the Yankees, wrote: "The Yankees traded Chase to Chicago for a bunion and an onion." Rollie Zeider was famous for his bunions—Chicago writers like Dryden and Fullerton were always kidding about Zeider's bunions. And an "onion" was a "lemon."

What struck me then and has remained with me since was that the American League must have known the Chase record and the suspicions underlying what Chance told Broun and me. But instead of disciplining Chase or calling for an investigation, they let Farrell trade him to a club that was much higher in the standings. The other thought I got out of it was that other players saw Chase get away with it and sure-

Hal Chase: speed and grace personified.   International News Photos

ly thought, "Why don't we give it a try?"

Before I detail the rest of Chase's strange career, let me say a word about his fielding, which I studied hard. As a glove man (when the mood was on him), only Sisler and Terry have come close to him. His range was incredible because of his speed. No other first baseman played so far off the bag. As a man charging in on a bunt he was fantastic. I have seen him field bunts on the third-base side of an imaginary line between home plate and the pitching rubber, and make his left-handed whiplike throws to third, to second, or to first as the occasion required, all in one apparently seamless motion. He was speed and grace personified.

How did he throw games—if, as is generally agreed, he did? His neatest trick (I think) was to arrive at first base for a throw from another infielder just a split second too late. A third baseman, for example, must throw to the bag, whether the first baseman is there or not. Chase, playing far off the bag, probably could have got there in time, with his speed. But if he wanted to let one get away . . . maybe if he moved just a bit lazily toward first for a step or two? He would then speed up and seem to be trying hard. But it would be difficult—it would take a suspicious-minded person like Chance—to charge him with anything but an error if a well-thrown peg slipped off the end of his glove.

After about two and a half seasons with the White Sox, Chase jumped to the Buffalo Federal League club. He made the move under a stipulation that perhaps was amply justified in Chase's case. The standard big league baseball contract had a ten-day release clause, giving a club the power to release a player with ten days' notice. Chase argued that this rule, to be a fair contract, had to hold for the club as well as for the player. So he notified Charles Comiskey, the White Sox owner, that in ten days he would leave the White Sox. It went into the courts, and the judge ruled that what was good for the goose was also good for the gander.

After Chase began playing in the Federal League, I heard continual rumors of strange things going on. His name often came up in connection with suspicious games. So when the Federal League went out of existence after the 1915 season and the best players were auctioned off to Big League clubs, no American League club wanted to touch Chase. But Garry Herrmann of the Reds bought him from Harry Sinclair, the oil millionaire, who under the peace treaty could dispose of all the players except those of the Chicago Whales, the St. Louis Blue Feds, and the Ward brothers' Brooklyn Feds.

In 1916 Chase led the National League in hitting. He was never a great hitter, but he was a good one—probably as good a hitter as he wanted to be, as Jim Price once said of his fielding. Even during Chase's big batting year I heard talk that Hal and his manager, Christy

Mathewson, were not hitting it off, and there was also talk that Matty suspected Chase's loyalty. But nothing came to a head until late in the war season of 1918. Then, just before he went into the army and overseas, Christy made charges to the Cincinnati press and to the National League president, John Heydler, that Chase had thrown some games.

Heydler attempted a full-scale investigation and had Chase come before him for a personal confrontation. He went to Boston to investigate a well-known gambler with whom Chase supposedly had a close association. The National League president felt handicapped by the fact that Matty was overseas and communications between them had broken down completely. While the trial was going on, John McGraw annoyed Heydler by stating that if Hal was vindicated, McGraw had a position for him at first base. "Here I am trying to prove the charges that Mathewson, McGraw's close friend, has made against this man, and McGraw already is offering him a job," Heydler complained.

In off-the-record talks Heydler told me that he felt Hal was guilty. "But I have no proof that will stand up in a court of law." In the end, just before the teams left for 1919 spring training, Heydler acquitted the great first baseman. He said in his statement that with Mathewson unavailable, he could not make Matty's charges stand up.

At the time of the Chase trial, Sgt. Gabby Street, just returned from service, spent some time in the backroom of the Yankees' Forty-second Street office, which was a hangout for New York baseball writers and former players. Street was a Yankee catcher in 1912 when Chase was player-manager. The conversation this day naturally turned to Chase. "A strange character, a very strange character," said Gabby. "A fellow I never want to meet in a card game. Shortly after I joined the club in 1912, Hal was in a poker game with five or six of his players. I wasn't in the game, just kibitzing in back of them. I knew Chase had the reputation of being a sharp player, so I stood behind his chair. Hal didn't seem to object. Chase played his cards conservatively, frequently passing. But then, suddenly, when a big pot had built up, Hal raised every time it was his turn to bid. I noticed he had three kings. Then I looked again and he had four kings. The additional king must have come from a sleight-of-hand operation, for Chase was famous for his speed and agility. I never knew where that extra king came from, but later I saw a low card disappear out of Chase's hand with the speed of a magician's trick. He must have had the king early and whisked it out when it would do him the most good." Naturally, Chase raked in a big pot.

Chase was with the Giants on the 1919 training trip to Gainesville, Florida, and in early practice games he played first base with his usual grace and dexterity.

The National League race quickly developed into a contest between the Giants and Pat Moran's upstart team in Cincinnati. The Reds took the lead for good by taking four out of six games in a thrilling, three-straight double-header series before capacity crowds at the Polo Grounds. The Giants never could catch them after that series.

However, mathematically the New Yorkers were still in contention in middle August when the surprising statement came out of Cincinnati that Manager McGraw of the Giants had suspended indefinitely both first baseman Hal Chase and third baseman Heinie Zimmerman. The Giants front office was very close-mouthed about it, but it soon developed that "indefinite suspensions" actually meant permanent expulsions from Big League baseball.

John Heydler explained it to me: "I never was satisfied with my earlier acquittal of Chase. I was unconvinced. Eventually I got a signed affidavit from the Boston gambler and a photographic copy of Chase's canceled check for five hundred dollars given him by a gambler as pay for throwing a game in 1918. I took this evidence to Charles Stoneham (owner-president of the Giants) saying, 'When I permitted Chase to play early last spring I said I had no real proof of Hal's throwing a game. Now I have that proof.' I handed him the affidavit and Chase's canceled check and then told Stoneham, 'Please notify your manager that Chase will not play in any future game with the Giants.' Stoneham said, 'If that is the way it is, that's it.' He took it quietly, saying, 'John, you had no other choice.'"

The big Zimmerman, 1912 National League Triple Crown winner (leading batting average, most home runs, most runs batted in) was still in 1919 a dangerous hitter.

I never heard of any direct charges filed against him, and so I tried to get from McGraw the real reason for Heinie's banishment. McGraw seemed reluctant to discuss it, but eventually said, "I was disgusted with some of his play on our last 1919 western trip. It didn't look as though he was doing his best." Zimmerman, a native New Yorker who learned the plumbing trade in the Bronx, never asked for a hearing or tried to get reinstated into baseball. He just dropped completely out of sight.

In Cincinnati, Lee Magee, born Leopold Hoernschemeyer, who played second base for the 1918 Reds, also fell with Chase. Magee, a native Cincinnatian, tried to win vindication in a civil court, but even the jurors in his hometown decided he was crooked. By this time Judge Landis was in power, and he decreed Magee ineligible for any future job in organized baseball.

During the investigation that followed the later Black Sox scandal and at the trial of the accused Black Sox octet, Hal Chase's name frequently came up as one who had knowledge of the fix. Some said he was the contact man between the erring ball players and the gamblers.

Others thought he was the mastermind behind baseball's worst scandal.

After Chase had been banished from organized baseball he picked up a few dollars here and there by playing semipro ball in the mining towns of northern Mexico, Arizona, and New Mexico. A man who saw Chase play when he was well over forty said that Hal still had the old grace and skill.

Chase eventually died in dire straits on May 18, 1947, at the age of sixty-four. What a waste of skill and artistry, and of a lifetime! He could think and move like a flash. Even at the age of thirty-five, Prince Hal had a clean, boyish face. Nature fitted him out to be a superstar. But alas! As Jim Price told me in 1911, he was born with a corkscrew brain.

It is also hard to avoid the conclusion that some, maybe much of the blame for Chase's corkscrew behavior belongs on the men who made up the early governing body of baseball—the National Commission. The three members were Garry Herrmann, chairman, who was also president of the Cincinnati Reds; Ban Johnson, president of the American League; and a succession of National League presidents in those trying years. Three of the most respected managers in baseball, George Stallings, Frank Chance, and Christy Mathewson, accused Chase of crookedness and throwing games. But Chase continued in the majors, undeterred, until 1919, six years after Chance first told Heywood Broun and me that Chase was throwing games on him in New York.

How many good young ballplayers may have said, "Chase gets by with it, year after year, so why shouldn't we pick up a little extra money when the chance is offered us?" And how many, when tempted, fell?

9

BASEBALL'S BIG BLACK BLOTCH: DIRTY BUSINESS IN THE 1919 WORLD SERIES

Prior to 1919, most officials and fans considered baseball in the same class as one of the bath soaps advertising itself as "99.44% pure." However, one club owner once admitted to me that "ballplayers, after all, are strictly human, and you will probably find a rotten apple in every barrel."

John Heydler, president of the National League, began to discover more than one rotten apple in his barrel at the end of the 1919 season, notably Chase, Zimmerman, and Magee. But suspicion also lighted on veteran pitcher Claude Hendrix, then of the Chicago Cubs, and infielder Gene Paulette, then of the Philadelphia Phillies. Both, along with Joe Gedeon, second baseman for the American League's St. Louis Browns, would ultimately be bounced by Judge Landis. In addition to these, John McGraw told me later that Buck Herzog, his second baseman in 1917, had sold him out in the 1917 Giants–Chicago White Sox World Series by consistently playing out of position for White Sox hitters—but he couldn't prove it and so had filed no charges.

That individual players might be tempted was well known to most baseball writers. But the notion that gamblers could "buy out" an entire team for a World Series was so beyond belief that we baseball writers, in our bull sessions, never even considered it. However, the inconceivable became not only possible, but an actuality.

All this occurred in the 1919 Cincinnati–White Sox World Series, won by the Reds five games to three, when eight Chicago players plotted to let Cincinnati win. There was suspicion of foul play during the Series itself and immediately afterwards, but the full plot was not exposed until almost a year later in the last week of the 1920 major league season.

The culprits in the scandal were among the top-ranking stars of baseball. The ring leader of "the unholy eight" was Arnold (Chic) Gandil, a hard-hitting first baseman. Then there were (Shoeless) Joe Jackson, almost illiterate but one of the great natural hitters of the game; George (Buck) Weaver, an All-Star player whether he played third base or shortstop; Eddie Cicotte, a talcum-powder ball specialist, who won twenty-eight games in 1917 and twenty-nine in 1919; Claude Williams, an almost equally successful left-handed pitcher; Oscar (Happy) Felsch, a fast, slick-fielding center fielder with a lifetime batting average of .290; Charles (Swede) Risberg, a shortstop with a great range; and Fred McMullin, formerly regular third baseman but used in 1919 as utility infielder.

Before the club was broken up, it was considered one of the greatest teams ever put together. In fact, Ed Barrow, general manager of the Yankees at the height of their glory in the 1920s and '30s, rated the White Sox of 1917 and 1919 as among the greatest teams of all time.

My prognostications before the Series, syndicated by the Al Munroe Elias Bureau, had the White Sox winning in six or seven games. In that year the winner had to take five out of nine. Hugh Fullerton of Chicago, who, like me, juggled baseball statistics and had a reputation for picking winners, also went along with the Windy City team. The American League, furthermore, had won eight out of the nine most recent World Series. We couldn't see how the Reds could start evening things up for the National League.

Dan Daniel and I covered the Series for the New York *Morning Sun*. It was the first Series after the close of World War I; baseball had enjoyed a fine postwar season and there was wide interest in this conflict between the supposedly invincible White Sox and the Reds.

World Series headquarters were at the Sinton Hotel, Cincinnati, but Daniel and I were tardy in getting our reservations and were assigned rooms in the Metropole Hotel, which even in ordinary times was a hangout for gamblers. We saw at least a dozen in the lobby as we checked in. To our surprise, they had money to bet on the Reds. "Buddy, do you want to bet a little money on Chicago?" they asked us. "We are offering six to five on the Reds."

That puzzled us. I said to Dan, "I figured it would be at least seven to five on the White Sox. Do they know something that we don't know? Has Cicotte come up with a lame arm?"

The 1919 Chicago White Sox. Left to right, front row: Lynn, Risberg, Liebold, Kerr, McClellan, Williams, Cicotte. Middle row: Schalk, Jenkins, Felsch, Gleason, E. Collins, J. Collins, Faber, Weaver. Back row: Jackson, Gandil, McMullin, Lowdermilk, James, Mayer, Murphy, Sullivan, Wilkinson.

We soon learned that something *was* wrong, especially with Cicotte. Manager Kid Gleason naturally started Cicotte, and the Reds belted him as though he were a rookie. The Reds won hugely, 9–1, with the Cincinnati left-hander Dutch Ruether holding the White Sox to six hits. The odds at the Metropole after the game jumped to 8–5 on the Reds. That evening I heard Hughie Fullerton say, "I don't like what I saw out there today. There is something smelly. Cicotte doesn't usually pitch like that." During the season Cicotte's earned run average was 1.82, and he completed all but four of the forty games he started.

After the game, catcher Ray Schalk told Chicago writers that Cicotte had repeatedly crossed him up, paid no attention to his signs and often pitched a delivery opposite from what Ray had signaled. Despite such evidences, I felt Cicotte had just had an off day.

The Reds also won the second game, 4–2, with left-handed Slim Sallee defeating Chicago's Claude Williams. It was an odd game because Williams, the loser, gave up only four hits while Sallee was stung for ten.

As I saw it later on, Williams had decided to lose, but in a smart way. In one inning Williams walked three of the Reds, then allowed Larry Kopf, weakest hitter in the Cincinnati lineup, to hit a damaging two-run triple, after which the National League batting champion, Eddie Roush, singled in another run. Outside of this inning, Williams retired the Reds almost as fast as they came up. In the remainder of the game he gave up only two stray singles. White Sox fans murmured, "Poor Claude. He had all of his stuff. The breaks of the game just went against him. Any other time he pitches a four-hitter, he wins easily."

After the two defeats in Cincinnati something happened on the World Series train back to Chicago that John Heydler told me only several years after the Series. It was around midnight when Charles Comiskey, White Sox president, knocked at the door of Heydler's stateroom. "Who is it?" asked John, who had already retired, well pleased with his league's lead.

"It's Charlie Comiskey. I've got something I must tell you." After Comiskey was seated, he said "Kid Gleason tells me he can't exactly put his finger on it, but he knows that something has been going on. 'Funny business on the part of his players in the first two games' is the way he put it. I can't go to Herrmann [president of the Reds] and I can't go to Johnson, because you know we feud and haven't spoken in years. So I had to come to you [as the third member of the national commission directing organized baseball at the time]." Eventually Heydler dressed and called at Johnson's compartment in the same car. It was then after one A.M.

Ban was a drinking man, and the World Series usually was a drinking holiday for him. He was in a drunken sleep when he was awakened, and in an irritable mood as he listened to Heydler retell Comiskey's story. When Heydler finished, Ban snapped, "That is the yelp of a beaten cur."

"What was I to do after that?" Heydler asked me rhetorically. "The team from my league was leading, two games to zero. With Johnson doing nothing, was I supposed to give the American public a story that the White Sox had handed us the two games we won?" In fairness to

Johnson, when the story of the Big Fix evolved and he finally was convinced something was wrong, he was relentless in his campaign to bring the crooked ballplayers to justice.

There was a halt in the Reds' victory march when in the third game little Dickie Kerr shut out the Reds, 3–0. There was a story bruited around that another syndicate group had reached the Reds. But perhaps the White Sox won the third game because Kerr was one of the Chicago "lily whites" not in on the fix. Long afterwards, Eddie Roush told me that a Reds pitcher, Hod Eller, had been under suspicion, but when Ed questioned him after game three about possible involvement with gamblers, Eller had denied it. (He later won games five and eight). Not even the most suspicious of us writers ever truly understood this game.

By the time Cicotte's turn to pitch had come around again, he realized he had pitched too poorly in the first game. He confided to a fellow plotter, "We've got to look good in losing. We must think of our 1920 contracts." This time he contrived to lose by only 2–0 and was helped by Jimmy Ring's shutout pitching. But he failed to follow his own advice. Cincinnati scored its two runs in the fifth inning, thanks largely to Cicotte's bungling. Cincinnati's Pat Duncan tapped to the pitcher, and though it looked like an easy play to first, Cicotte threw without steadying himself and his wild throw hit the grandstand as Duncan pulled up at second base.

Kopf singled to left and Duncan headed for home. Jackson, one of the plotters, actually made a beautiful beeline throw to the plate. It looked as if Kopf would be out by ten feet. However, Cicotte put his glove down at the ball as though he was taking it for a cutoff play, but he only pushed Jackson's throw into foul territory. This enabled Duncan to score easily. Kopf took second base on the error and scored on Greasy Neale's single. Even now, I can see that play as though it happened yesterday, and I thought at the time, "What a stupid thing for Cicotte to do."

The following Monday there was another strange game in Comiskey Park. More or less duplicating his first game, Claude Williams again held the Reds to four hits but this time lost to Hod Eller, 5–0. Hod set a World Series record by striking out six Sox in order in the second and third innings. After we learned that the Series had been fixed there was doubt whether this feat belonged in the record book. We weren't sure whether the Sox were swinging for hits or for outs.

The Reds returned to Redland, leading four games to one. In Cincinnati there was little credence to stories printed in Chicago and New York that there was something suspicious about the Red victories. The fans only knew that their team was one away from their first World Series victory, and they liked the full taste of it.

The crowd of 32,000 eager for the kill saw the White Sox fight back from a 4–0 deficit to win another for honest Dickie Kerr by 5–4, the "unholy octet" hitting the ball ferociously in the sixth and tenth innings. Now the rumors of other gamblers wanting the White Sox to win began to spread.

Before only 14,000 Cincinnati fans at game six, Cicotte finally broke into the win column. He now pitched as well as during the regular season, and prevailed easily, 4–1.

Just why were the Sox permitted to win games six and seven? There were two explanations: One was that another syndicate of gamblers had entered the picture and wanted the White Sox to win. The second reason was that the fixers hadn't paid the money they had promised. Gandil, the ring leader of the "unholy octet," had been taken care of on the side and so had his lieutenant in the fix, Swede Risberg. Jackson, Cicotte, and Williams had sacks of cash under their pillows, but there was only $5,000 in each; they had expected at least $10,000. Others had fared even worse.

In the meantime most Chicagoans took these wins, especially Cicotte's, as signs that the great White Sox had tried all the way, and now things were suddenly breaking for them. One more win for Chicago would tie it up at 4–4 and leave the outcome hanging on a ninth game also scheduled for Chicago. That ninth game was never to be. I could tell that before a ball was pitched in Comiskey Park. I went to the men's room before going to my seat in the press box. Three disgruntled gamblers were talking as I came in, saying things such as, "The Reds could still lose this and we don't know how we stand." "Anything can still happen," and "It doesn't look good!" Then a fourth joined them, full of cheer and joy. "Everything is okay, boys—nothing to worry about. It's all in the bag. Williams will pitch and it will be all over in the first inning."

How right the man was! According to what I heard later, some Chicago gangsters had threatened to kill the left-hander if he pitched a victory; they said he would be shot right in the pitcher's box.

Claude started off as a man scared. After retiring Morris Rath, the leadoff hitter, Daubert, Groh, Roush, and Duncan stung him for successive clean hits. Unhappy Kid Gleason rushed in reliever Roy Wilkinson, but Cincinnati had five big runs on the scoreboard. The Sox rallied for runs here and there, but Cincinnati won the clincher, 10–5.

The Series was over, but its repercussions sounded for months, years, even until today. Ray Schalk, who had said that both Cicotte and Williams crossed him up or ignored his signs, disappeared in the north woods for a ten-day trip. When he emerged he claimed he had been misquoted and refused to say anything more.

Comiskey offered $10,000 to anyone who could give him informa-

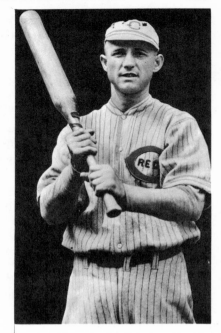

Heinie Groh and his famous bottle-shaped bat, designed to let his hands slide upward for bunting and hit-and-run hitting to spots.   C.M. Conlon

tion that any of his players had done anything crooked in the series. A poor boy who had grown rich in baseball, he was in danger of losing perhaps $1,500,000 (1920 prices) in star ballplayers. While Comiskey later helped in the prosecution, he didn't particularly want to see his lifetime earnings go down the drain. Yet, many writers and fans regarded him as the real culprit of the "Black Sox" Scandal because of his pinch-penny handling of his players. While Eddie Collins received $12,000 a year as a result of a holdover contract from the Federal League war, Jackson, a lifetime .350 hitter, received $8,000, and Cicotte, twice a near thirty-game winner, was paid only $6,000 for his 1919 efforts.

The Sporting News, in its issue immediately after the Series, defended Comiskey, Kid Gleason, and their players. It ridiculed any thought of a fix and referred to those who talked of one as slimy creatures always ready to suspect and malign. Soon they changed their point of view and became relentless in pursuit of the crooks.

Announcement of the indictments was like an atomic bomb dropping on our national game. A young boy who worshipped the White Sox confronted Jackson with words that rang throughout the country:

"Say it ain't so, Joe!" Col. Huston, Yankee half-owner, kept repeating, "A sweet young lady turned whore."

The Illinois State Attorney had signed confessions from Jackson, Cicotte, and Williams, and Felsch confessed his guilt to a number of newspapermen. Arnold Rothstein, the New York gambler and underworld character, was believed to be the money man behind the fix. Rothstein testified in court that he had been approached by Abe Attell, the ex-featherweight champion, and Bill Burns, a former second-string pitcher with the White Sox. Rothstein said he wanted none of it and even testified that he had made a bet on the White Sox to win.

Before the case came to trial there was a change in the office of the Illinois State Attorney, and shortly thereafter all papers in the case, including the confessions of Cicotte, Jackson, and Williams were stolen. It generally was believed that members of the Chicago underworld stole the papers to protect the indicted players and their gambling associates. Rothstein was subsequently rubbed out by a rival mob.

The new state attorney told Ban Johnson, "There was nothing for me to do but drop the indictments procured by my predecessor, inasmuch as, with the records gone, we have no case against these men. When we get new evidence it will be necessary to build up an entirely new case against your former ballplayers."

Johnson, who had once said Comiskey's and Gleason's suspicions were the yelps of beaten curs, worked like a beaver to gather new evidence. He traveled ten thousand miles following leads and digging up new evidence. He pursued Bill Burns, one of the fixers, into the mountain country of Northern Mexico and induced him to come back to Chicago. Burns eventually turned state's evidence, and was one of prosecutor Crowe's strongest witnesses.

The State of Illinois brought in new indictments, charging criminal conspiracy against the men named in the first indictments and adding five additional names, all midwestern gamblers that Johnson had tracked down.

However, after hearing a month's worth of evidence, the Chicago jury on August 2, 1921, brought in a verdict of "not guilty." It was said that some of the jurors felt the players had thrown a few games but this was not necessarily a criminal offense. A rather disgusting aftermath of the trial came on the evening of the verdict when the jury together with the tried Black Sox celebrated the acquittal with a hilarious party in an Italian restaurant on Chicago's West Side.

The acquitted players escaped the penitentiary, but they really had no cause for merriment. Commissioner Landis, elected in November 1920, saw to that. He issued a statement saying, "Regardless of the verdict of juries, no player that throws a game, no player that entertains propositions or promises to throw a game, no player that sits in on a conference with a bunch of gamblers in which ways and means of throwing a game are discussed and does not promptly tell his club about it, will ever again play professional baseball."

One of the players who stoutly maintained his innocence of any wrongdoing was George (Buck) Weaver. He cited his averages to show that he constantly was playing his best, hitting .333 and fielding magnificently. He enlisted the support of the Chicago District of the Masonic Brotherhood and 20,000 Masons signed a document requesting Judge Landis to permit Weaver to continue at his livelihood.

Landis called Weaver into his office in Chicago. The commissioner said, "Buck, I'm going to ask you only two questions: Did you sit in on a conference with gamblers and dishonest players who thought of ways in which to throw the 1919 Series?" Weaver replied, "Yes, I did, Judge, but during the Series I played my best." Then Landis said, "Three days before the Series there was another conference—were you there?" Weaver again replied, "I did attend that meeting, Judge, but I played my best throughout the Series and I didn't get a penny out of it." Landis retorted, "If you attended two such meetings, you knew everything that was going on; and if you did not so inform your club, I hold you as guilty as the actual plotters and the men who took money for throwing the Series."

The Judge ran the curtain down on a sleazy scene. Babe Ruth, already sticking his head out from the wings, would in the next scene make sports fans forget almost overnight what had just happened.

10

JUDGE LANDIS: SAVIOR
OF BASEBALL

Judge Kenesaw Mountain Landis, elected commissioner of baseball by the club owners after the Black Sox scandal, was generally regarded as the savior of baseball. Some thought the true savior was Babe Ruth, the big man with the magic bat who in 1920 pushed the major league home-run record of 29, set by Ruth himself in 1919, to an unbelievable 54. The Babe deserved at least equal billing with the Judge as the one who ushered in a new era in baseball's history; but it was Landis whose accomplishments turned the Black Sox disgrace to constructive use.

Though he was a small in height (5 feet 7 inches) and weight (about 125 pounds), Landis was a big man—a great man—who lifted up the national game with his own hands and the very tone of his voice. When the Judge threw his weight around, he had the heft to topple anyone—players, league presidents, and all club officials—who didn't toe the line, often a line that he himself drew.

He was born on November 20, 1866, at Millville, Ohio, and was baptized Kenesaw Mountain Landis. He was given this odd name because his father, a surgeon in the Union Army, had been wounded in the battle for Kennesaw Mountain, Georgia, during the Civil War. Landis was as hard on offenders in civil courts and later in baseball as a chip of granite from Kennesaw Mountain, and when he reached a decision he was as firm as the mountain itself in making it stand.

Landis held his lofty position as commissioner of baseball from the time of his election in November 1920 until he died November 25,

1944, a week after he had been elected to a fifth term. Though he was the shortest of all baseball commissioners, he towered over all of his successors: Senator Albert (Happy) Chandler, Ford Frick, General William D. Eckert, and the present commissioner, Bowie K. Kuhn. None of the men who succeeded him has had anything like the Judge's czarlike authority and domination.

The club owners willingly gave Landis all the power he demanded when he first came into the baseball picture. At the time the owners were running scared; they were thinking of saving their game and their own financial hides. Landis as a judge projected an image of toughness and integrity at a time when everyone in baseball recognized that the public needed renewed trust in the decency of the game and a diversion from the stench of the Black Sox scandal. The new home-run king, Babe Ruth, helped by giving the fans a new untarnished hero. Landis, on his part, thoroughly won the fans to his side by his forthright early decisions stemming from the trials of the guilty White Sox players.

Landis had remarkable charisma; he stood out in any gathering he attended. Along with all the virtues of an honest federal judge, he had many of the foibles of the ordinary man. He was intensely patriotic and had loved baseball since he was a small boy. I think he was totally honest, but he was vain, egotistical, domineering, and a show-off. He swore like a trooper, chewed tobacco, and was fond of bourbon whiskey. He had great respect for the law and for himself as a person entrusted with the enforcement of the law, whether it be that of the government or of baseball. Some writers doubted his sincerity, thinking it contradictory that a man who could drink bootleg liquor behind the scenes would sentence a man for twenty years for violation of the prohibition amendment and the Volstead Act, as Landis had done. To understand the seeming contradiction you had to understand that Landis on the bench was a totally different man from Landis in the golf clubhouse.

My acquaintance with Landis was good, for I was chairman of the New York chapter of the Baseball Writers Association in the first four World Series under his commissionership, the first three of which (1921–23) were held entirely in New York, the last (1924) being a Washington–New York contest. It was my responsibility, subject only to an appeal to the commissioner, to distribute some 500 seats set aside by the New York clubs for baseball writers—about 150 in the press box, and the rest good seats in front rows of the grandstand. Telegraphers and accredited photographers also had to be provided for.

In 1921 both the Judge and I were new to this responsibility. Inevitably some of the news associations and big-name newspapers complained to Landis that I had shortchanged them, and men from the smaller cities, assigned grandstand seats, demanded seats in the press

Kenesaw Mountain Landis, a portrait taken at the time of his election as Commissioner.   Moffett, Chicago

box. Many a time just before the Series opened, Landis would phone me to come to his room to discuss the appeals from my ticket assignments. In the process a mutual respect grew.

After the ticket business had been settled, the Judge decided that the president of the Baseball Writers Association should automatically be the chief scorer of the World Series games, setting a precedent that still holds. I objected, for by so ruling, Landis was bumping off the existing three-man scoring team including my good friend Joe McCready. Furthermore, I had during the Series been elected president of the Association and so this decision would make me chief scorer the next year. "You won't hold the presidency all your life, Fred, so don't be embarrassed," was his final word on the subject.

Since I remained president through the 1924 Series, I was chief scorer of the World Series in 1922, 1923, and 1924. The other two men were the official scorers chosen by the chapters of the cities participating in the Series. I received $400 per Series, the other two $300. Today each man receives more than $1,000.

At the end of the 1921 Series I was in the Judge's suite when Babe Ruth telephoned in response to a message from Landis. Landis had waited hours for Ruth to return his call and was in a disagreeable mood. I could tell that the telephone conversation was heated, and then I heard Landis say, "I absolutely refuse to give you and your companions permission to make that trip!"

Babe must have replied that he intended to make the trip with or without permission, for Landis hung up on him with a loud bang and began pacing up and down. Out came a string of profanity: "Who the hell does that big ape think he is? That blankety-blank! If he goes on that trip it will be one of the sorriest things he has ever done!" The Judge had been challenged.

When I left Landis, I hurried to Col. Huston, part-owner of the Yankees, in a nearby hotel and told him the Judge had said he would make an example of Ruth if he disobeyed orders. It would obviously hurt the club if other Yankee players followed the Babe's lead.

Huston told me later that the only way he could catch up with Ruth (the Series being over) was by going to Grand Central Station that night to catch Babe as he embarked for Buffalo on the first leg of the projected barnstorming trip forbidden by Landis to all participants in the recent World Series. This exhibition tour of Ruth's was planned before Christy Walsh became his agent, and Babe was entirely on his own. Huston said that he had argued long and loud, but the Babe remained determined. "The games have been advertised," Ruth said. "We have to fulfill our commitments."

Ruth, Bob Meusel, and the young pitchers Bill Piercy and Tom Sheehan made the trip. (Sheehan could do so without breaking the rule

Judge Landis with owners (left to right) Jacob Ruppert and Tillinghast Huston of the Yankees and Harry Frazee of the Red Sox. *Herald* Staff Photo

because he had come up to the Yanks too late in the season to be eligible for Series play.) Huston did succeed in changing the minds of Wally Schang and Carl Mays, who were booked to go.

Landis was as good as his word in his punishment—severe. Ruth, Meusel, and Piercy were suspended for the first forty days of the 1922 season.

My association with Landis became even closer during the 1922 World Series. This was the Series in which George Hildebrand, the plate umpire in the second game, called it off in the bottom of the tenth inning, "on account of darkness." At 4:30 P.M., it was a pleasant, sunny, early October afternoon and there was still a long half hour of ample daylight. The fans were outraged. They had seen Bill Klem, veteran National League umpire, come in from his position on the bases to talk to Hildebrand. Klem was the real culprit. He told Hildebrand of a

World Series game in Boston in 1916 in which there was enough light when the fourteenth inning started, but it was so dark in the bottom half of the inning that Brooklyn fielders could hardly see the ball as the Red Sox scored their winning run. After Hildebrand went over to the commissioner's box for a brief chat with Landis the game was called off—not, Landis told me, on anyone's decision but Hildebrand's.

As the Judge and Mrs. Landis and a visiting British dignitary who was their guest walked across the field toward their car parked on Eighth Avenue the fans got "on" Judge Landis. "Trying to make more money for the club owners, eh, Judge?" was a typical slur. The British guest made it even worse when he exclaimed, "My God, Your Honor, I believe they are giving you the bird!" Landis was so upset and angry that a few hours later he called reporters to his suite at the Commodore and announced that the entire gate receipts for the second game would be given to charity.

An evening or two before this the Judge and Mrs. Landis had invited Mary and me to have dinner with them at the Commodore. Mrs. Landis, who called her husband Squire, was a gracious person and we enjoyed our evening thoroughly. Trying to repay the "Squire and Mrs. Squire" for their dinner, I invited them to join us in seeing Earl Carroll's "Vanities" right after the fourth game. This was regarded as a daring show for the early 1920s, featuring a nude draped around the swinging pendulum of a large clock. In the second act one scene offered eight little carousels, each with a bare-breasted damsel curtained by the flimsiest of gauzes. We were way up front—ringside, one might say—almost close enough to touch one of these beauties as the carousels whirled around in an eye-filling dance number.

Will Rogers was the show's star, and much of his humor was related to the leading characters in the World Series. After kidding Babe Ruth for his miserable .119 batting average and Miller Huggins for his unsuccessful five-star pitching staff, he got around to the Judge and the game "called on account of darkness in the middle of the day." Landis laughed, or pretended to, but I was quite aware that he didn't think it was funny.

After the performance I couldn't resist asking him how he liked the show. "Bully, bully!" he replied. "They surely had some pretty lasses. But the next time I meet Will Rogers I will try to impress on him that I do know the difference between daylight and darkness."

I asked Mrs. Landis the same question. "I always like Will Rogers," she replied, "even when he kidded the Squire. But I must admit I would have preferred it if the young ladies had worn a little more underwear."

After the last game of the 1924 Washington–New York World Series I was alone with Landis for a few moments on a little balcony outside

Walter Johnson, 1924.
NYH Service

his room in the Raleigh Hotel in Washington. Below us on Pennsylvania Avenue snake-danced a joy-maddened crowd: Washington's beloved Senators had just won the deciding seventh game, and Saint Walter Johnson had been the winning pitcher in a twelve-inning cliffhanger. It was not only Washington's first World Series victory but also its first major league pennant. Congressmen, department heads, merchants, barbers, bootblacks, janitors, office secretaries—all joined in the frivolity. They blew trumpets and beat drums—some beat wash basins with large spoons. Anything that could make a noise was being used in this joyous paean of victory.

Landis put his hand on my shoulder and looked directly in my eyes as he said, "Freddy, what we are looking at now—could this be the highest point of what we affectionately call our national sport? Greece had its sports and its Olympics; they must have reached a zenith and then waned. The same for the sports of ancient Rome: there must have been a year at which they were at their peak. I repeat, Freddy, are we looking at the zenith of baseball?"

Looking back, I feel that Washington's affection for its 1924 team was baseball's finest moment up to that point. But Landis lived to see other demonstrations as big and delirious: St. Louis greeting its first

National League pennant and then its first world championship in 1926; Detroit's crazy happenings after the Tigers won the 1935 Series from the Cubs; Cincinnati's demonstration at its first on-the-level victory, over the Tigers, in 1940—these are some that must have renewed his faith in the game and its hold on the American public before he died in 1944.

Judge Landis had his likes and dislikes in baseball. He seemed to have a contempt for most of the club owners, who nevertheless repeatedly renewed his contract. His dislike for Ban Johnson, the American League president, was surpassed only by Johnson's undying hatred of the Judge.

Landis didn't like Branch Rickey. Most baseball men thought Rickey's development of a chain of "farms" for younger players was a step forward for baseball, and they hastened to copy it. Landis, on the other hand, called it a damnable thing. "It will be the ruination of the individual minor league club owners," he said. Indeed, the farm system did change the complexion of the minor leagues, but it was the televising of big league games that ultimately reduced the number of minor leagues to but one fifth of the number that operated in 1950.

After hours, when the Judge could feel free to let his shaggy hair down, he liked to imitate the speech, grammar, and mannerisms of the clubowners who employed him. He could do an amusing takeoff of Barney Dreyfuss, president of the Pittsburgh Pirates when Landis came into baseball, and he caught perfectly Sam Breadon's East Side New York accent. He was especially devasting on William F. Baker, a former New York police commissioner who operated the Philadelphia National League club with pinch-penny penury when the team was known as Phoolish Phillies. Baker raised the ire of the Judge by his cheap treatment of one of his own managers, Wild Bill Donovan, who—it so happened—had been one of the Judge's favorite players as a pitcher for several teams, notably the Detroit Tigers. Baker had fired Donovan for a multiplicity of reasons which Landis termed absurd. Baker only paid Donovan up to the date he fired him. The Judge was not a man to hold back his criticism of owners just because they hired him.

It was at a party held by George Weiss for Donovan in 1922 that we New York writers learned that Landis, the tough judge in cases of violations of Prohibition, would join in alcoholic frolics now that he had left the bench. Weiss then owned the New Haven club in the Eastern League (class AA) and Donovan had won a pennant for him. Then in a brief three-game series Donovan had beaten the strong Baltimore International League (class AAA) champions, two games to one. Donovan had managed the Yankees for Ruppert and Huston in 1915–17 and was popular with the New York writers.

Our group, including Babe Ruth, Col. Huston, and Judge Landis, climbed aboard a parlor car for the event in New Haven. Bugs Baer, amusing writer and cartoonist, developed a sore throat and couldn't deliver his expected speech. I got tapped to pinch-hit for Baer and pleased the audience when I pointed out that if the new Yankee owners, Col Huston and Col. Ruppert, had only bought all those Red Sox players—Ruth, Mays, Hoyt, and the rest—a wee bit earlier, we would all be in New York now, celebrating a Donovan American League championship.

At the party there was Prohibition liquor hidden at different tables. Ginger ale was served openly, but the guest had to spike it with Scotch hidden under the table from the Judge's view. When the dinner broke up about 11:00 P.M., Weiss took a smaller group, including the Judge and me, to an upstairs room, where a martini awaited each person at his seat. How would Judge Landis react? Would he bawl out Weiss? Leave the party? Landis seemed to sense the tenseness. After everybody was seated he got up, raised his glass, and said, "Gentlemen, let us drink to the Eighteenth Amendment." That broke the tension, and we had a high old time until we returned to our parlor car at 1:30 for the trip back to New York.

I played numerous rounds of golf with Landis because in his first decade as commissioner he would spend the month of March at the Belleview Biltmore in Clearwater, Florida, not too far from my home in St. Pete. For his size and age he played respectable golf, staying in the middle of the fairway, and he usually scored about 95. When he used 100 strokes he felt bad, and his profanity would achieve its highest levels. On occasion he would also give lessons in profanity to other golfers whose scolding of their golf balls he regarded as inadequately expressive and not likely to command the respect of the ball.

Once in Clearwater George Herbert Daley and I defeated Landis and John Orr, then a part-owner of the Cincinnati Reds, and wound up the large winners of twenty-five cents apiece. "You have to give us a chance to win back some of the money you took from us," the Judge insisted.

So we set a date at the old Jungle Club course in St. Petersburg. The sky looked threatening when we all arrived at the first tee, but Landis would tolerate no delay, let alone chickening out. It began raining when we were on the fourth hole; by the time we reached the sixth tee it was pouring. Furthermore it was downright chilly. We held a conference: Landis and Daley voted to continue, Orr and I to quit. So we flipped a coin, Orr and I won, and we started back for the clubhouse. We hadn't gone 150 yards when we met two stockily built Amazons wearing foul-weather gear and carrying their own bags over their shoulders. Landis couldn't stand it. "Are you two sissies going to let

Judge Landis. On a golf course he hated to lose even a quarter. AP Photo.

those two ladies enjoy this golf course by themselves?" he remarked disdainfully.

Orr and I yielded and returned meekly with Landis and Daley to the sixth tee. In the most miserable of conditions we slogged our way for the full eighteen holes. Judge Landis was just as wet as any of us but he was wearing a smile of beatific satisfaction. He had got in his daily round despite the elements. And he had won back his quarter.

11

THE TRAGIC CAREER OF CARL MAYS

The 1921 World Series—the first between the two New York teams—has always intrigued me, especially the part played in it by Carl Mays. Carl was without much doubt the best underhand pitcher in the history of baseball. He won twenty-six games for the Yankees in 1920, and he followed that up with twenty-seven wins in 1921. In the latter year he completed thirty games in a 154-game schedule, an American League record that only Catfish Hunter has come close to in modern times.

Mays started the 1921 Series brilliantly, pitching a five-hit shutout and winning, 3–0. The next day his teammate Waite Hoyt pitched another 3–0 shutout, getting the Yanks out in front of the McGraw men by two games. It was a five-out-of-nine Series. In the third game the Yankees pounded Fred Toney out of the box with four runs in the third inning—a beautiful cushion for their own pitcher, Bob Shawkey. As the Yanks ran up the lead, I looked toward one of the boxes used by the owners of the Giants, and I saw Judge McQuade, treasurer and part owner, refusing to watch the game any longer. He sat bent over, his forehead resting on the wall of the box, as though he had been given a death sentence. But his despondency did not last long, for the Giants came right back in their half of the third, knocking Shawkey out and tying the game. The tie remained until the seventh inning, when the Giants scored an incredible eight runs without the benefit of an error. wound up with twenty hits for the day, and won 13–5.

127

Carl Mays.   NYH Service

Now it was up to Mays again to get the Yankees out in front and keep the series from being evened. Again he opposed Phil Douglas, the big spitball pitcher of the Giants. It was a tight game for seven innings. Mays had pitched hitless and runless ball for five innings, then yielded harmless singles in the sixth and seventh. The Yankees had gone ahead, 1–0, in the fifth, on a home run by Babe Ruth. Then came a crucial inning—and a tragic one—for Mays. All of a sudden the Giants' bats went bang! bang! bang! In a few moments they had four hits, including a triple by Emil (Irish) Meusel, a double by George Burns, and three runs.

The story of the game centered around the blow by Emil Meusel that drove in one run, Irish himself scoring a moment later. Just before the Meusel hit, Manager Miller Huggins had signaled from the bench for a fastball. But Mays disregarded the instruction. Instead he pitched a slow-breaking curve. Later he justified himself by saying that earlier in the game he had retired Meusel on just such a pitch. This time, however, Irish drove it to the wall, and the Giants soon had three runs. In the ninth inning the Giants continued to hit Mays, three more hits bringing in another run. The Yanks scored one in the bottom half of the ninth, but the game was gone and the Yanks left the field a dejected 4–2 loser.

On the night of this game, toward midnight, George Perry, who was helping me in my role that year as chairman of the arrangements and hospitality for the national press, came to me at the pressroom in the Commodore Hotel with a man whose story he wanted me to hear. The man happened to be a prominent player in a number of Broadway shows of that time.

The actor's tale went something like this: At the start of the eighth innings, Mrs. Mays, sitting in the grandstand, flashed a signal to Carl by wiping her face with a white handkerchief. Some persons, he said, who regarded a Giants' victory in the Series as absolutely necessary for their welfare, had offered Carl a rather substantial sum in cash if in close games he would serve up enough hittable pitches to lose the game. Mrs. Mays was to be the one who, by the prearranged handkerchief signal, would advise her husband that the money had been handed over.

It was only a year after the Black Sox scandal had exploded, bringing about life expulsion for eight players. And since then the new commissioner Judge Landis had banished for life such other players guilty of misconduct as Claude Hendrix, Joe Gedeon, Hal Chase, Heinie Zimmerman, and Eugene Paulette. Could such a high-salaried star as Carl Mays join these culprits? It didn't seem possible.

However, I knew what I had to do—inform Judge Landis and the owners of the Yankees. I thought it best to have the actor tell his story first to Col. Tillinghast Huston, who was half-owner of the Yankees and very close to the 1921 writers covering his team. Huston had rooms for the Series in the Hotel Martinique, at Thirty-first Street and Broadway. When the actor and I reached the Martinique, we went right up to the Huston suite. Some member of the Yankee front office staff let us in. In the bedroom we found Huston sleeping on one bed and Harry Frazee, the Red Sox owner, on another. Both were fully dressed and snoring like drunken sailors. Empty whiskey bottles were on the dresser, and the room reeked of stale liquor.

I awakened Huston with some difficulty and introduced the actor, saying, "I'll let this man tell you his story."

The actor told Huston the same story he had told me a half hour earlier. "This doesn't look too good for our club," said the Colonel. "Have you brought it to Judge Landis's attention?"

"No," I said, "I wanted to tell you first, but Judge Landis's quarters at the Commodore are our next stop."

So Huston, Perry, the actor, and I hopped a cab to call on the commissioner back at the Commodore Hotel, next to the Grand Central Station. In retrospect this sounds like a badly plotted TV melodrama, but we went right up to his suite and pounded on the door. I guess I was thinking that if I telephoned the room first, it being after midnight, the Judge might say to wait until the following morning. I was worked up to my responsibility, as I saw it, that we had better get quick action.

After several knocks Landis himself finally appeared, in a flannel nightgown. "What in the hell do you fellows want at this hour of the night?" he growled, eyebrows lowered.

"Judge," I said rather apologetically, "here's a man who thinks the game yesterday wasn't entirely on the up-and-up. He thinks Mays let up in the last two innings."

The Judge snapped to full attention, took the actor into one of the bedrooms, and pumped him for nearly half an hour. Huston, Perry, and I cooled our heels in the suite's anteroom. When Landis and the actor reappeared, the Judge told me directly, "I am making a full investigation of this man's story. I have already called up the detective agency that my office employs from time to time, and they will keep their eyes on Mays for the remainder of the Series." And then after a pause, "Freddy, don't you use this in your paper until there are further developments."

At the end of the Series, Landis, who had seen me several times that week for various reasons, told me the detective agency had been unable to find anything that would incriminate Carl Mays or corroborate the actor's story.

If that had been the end of the Mays incident of the 1921 World Series I would not be writing about it today. But there was an aftermath—a conversation seven years later that brought it all back to me. It happened at Dover Hill, a hunting lodge which several club owners shared near Brunswick, Georgia. I had visited there several times and this time I went with Harvey Traband, secretary of the National League. In the living room one night we were all in front of a big log fire—Col. Huston; Wilbert Robinson, manager and president of the Brooklyn Dodgers at that time; Harvey Traband; Frank Grayson, a Cincinnati baseball writer; our wives. The drink for the night was Coca-Cola and rum, and Uncle Robbie and Huston took frequent quenches of this southern Prohibition drink.

Some time in the evening, after Huston had imbibed more than a little, he turned to me and said, "Freddy, I am going to tell you the damnedest story a baseball owner has ever told a reporter." Every time he repeated this remark, Uncle Robby would sh-sh-sh him and say, "No, no, Colonel! Don't tell him! Don't tell him!" But Huston would return to the subject. As the rum and Coca-Cola had its effect, some of the people in the room gradually disappeared and Robby fell asleep. Only Huston, Grayson, and I were left. Grayson, still consuming Coca-Cola and rum, tried to stay awake to hear the story that Huston apparently intended to tell me, but finally he too fell asleep. So I said to Huston, "Now that we're alone, what is this story you're holding back on me?"

"I wanted to tell you that some of our pitchers threw World Series games on us in both 1921 and 1922," he mumbled.

"You mean that Mays matter of the 1921 World Series?" I asked.

He said, "Yes, but there were others—other times, other pitchers." By now he was almost in a stupor and stumbled off to bed.

I suppose as a good reporter I should have stuck around the next morning and pressed Huston for specifics—names, dates, and all that. But I didn't. Huston hadn't appeared before Traband and I were scheduled to leave to play golf at Sea Island, Georgia. After our game we continued north. (When I next spoke with Huston alone a year or two later, he would say only that he stood by what he had told me at Dover Hall.)

Upon arriving back in New York where I kept my baseball books in my den, I looked up Mays's record in the 1921 Series. It struck me as odd that all the destruction wreaked on Carl by the Giants had happened in those two innings in which the actor had suspected foul play. In three games, Mays pitched twenty-six innings in which he gave up 20 hits. In two of those innings, the Giants scored 4 runs on 7 hits. In the other twenty-four innings they scored only 2 runs on 13 hits, and one of those runs was unearned.

I pursued the matter no further. But then, several years later, it popped up again in a conversation with Miller Huggins. Hug and three or four of us writers were discussing the sore straits of some retired players of great ability. There was no Baseball Players Association then and no fat one-thousand-dollar monthly retirement check.

Huggins said, "Any ballplayers that played for me on either the Cardinals or Yankees could come to me if he were in need and I would give him a helping hand." Then after a pause, "I make only two exceptions, Carl Mays and Joe Bush. If they were in the gutter, I'd kick them." And he got up from his chair and demonstrated how he would kick them. I thought to myself, "How can such a kindly gentleman carry such a deep hatred?" Before I could ask a follow-up question, the conversation had moved on to ballplayers specifically in need.

I was sure he was thinking, first of all, of the Mays game in 1921. As for Bush, I was reasonably certain he had in mind, perhaps only as one example, a game in the 1922 World Series. I was the chief scorer that year and followed every pitch intently. In both the first and fifth games Bush carried a small lead into the eighth inning. In both games he allowed three runs in the eighth and lost. In the second of these, Manager Huggins ordered right-handed Bullet Joe to walk left-handed batter Ross Youngs and take a chance on right-handed George Kelly. Bush turned toward Huggins and yelled from the mound, "What for, you stupid . . . [incredible obscenity]?" His voice carried throughout the press box and must have been heard by at least a thousand box holders. After sullenly walking Youngs as ordered, Bush pitched the next one "right down the pike" and Kelly belted it for a line-drive single, turning the game around.

Mays's career with the Yankees went downhill in the two years that followed the 1921 World Series. It was not a good year for the Yankees in 1922, though they did beat the St. Louis Browns by one game for the American League championship. It also was an off season for Mays, who dropped from 26–11 in 1920 and 27–9 in 1921 to a mediocre 13–14 with a first-place club.

In 1923 Huggins really made Mays suffer. While Carl claimed he was in fine physical condition and that his arm felt as strong as ever, he got almost no work, despite the fact that he was probably the highest salaried pitcher on the club. Sometimes two or three weeks would go by, and then Huggins would let him finish a losing game. His record was 5–2, but he was used in only eighty-one innings. Carl would ask the reporters, including me, "What's wrong with me? Why doesn't Huggins pitch me?"

When we questioned Huggins, his reply was, "Why should I use him? I'm winning an easy pennant without him. I'm pitching Waite Hoyt, Herb Pennock, Joe Bush, Bob Shawkey, and Sam Jones. They are all delivering for me. Why should I break the rhythm of an effective rotation?"

Hug took satanic joy in one of the two defeats charged to Mays in

Fred Lieb and Miller Huggins discussing Ruth's indefinite suspension in 1925.   Charles M. Conlon

1923. It was a July game in Cleveland when Huggins started Mays against George Uhle. While winning, 13–0, the Indians whacked 20 hits, and though Carl pitched until his tongue hung out, Hug made him take the humiliating beating for the full nine innings. Hug said, "He told me he needed lots of work, so I gave it to him."

Carl explained his poor showing thus: "He pitched me maybe two innings here, one inning a week later. So even though I have a sound arm, I am in no shape to pitch a nine-inning game. A strong-armed pitcher like me needs to work every fourth or fifth game to have his stuff."

After the 1923 World Series, which the Yanks won four games to two without Mays pitching an inning, the Yankees asked for waivers on Carl. None of the seven other American League clubs claimed him, which surprised me, and Mays was sold to the Cincinnati Reds for $7,500, then the interleague waiver price.

Huggins wrote to Garry Herrmann, president of the Reds and Miller's former boss when he played second base for the Reds, "I may be sending you the best pitcher I have, but I warn you that Carl is a troublemaker and always will be a hard man to sign."

Mays proved he was as good a pitcher as ever by winning twenty games for Cincinnati in 1924 and again in 1926. But why did no American League club pick up Carl for the within-the-league waiver price of only $5,000?

I cannot judge Mays, even with the perspective of fifty-six years. I know that Landis cleared Carl after one of the nation's best detective agencies said they could find nothing suspicious in October 1921. And I know how merciless Judge Landis was in dealing with players who were only indirectly connected with the throwing of a ball game. I know, too, that even the greatest pitchers—Christy Mathewson, Walter Johnson, Bob Feller, Warren Spahn—have for an inning or two in a crucial game lost their stuff and taken a cruel pounding. It could have happened to Carl Mays.

Fewer than a dozen people knew Mays was investigated in the last four games of that Series. As Landis requested, I printed nothing about it at the time.

However, in 1949 I did give this story a briefer telling in an earlier book of mine, *The Story of the World Series*. Mays was still alive and active as a big league scout when my book and its later revised editions appeared. If he read it, he never wrote to give me his side. He died in 1971.

I knew both Carl and Mrs. Mays reasonably well in Carl's years with the Yankees. Mrs. Mays and my wife were the only women on the 1920 Yankees' special train to their Jacksonville training camp. The ladies quickly made friends and the four of us attended several Sunday afternoon musicals. Mrs. Mays was a graduate of the Boston Academy of Music—a talented and attractive person, the last person I could imagine to serve as signal giver in a conspiracy to throw a ball game.

Carl Mays's story is even more poignant in light of an earlier bitter incident on August 16, 1920.

The weather was hot and sultry in the Polo Grounds that afternoon. Two clubs which had never won an American League pennant, the Cleveland Indians and the New York Yankees, were battling for their first championship. Both managers, Miller Huggins and Tris Speaker, had started their best pitchers, Carl Mays and Stan Coveleski, a spitballer who in a decade (1916–25) won 193 games. Mays was unsteady in the early innings, and the Indians led, 3–0, when Mays faced Ray Chapman, star shortstop, Cleveland's first hitter in the top of the fifth inning.

With a count of one strike and one ball on the batter, Mays let go a pitch with results that would haunt him for the rest of his life. It was high on the inside, designed to prevent Chapman from attempting a drag bunt, one of Ray's specialties. Sitting in the old downstairs press box, not much more than fifty feet behind the umpire, I had a perfect view of the action. A right-handed hitter, Chapman crouched over the plate more than any other batter of his era. I saw Mays's "submarine" pitch rise, from the near-ground level where it was delivered, on a straight line towards Chapman's head. A batter has about a half second to react to a ball that may hit him. As soon as Ray was hit I thought, "Why didn't he react, duck, throw himself to the ground?" But he didn't. He froze.

There was a sickening thud as the ball hit the left side of Chapman's head at the temple. He got up after a few seconds, and I could see the left eye hanging from its socket. With a ball player's instinct, he took two steps toward first, then fell in a heap. He never regained consciousness. Cleveland players carried him to the center-field clubhouse, and from there he was rushed to a downtown hospital. He died at 3:30 A.M. the next morning, the only big leaguer to be a fatal victim of a pitched ball.

Mays continued to pitch until the eighth inning, when Sammy Vick pinch-hit for him. At the time few people knew of the seriousness of the accident. In 1920 television was a generation away and even radio was in its infancy. The morning papers merely reported that Chapman still was in a coma in the hospital. Mays himself did not learn of Chap-

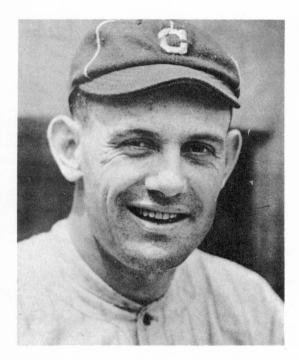

Ray Chapman, Cleveland shortstop—the only player ever to have been killed by a pitched ball. Western Newspaper Union

man's death until ten o'clock the next day, when Mark Roth, the New York team's traveling secretary, brought word to his apartment.

Manager Miller Huggins, a law-school graduate familiar with the legal technicalities, took Mays to the police station nearest the Polo Grounds to file his personal report of the incident. Later Carl was summoned to the office of the district attorney of Manhattan for an interrogation. The pitcher was absolved from any guilt, and Chapman's death was officially listed as accidental.

Mays had little to say about the accident, except that he thought Chapman should have thrown himself to the ground. When his turn to pitch came around again, he was ready and hurled a winning game.

But when the news of Chapman's death became known to the general public, they vilified Mays. Most of the Cleveland players I interviewed on their bench the next day were bitter. "Mays should be strung up," insisted Doc Johnston, the Indians' first baseman.

Tris Speaker was easier on Mays than most of the rest. As the batter-on-deck at the time of the fatal pitch, he was perhaps better qualified to discuss it. Tris told me: "I don't think Mays deliberately threw at him. There was time for Chappie to duck when the ball was coming at him, but he never moved. It was a tight pitch, high and on the inside, but we are trained to duck when such a pitch is coming at us."

What made it tougher for Mays was that he had a long-standing reputation for throwing so-called bean balls. When Carl was on the World Champion Red Sox of 1915, 1916, and 1918, he and left-hander Dutch Leonard were notorious for throwing toward a batter's head now and then. That was the way the Boston manager, Bill Carrigan, liked them to pitch.

Mays felt he never lived down the Chapman accident. Late in his life I heard him say, "I won over two hundred big league games, but no one today remembers that. When they think of me, I'm the guy who killed Chapman with a fastball."

Mays and his biographer, Bob McGarigle, felt that only the death of Chapman in 1920 kept Carl out of the Baseball Hall of Fame. As a member of the Hall of Fame's Veterans Committee for over a decade, I know that this is not so. Carl Mays's name has frequently come before the committee, but no one has ever brought up the Chapman tragedy as a reason why Carl should not be in the Cooperstown shrine. Rather, the question mark has often been his performance in the Series of 1921.

I am not suggesting that Mays be given a break. But I would like to enlarge upon the compliment Huggins paid Mays for his pitching ability when he waived him to Cincinnati: "I may be sending you the best pitcher I have. . . ."

Consider these figures: 130 games won in a six-season stretch, 1916–21. Back-to-back seasons, 1920–21, 53 games won. Overall rec-

Tris Speaker setting out for a fly ball. Many regard him as the greatest center fielder in the history of baseball. AP Wirephoto

ord, won 207, lost 127. Winning percentage, .620. Lifetime ERA, 2.92.

Carl's pitching teammates on the Yankees, Waite Hoyt and Herb Pennock, are safely in the Hall of Fame. Though each won more games than Carl, neither was close to him in winning percentage and both trailed him badly in the ERA statistic, Hoyt with 3.59, Pennock with 3.61.

Flaw in his character? Bad luck? Slander? No one can say for sure.

12

A GAMBLE FOR RAIN—
FOR MATTY

I was never much of a gambling man but in 1921 I took a gamble for rain—and won. It was in connection with the Christy Mathewson Testimonial Game at the Polo Grounds on the last day of the season. The scheduled game was between the New York Giants and old Boston Braves and nothing was at stake, for the Giants had clinched the National League pennant ten days earlier.

The story behind this first of all testimonial days for the benefit of a player began three years earlier. Late in the shortened season of 1918, Mathewson, the former pitching ace of the Giants with a lifetime record of 373–188, had resigned after two and a half seasons as manager of the Cincinnati Reds to become Captain Christopher Mathewson of the Army's Chemical Warfare Division. He was promptly sent to France. After the Armistice of November 11, 1918, he was ordered to inspect some of the trenches abandoned by the surrendering Germans. Unknown to Matty, there still were pockets of poison gas in the bunkers under covered portions of the trenches. Perhaps the gas had been fired by the Allies during the last days of the war, or perhaps it had been intentionally left by the Germans. In any case, Matty took a little of this into his throat and upper lungs and immediately suffered severe coughing spells.

After the Armistice Garry Herrmann, the Cincinnati president, had every intention of reestablishing Mathewson as manager. According to Herrmann he had sent several cablegrams to him in France inquiring as to his availability, but received no answer. So on the eve of the 1919 training season, Herrmann named Pat Moran, former Philadelphia Phillies manager, as his team leader.

When Mathewson did return after hospitalization in France, he said he had never received the Herrmann cablegrams. John McGraw then named his former star as number one coach and assistant manager of the Giants, and Christy reported to the Giants' camp in Gainesville, Florida. Early in the season the coughing spells began seizing him again. Physicians promptly diagnosed it as tuberculosis. He and his beautiful wife Jane were promptly hustled off to Lake Placid, New York, where he was put under the care of Dr. Edward Trudeau, a lung specialist and founder of a famous tuberculosis sanatorium.

Mathewson had been a good businessman, and though he never made ten thousand dollars a year before the 1914–1915 Federal League war (which raised everyone's salaries), his savings were well invested. Until now Christy and Jane had had a modest nest egg for the future. He had made a few extra bucks by endorsing sundry products, and he did a little writing, much of it ghosted by Jack Wheeler. It makes me laugh when I contemplate the few thousands a star of Mathewson's caliber garnered then as compared with the side money which goes to-day to such stars as Johnny Bench, Catfish Hunter, and Tom Seaver. In contrast to their tens of thousands of dollars per "job," Mathewson's pay was dimes and nickels.

Some of Matty's friends and admirers wanted to do something for their hero, and so the testimonial was organized. As chairman of the New York baseball writers at the time, I was tapped for the chairmanship of the testimonial committee. Harry Stevens, the caterer at the Polo Grounds and numerous other ball parks and racetracks, pledged himself, his boundless energy, and his organization to the Matty game. Stevens also contributed some good ideas, the best of which was a Christy Mathewson Souvenir scorecard and book. "I'll make it the best ever given to an American athlete or actor," Harry said. "Nothing we can do is too great for Matty. I really love that guy—the salt of the earth." I suggested to Harry that each of the active New York baseball writers be given an illustrated page in the book in which to write of some phase of Mathewson's life or baseball career.

Two or three weeks before the testimonial game I was approached by an energetic salesman from one of the larger insurance companies. He wanted to insure the Mathewson testimonial game for $25,000 against rain. My first reaction was that we would have to pay out too much of the game's receipts if it came off on a fair day. However, the insurance man was persistent and persuasive. He had a table showing how often it rained in early October in New York. "I don't have to tell you about the 1911 World Series which was held up for a week in Philadelphia," he said. "On most of those days it also was raining in New

York," he added with a significant look at me. I well remembered that wretched week a decade earlier.

"Think of poor Matty, if it does rain on October first," he continued. "It's the last day of the season, with the World Series right afterwards. There can be no postponement. And, there would be no one to buy those beautiful souvenir programs or bid for your autographed baseballs. Matty would get nothing, absolutely nothing. But, if you insure the game, he would get a snug sum, probably better than the gate receipts."

I signed the insurance contract. McGraw was vastly displeased, especially about the company's ten percent of the $25,000, but I stood my ground. "That's Matty's money you're giving away," he said with undisguised scorn.

Then I thought up another gimmick to bring some longtime fans to the park—a pregame five-inning exhibition between the new 1921 National League Champions and an old-timers team made up of the Giants' world champions of 1905. I can still hear McGraw snap, "That's bush!" meaning it was a "bush" (minor league) idea. But I eventually won out on that one, too.

Billy Gilbert, Giants second baseman of that great 1905 team, helped

Fred Lieb and John McGraw at the Polo Grounds during the 1922 Giants-Yankees World Series

out importantly. Between us we enlisted Art Devlin, Mike Donlin, Joe McGinnity, George Wiltse, Frank Bowerman, and a few others. We eventually filled out the old-timers' lineup with players from the Giants National League champs of 1911, 1912, and 1913: Larry Doyle, Georgie Burns, Chief Meyers, and Red Ames. The event brought together a lot of once-familiar faces.

The wildest idea for the Matty Day events was an offer to stage a rattlesnake race. No less than Heywood Broun called and asked me to meet him and Christopher Morley for a luncheon. Morley was a sophisticated columnist on the New York *Evening Post,* then regarded mostly as a financial newspaper. Its circulation was only 25,000, but it was read by the intelligentsia of the greater New York area, largely on account of Morley's charm, wit, and sarcasm.

At this time, Morley was devoting a good bit of space in his column to his racing rattlers. He lived in northern New Jersey where he had sufficient space to train and race his reptiles, and now another man had challenged him. At our luncheon, Morley and Broun proposed that we use the Polo Grounds as an arena for these races; they thought a perfect time would be the interval between the exhibition game and the regularly scheduled National League game on Matty Day.

"It would be good for an additional five to ten thousand in attendance," argued Broun with a straight face. "You don't think too highly of our plan, do you?"

"That's right," I said. "I believe it would be making a circus out of our tribute to a great athlete." That idea was one I was *sure* McGraw would veto!

Eventually, Matty's big day arrived. The Giants had committed their full share of the home club's receipts to the Matty fund. But George Washington Grant, owner of the Braves, was in no mood to be generous. His club was suffering from financial heebie-jeebies, and he was out to get all of the visiting club's share of the enlarged gate receipts.

The day started out beautiful—warm, pleasant and sunny. During the intermission between games we auctioned off three dozen balls signed by Mathewson and all the 1921 Giants. Harry Stevens put some of his most eloquent peanut, hot dog, and scorecard salesmen to work drumming up bids throughout the stands.

The prize baseball was autographed by Mathewson, President Harding, Vice-President Coolidge, Governor Miller, Babe Ruth, Walter Johnson, Ty Cobb, George M. Cohan, Richard Mansfield, and several other actors, athletes, and politicians. It was the most autographed ball I ever saw and I auctioned it off myself from the concrete roof of the Braves' dugout. It finally went for $450 to a persistent man whom I didn't know. He told me he did not have $450 with him, but would promptly send a check.

Two days later I asked the treasurer whether he had received the check and he said he hadn't. I asked again after a week, after a month, after three months, and the answer always was no. So our prize ball went to a deadbeat. It was the only unpleasant thing in an otherwise beautiful day. If anybody knows where this ball is today, I will pay $450 for it.

By the time they started the Giants-Braves game, clouds had gathered in the east and the skies were becoming ominous. After one scoreless inning the heavens opened. What came down was no mere shower, but such a rain as to convince everyone quite early that the contest could not be resumed. We had in the till not only the gate receipts from a crowd of 18,000, but also the $25,000 no-game rain insurance. After the umpires officially called off the game, it was announced through the public address system that any fan who wanted to get his money back should bring his rain check to the Giants office at the end of the World Series. Only 4,000 called for the refund.

Promptly the next morning the insurance man called to hand me a check for $25,000 made out to Frederick G. Lieb, Chairman. He told me how happy the company was to pay out the money because of the good publicity they were getting. The $25,000 was the biggest check I had handled up to that time, and I promptly proceeded to lose it. When I arrived home that night and tried to show the check to Mary, I simply didn't have it. That afternoon I had stopped off at the Giants' offices to pick up some World Series tickets for friends and had shown the check to some of the office girls. The next morning it was found lying on top of a secretary's desk.

Exactly how much money the Mathewsons received from the game I was never told, but it was in the neighborhood of $45,000, the equivalent of $200,000 today. Aside from the insurance money, the Giants' share of the gate receipts yielded around $15,000, profits from the one-dollar souvenir score books were $5,000, and another $5,000 came from autographed baseballs and personal checks sent to the fund by friends of Mathewson in Wall Street and the theatrical district. I was told it was the largest amount ever raised for any actor or athlete up to that time. The Mathewsons were genuinely grateful for the gift and for my part in it. Matty wrote me: "The amount is far above our expectations, and I know what a break you gave us when you insured the game."

I do not think Mathewson as a pitcher was as fast as Walter Johnson, Rube Waddell, Bob Grove, Bobby Feller, or Nolan Ryan when Ryan was at his best. But he was fast, and he had amazing control. He once went sixty-eight consecutive innings without issuing a base on balls. He had an extra pitch, called the fadeaway (I think Boze Bulger so named it). This can best be thought of as the same as Carl Hubbell's

left-handed screwball, but pitched by a right-hander. It broke outward
and away from left-handed batters, down and in on right-handed, exactly the opposite from a right-hander's curveball. Sometimes when he
threw it, it didn't curve but suddenly plunged, as does a tennis ball
rolled across and off a dining-room table.

Prior to the testimonial game, I knew Mathewson well enough only
to say, "Hello, Matty," when I met him in hotel lobbies and trains. He
was not a great one to talk with reporters, especially the younger ones.
After the testimonial game, he became really cordial. I remember particularly a conversation after the Giants lost that harrowing twelve-
inning seventh game of the 1924 World Series. We ate dinner together
in the Pullman compartment on the train back to New York, chatted
about many things, but always returned to the subject of the game and
the World Series that McGraw had just lost to Bucky Harris, the young
manager of the new Washington world champions. Particularly on
Matty's mind was the unhappy Hank Gowdy incident, which he called
an unforgivable mistake.

As Gowdy, an experienced catcher for the Boston Braves and Giants,
started after a foul in the last half of the twelfth inning with the score
tied, 3–3, he caught his left foot in his mask, which he had carelessly
tossed to the ground near his feet. The mask held on like a bear trap,
and as Hank tried to shake it loose, the easy foul pop fly fell safely to
the ground. His batting life saved, little Muddy Ruel hit the next pitch
to deep right field for a double, and he scored the winning run a few
minutes later when a ground ball took a crazy hop over the head of the
boy third baseman, Freddy Lindstrom. The combination of lucky
plays meant a day of delirious happiness for Washington; for partisans
of the Giants, it brought sorrow, despair, and recrimination.

In 1923 Judge Emil Fuchs, who had acquired the Boston Braves
from George W. Grant, asked Mathewson to serve as president of his
club. The job was more or less window dressing. Fuchs told Mathewson that he could continue to live in Lake Placid, and he need only
come to Boston whenever he felt his health permitted it. Fuchs would
consult him on player salaries, player trades, and new players to be acquired, and he, Matty, would be the voice of the Boston club in league
meetings.

In retrospect, I think it would have been better if he had not accepted. The treatment of tuberculosis had not yet advanced to the point
where, a generation later, Red Schoendienst of the Milwaukee Braves,
later manager of the Cardinals, could conquer the disease so well that
he could return from treatment to play four more seasons and then
serve as a manager for twelve more years.

I next caught up with Matty when the Yankees moved their spring
training camp from New Orleans to St. Petersburg in 1925. The Braves

were already there, having pitched their training camp in the Sunshine City in 1922. That spring I enjoyed several lengthy talks with Mathewson. I came to respect his mind and his ability to express himself. Then during the 1925 season, when McGraw was trying to win a fifth straight pennant in New York, we heard that Mathewson had suffered a relapse and wasn't doing well. Nevertheless, everyone at the 1925 Pirate-Washington World Series was shocked at the news that the great pitcher, the idol of the fans for the first two decades of this century, had died at Lake Placid. National League President John Heydler, McGraw, Fuchs, and other baseball men left the Series to attend Matty's funeral.

Long after Mathewson's death I have been asked, "Why was Mathewson loved so much? Did people really love him as much as sports writers of his day alleged?"

Fans regarded him as the all-American boy. (Tom Seaver in his younger days enjoyed this kind of reputation.) Matty didn't play Sunday baseball because of a promise he once made to his mother. But that didn't mean too much in New York at that time, for in Matty's day there were only three big league clubs that permitted Sunday baseball: Chicago, St. Louis, and Cincinnati. He was a consistent Episcopal churchgoer. Though there were other college men in big league baseball in Matty's time, Sir Christopher of Bucknell was the best known and most outstanding graduate. There is today a big Christy Mathewson Memorial Gate at the entrance to Bucknell's Athletic Field. He was happily and devotedly married to a lovely and intelligent wife.

Mathewson had three nicknames: Christy, Matty, and Big Six. One said Christy Mathewson, but not Matty Mathewson. His wife and the New York fans called him Matty, a general term of endearment for their hero. His Giant teammates invariably spoke of him as Matty. Big Six was a name created by some sports writer before I arrived in New York and it was only used in baseball stories, as Joe DiMaggio is called the Yankee Clipper in print. "Big Six" had two bases: Matty was a "big six," standing 6 feet 1½ inches, and there is an important typographical union in New York called Big Six. The very name suggested power.

There was a legend that Matty didn't drink or smoke. He did take an occasional drink and he smoked cigarettes, but he was not a chain smoker. He did swear on occasion and he loved to gamble. He was good at card games of any sort and usually won—he was smarter, had a quicker mind, and knew cards and percentages better than most of them. He studied opposing card players much as he studied batsmen when he was pitching, and this gave him a decided advantage.

Once in a dice game when his luck wasn't so good, he threw a $1,000 bill on the floor and said, "Fade that if you dare!" No one took up the challenge. McGraw had been tipped off about the game, and ultimately

Christy Mathewson in the latter part of his pitching career.

broke it up, fining each of the lesser players $10. For Mathewson the fine was $100. Though McGraw and Mathewson were close personal friends, the manager was very stern on this occasion, saying, "It will cost you one hundred dollars because you should have set a better example for these men who don't have your intelligence."

The son of English-born middle-class parents, Matty had the reserve and reticence of the British gentry. He disliked having people—even teammates—close in on him. When a train carrying the Giants stopped at a smaller city, Mathewson, playing cards beside a window seat, would pull down the shade of the Pullman so that none of the people on the train platform could see him. In this respect he was entirely different from the budding American League star, Babe Ruth. When a Yankees Special pulled into a smaller town, Babe would jump from his card game, climb down onto the platform and immediately yell, "Hello, kid," to any strangers within earshot.

Larry Doyle told me that Matty had once humiliated him by refusing after a game to speak to some friends of Larry's who had come a long distance just to see their hero pitch. On occasion Matty could be standoffish. Despite this trait, Christy Mathewson for fifteen years was the most admired player in baseball, the one fathers would take their sons to see pitch on their first visit to a ball park. His pitching records speak for themselves. I doubt if there was a dissenting voice anywhere in the land when he was elected, with Wagner, Cobb, Johnson, and Ruth, as one of the first players to be enshrined in baseball's Hall of Fame in Cooperstown, New York.

13

THE BIG BAMBINO

With the exception of King David of Israel, whose slingshot knockout of Goliath is recorded in millions of Bibles printed in hundreds of languages, George Herman "Babe" Ruth was the most publicized athlete who ever lived. Babe Ruth surely was the best known and most loved sports figure of America. In the golden decade of American sports, the 1920s, he was the hero of boys from the ages of three to ninety-three and of many of their mothers, wives, and daughters.

A candy manufacturer cashed in on the man of the day with a popular chocolate bar, "Baby Ruth" (without getting the permission of the Ruth clan), much to the distress of Ruth and the late Christy Walsh, Babe's agent and publicist. Kids, however, had no problem distinguishing between Babe Ruth and Baby Ruth. Their fathers and grandfathers worshipped at Ruth's shrine, Yankee Stadium in New York, a stadium I dubbed in a moment of inspiration in the spring of 1923 The House That Ruth Built. In World War II American soldiers and Marines, shouting at Japanese soldiers across the mud and mist of some South Pacific island, yelled, "The hell with Emperor Hirohito." The Japanese, thinking to strike back at the Americans' most vulnerable spot, called back, "The hell with Babe Ruth."

Even when the Babe was in the wrong, everyone made it all right. One night when the Babe was driving the wrong direction down a one-way street on New York's East Side, he was stopped by a police car. As Ruth was bringing out his driver's license, the officer recognized Babe's moonlike face. "Oh, it's you, Mr. Babe," said the officer. Instead of rebuking Ruth for dangerous driving and giving him a ticket, the cop said gently, "Just follow me, Mr. Babe, and we'll see you get out of this mess without an accident." With his lights flashing and siren wail-

Yankee Stadium, "The House That Ruth Built," on its opening day in 1923.

ing, the cop guided Ruth to a point where Babe would be moving with the traffic.

At least as late as 1930, Ty Cobb and Hans Wagner generally were regarded as the greatest players of all time. However, now that Ruth's contributions to baseball can be fully evaluated, Mr. Babe looms up as number one. Indeed, he was labeled baseball's top player by a committee of experts at baseball's centennial celebration in Washington in 1969. As time goes on since Ruth laid down his big bat in 1935, his stature continues to grow.

Though the durable and amazing Hank Aaron, then of the Atlanta Braves, erased Ruth's lifetime home-run record of 714 in 1974, to millions of fans Ruth still is the Sultan of Swat. Fans remember that when Babe Ruth opened the home-run era, homers were comparatively rare. When the Maryland farmer, Frank Baker, was nicknamed Home Run Baker, it was on the strength of leading the American League in homers in 1911–14 with 9, 10, 12, and 8 respectively. When the new thunderer, Ruth, hit a magnificent 54 in 1920 and 59 in 1921, each figure was greater than the home-run total of 13 of the sixteen big league teams in those years.

The 1969 committee that voted Ruth "the greatest" also stressed his ability as a defensive player. In 1915, his first complete season in the American League, he was the won and lost leader with 18–8 and a .697 average. In the next two years he was 23–12 (.657) and 24–13 (.649). In 1916 he had the lowest earned run average in the American League, 1.75, 14 points lower than the great Washington right-hander, Walter Johnson.

In the 1916 and 1918 World Series the young lefthander pitched 29⅔ consecutive scoreless innings, breaking the former record of Christy Mathewson by 1⅔ innings. Ruth was very proud of this record, which lasted until 1962 when another Yankee left-hander, Whitey Ford, stretched it to 33⅔ innings. Ruth hotly resented any accusations that he was just a hard thrower, not a pitcher.

Shortly after Ruth's death in 1948, Taylor Spink, publisher of *The Sporting News*, asked me to take the Ruth side in a debate with Harry Salsinger of the Detroit *News* on the subject "Who was the greater—Ty Cobb or Babe Ruth?" As a matter of fact, up to that time I myself had considered Cobb to be number one. In arguing for Ruth, I made my case on the larger meaning of the word "great." I pointed out that while Ruth had hammered out 714 home runs and had a lifetime batting average of .342, a remarkable combination, he had, more importantly, revolutionized the entire game of baseball. Rather than playing for one run via the sacrifice bunt and the stolen base, a team could now play for one, two, three, or four runs with one swing of a Ruthian bat.

Ruth also gave the game of baseball more publicity than it had ever enjoyed before. The Babe was known in Japan, the Caribbean countries, England, Ireland, and Italy. In 1925 there was a false report of Ruth's death and it immediately spread around the world. One newspaper in London printed a two-column obituary on the Babe's demise, telling of his popularity, accomplishments, and heroics. So great was his attraction that people who never had been inside a big league park and knew little of baseball paid their money at box offices just to see this phenomenon.

By attracting many more fans, not only to Yankee Stadium in New York, but also on the road, Ruth raised the pay of ballplayers all along the line, in both major leagues and the strong minor leagues of that period. Within two years after Babe turned the game into a home-run frenzy, the pay checks of the average players were up 33⅓ percent. Hall of Famer Waite Hoyt, a fellow player with Ruth on the Yankees of that era, quipped: "Every big leaguer and his wife should teach their children to pray: 'God bless Mommy, God bless Daddy, and God bless Babe Ruth.'"

Babe Ruth's first year in New York, 1920, was also the year of the Harding-Cox presidential race. During the campaign I received a telegram from Bill Veeck, Sr., president of the Cubs: "DROP EVERYTHING. TAKE NIGHT TRAIN TO CHICAGO. WILL MEET YOU IN THE STATION. IMPORTANT."

I showed the telegram to some of my colleagues in the press box that afternoon. They guessed I was being recommended for the job of secretary to Judge Landis. But when Veeck met me in Chicago, he had with him Will Hays, chairman of the Republican National Committee, and Albert D. Lasker, a big name in advertising in Chicago. Politics and winning votes for Harding were why I had been summoned.

Ty Cobb had come out for Cox. The Veeck-Hays-Lasker trio recognized in Babe Ruth, the new wonder boy of baseball, the answer to Cobb's statement. Harding was waging a front-porch campaign from his Warren, Ohio, residence, so I was asked to bring Babe there for an appearance. If I could bring it off, there was $4,000 in it for Babe and $1,000 for me. It didn't mean much whether Babe was a Democrat or Republican so long as he would have lunch and sit on the front porch with the candidate. At the time Babe had no agent. The offer was the equivalent today of $16,000 and $4,000, respectively—almost totally tax-free. So I broached the matter to Babe, who replied, "I'm a Democrat, but I'll go to Warren for the money."

As the pennant race tightened, neither Huggins nor Huston would allow Ruth to be taken out of the lineup to skip out to Warren for a day. In the meantime the Babe's interest in the visit to Harding and in the money was rising, and he asked me to see if I could get a part of the pay as an advance to bind the agreement. I passed this request along to

Veeck in a letter, and the next morning, before I was out of bed, he was on the phone saying, "Don't write anything in a letter about money in connection with this matter. Use the telephone."

We finally set up the trip to Warren for the day after the season's final game. But the scandal of the Black Sox broke in the last week and baseball generally was being clobbered. In the light of baseball's bad publicity, Lasker and Veeck cooled off on the whole subject and Ruth never made his appearance.

During the years that the Babe was in his prime, a professor at Columbia College gave Ruth a thorough physical examination, testing such measurable traits as the speed of his muscular and nervous reactions to various stimuli. The New York *Times,* in recording the professor's findings, gave the story the head "ONE MAN IN A MILLION." The report said nothing about Babe's IQ, but in twenty categories, Ruth ranked well above the average male. All of his five senses were keener and sharper than average. He also scored high in strength, response to stress, and reaction time. As I recall it, the professor explained: "Take twenty men off the street and you will find that several of them may score above average in two, three, or four of these tests, but it is only one in a million who will score above average in all twenty."

The professor admittedly did not go into Ruth's mind; he dealt largely at the level of physical reactions. Ruth probably had a low IQ. Certainly he couldn't remember names, so with every one it was "Hello, kid," no matter what the person's age.

When the Yankees played in St. Louis, the team often boarded their train home at Delmar, a suburb west of the city. Young Charley Devens, a halfback and pitcher at Harvard and a man with family and social background, was one of the first to show up at the Delmar station. He had been with the Yankees for about a month and had started three or four games. Soon Ruth and some of the regulars, Gehrig, Lazzeri, and Dugan, joined the early birds at the station. Pointing to Devens, Babe asked me, "Is that guy with us?"

I said, "Oh, yes, that's Devens, the pitcher from Harvard." The Babe looked blank. "He's started several games for the Yankees," I added.

"Yeah, I remember now," said Babe. "We don't get him many runs, do we?" Babe couldn't remember the face or the name, but he could remember an essential fact about the games he had pitched.

On one occasion he was talking to a group of players about Ford Frick (who later became baseball commissioner). For three or four years Frick had been Babe's ghost-writer for the Christy Walsh Syndicate. I was sitting several seats away in the Pullman car when Babe called to me: "What's the name of the guy that writes for me? It rhymes with 'quick,' thick,' 'Dick.'"

"The name is Frick, Ford Frick," I called back.

Babe Ruth and Fred Lieb in St. Petersburg, about 1923.

"That's it: I should have remembered it," was Babe's answer.

I wrote New York baseball the entire time that Ruth was in the big leagues (1914–1935) and during the full fifteen years he served with the Yankees (1920–1934). I often had occasion for talks with Babe. He was proud that he and I, each writing under his own by-line, were the only ones to pick the 1926 Yankees, a seventh-place club in 1925, to win the pennant. "Fred Lieb and I sure had our necks out on that one," he used to say. "But the team came through for us." Despite some obvious lacks in Babe's mental makeup, I refute the recent stories that make him such a numskull. Though his language invariably was colored with vulgarity and profanity, he often made intelligent comments on New York City and its politics, the Yankees, visiting players, and the chances of the other fifteen major league clubs.

Once when Ruth and I were guests of the Gehrigs at their home in New Rochelle, New York, I was surprised to overhear Ruth speaking German to Mom Gehrig. He spoke almost as well as Lou Gehrig, who was raised to talk German to his parents, and he even got some indelicate German words and phrases into his conversation. Ruth's parents were German and he spoke their language when he was home.

Ruth once admitted to me that he had been a pretty tough kid. He said he delighted in doing things that older people thought were bad. "We lived in back of a Baltimore saloon, and my mother often tended bar when my father was away," he said. "I learned early to drink beer, wine, and whiskey, and I think I was about five when I first chewed tobacco. I didn't particularly like the taste, but I knew it was supposed to be bad. There was a lot of cussing in Pop's saloon, so I learned a lot of swear words, some really bad ones. That's why they kept sticking me back in St. Mary's."

In the early stories of Ruth's career, writers had him in St. Mary's continuously from the age of seven to nineteen, when he was legally adopted by Jack Dunn, former owner of the Baltimore International League club. Through research that the late Bob Considine and I did in Baltimore in 1947 as background for *The Babe Ruth Story* we learned that Ruth was out of St. Mary's three times, but each time he was sent back by his parents, the Baltimore police, or his church. St. Mary's Industrial School was a semi-reform school, with bars on the windows, where they sent runaways, incorrigibles, and kids guilty of misdemeanors or from broken homes.

"If it wasn't for baseball, I'd be in either the penitentiary or the cemetery. I have the same violent temper my father and older brother had. Both died of injuries from street fights in Baltimore, fights begun by flare-ups of their tempers."

Babe was headstrong, easily provoked, and never could accept managerial discipline. He gave Miller Huggins, his pint-sized manager from 1920 to 1929, a miserable time. Hug's sister and housekeeper, Myrtle, told my wife: "Babe Ruth took five years from Miller's life." The midget manager died in the last week of the 1929 season at the early age of forty-nine.

In the four years when Joe McCarthy was Ruth's manager (1931–34), the two men had nothing to say to each other away from the ball park. A strict disciplinarian, Joe knew Ruth flouted all training rules. It was generally admitted on that team that there was one rule for Babe and another for the other twenty-four players. The owners and McCarthy knew and accepted the situation. They knew Babe still was hitting homers. There was the historic blow which became famous as Babe's "called" home-run shot at Wrigley Field, Chicago, in the 1932 Yankee-Cub World Series; and his two-run homer in old Comiskey Park, Chicago, in the first All-Star game in 1933.

Ruth did everything big. His appetite for food was enormous. I've seen him eat ten hot dog sandwiches, washing them down with beer, and then ask for more. He could drink the same way, since he had an

abnormal capacity for handling beer and liquor. While I never attended any of his well-known debauches, neither did I ever, in his years as
a player, see him stinking drunk. I've seen players on the field who
were obviously carrying hangovers from big nights before—Ray Caldwell, Rabbit Maranville, Paul Waner, Grover Alexander, Hack Wilson—and it affected their play, but never Ruth during the season.

The only time that Ruth showed the effect of a big night was in Palm
Beach on the 1920 Florida training trip. The Yankees, who trained in
Jacksonville that spring, ran down to Miami for a weekend three-game
series with the Cincinnati Reds, then the world champions. The two
clubs played Saturday and Sunday games in Miami and a third game
Monday in Palm Beach. It was deep in the Prohibition era, and the
Reds felt it was up to them to give Ruth and some of his buddies a full
taste of Miami's sordid nightlife. They treated the Yankee players so
royally that it was a quarter of a century before another Yankee club
scheduled an exhibition game in the Florida resort city.

For the Monday game in Palm Beach some circus seats had been
erected on a cricket field behind the Breakers Hotel. There were many
chairs along the foul lines. This was before the general public thought
of wintering in Florida, and the accents in the stands were Ivy League
and high society. Dressed in their summer outing clothes, the swells
made a pretty picture on a warm sunshiny afternoon. Many of them
came out of curiosity for baseball's new wonder man, Babe Ruth, who
in 1919 had hit an unbelievable twenty-nine home runs for the Boston
Red Sox. But only those who came early got a glimpse of the famous
Babe because in fielding practice before the game, Ruth, playing center
field, crashed into a large oak tree and knocked himself unconscious.
Four of Babe's new playmates, two at his head and two at his feet, carried the star to the hotel. No one had told Ruth about the big tree, the
only one out there, and perhaps he forgot to look.

One story written about Ruth—that he read with difficulty and never
looked at newspapers—is absolutely false. I know that he read the New
York newspapers with which I was associated, because he was quick to
tell me what he didn't like about my coverage or about the hit I didn't
give him.

Once when he was in an automobile accident—one of several—the
New York *Telegram* ran an editorial saying that Babe was a traffic haz-
ard and that if he didn't learn to drive more safely, the State of New
York should pick up his driving license. As I expected, Ruth was on me
as soon as I sat down in my press seat at the old Polo Grounds. "That's
a hell of a thing your paper printed about me yesterday," stormed the
Babe. "Intimating I was drunk, that I didn't know how to drive, and
saying my license should be taken away from me."

I admitted that I thought the man was a little hard on him and added,

"I'm not responsible for everything that appears in the *Telegram*. I write baseball, and he writes editorials."

"Well, if that guy doesn't take back what he wrote, I'll come down to your paper, look him up, and I'll punch him right in the nose." The editorial writer took nothing back, nor did Babe punch him in the nose.

My biggest disagreement with Ruth was over a play I didn't even score. It happened in the morning game of July 4, 1921, at the Polo Grounds. The Yankees were playing the Philadelphia Athletics and Ruth hit the highest infield fly—or any kind of a fly—that I have seen in nearly seven decades of watching big league ball. It went straight up in the air to about twice the height of the Polo Grounds roof. At its zenith, it was just a tiny white speck in the blue sky of a clear summer day. This monster pop fly came down in back of second base. Jimmy Dykes fidgeted around trying to get under the ball, but it skidded off his fingertips and fell to the ground while a grinning Babe Ruth stood at second base, mocking Dykes.

While I had been the official scorer for the first half of that 1921 season, George Daley of the *Morning World* took over on the Fourth of July. George scored it as an error, a muff for Dykes. When the inning was over, Babe sent Eddie Bennett, the little hunchbacked mascot, to ask me how I scored the play.

"I'm not the official scorer anymore," I said. "Tell that to the Babe, and tell him that Daley, my successor, has scored it an error for Dykes." (Had I still been scoring, I would have scored it as a double for Ruth because the ball was descending at line-drive speed.)

Soon Bennett was back saying, "Babe *knows* you're the official scorer, and he wants that two-base hit."

I told Eddie to tell Babe to fly a kite.

For two months afterward Babe crabbed about that hit, which he said I stole from him. Whenever we passed each other on a train, in the team's hotel, or in the locker room, he would repeat the same line: "Whatta you got to do in this league to get a hit?"

Finally, late in the season, he stood for a moment behind my chair in a Pullman bridge game, and out came that familiar refrain.

By this time I was really annoyed and I fairly shouted, "For God's sake, Babe, you've got to hit the ball out of the infield!" Ruth grunted a vulgarity, but that was the last time he mentioned the Fourth of July skyscraper.

I have said before that Ruth was a big man who did things in a big way. He ate big, drank big, hit big home runs, so it is not surprising that Babe had a big sex appetite. And this appetite was unquenchable. Babe was not a one-woman man. One woman couldn't satisfy him. Frequently it took half a dozen.

Ed Barrow, former Yankee general manager and later the team's

Babe Ruth as a superlative left-handed pitcher for the Boston Red Sox, 1915–19. Western Newspaper Union

president, once told me the story behind manager Miller Huggins's fining Ruth $5,000 and suspending him indefinitely in St. Louis in August 1925. "Huggins took that action after we had conferred at length over long-distance telephone. The club had just received a report from a private detective in Chicago that Babe had been with six different women in one night in Chicago."

Yet Ruth was ready to return to his work bench in St. Louis, the Yankee stop after Chicago. As the big Bambino was pulling on his work clothes in the Browns' clubhouse, Hug approached him, saying, "You need not dress today. You're not playing today, nor in the coming days. I am suspending you indefinitely."

"The team isn't winning many games these days," was Babe's response. "You won't win any without my big bat in there."

"I can count the games you've won lately on two fingers of my right hand," snapped Huggins.

Ruth did not get back into the club's good graces until he made a public apology to Huggins. The $5,000 fine was never repaid until after Huggins's death in 1929.

A believer in reincarnation, I always have felt that Ruth was a reincarnated African king or an Arabic emir with a stable of wives and concubines. Or, perhaps in a much earlier life, he lived in ancient Babylon, where they worshipped Phallus. Babe was inherently a Phallus worshipper. It cropped up regularly in his conversation. His phallus and home-run bat were his prize possessions, in that order.

In his early years with the Yankees, when he changed the structure of baseball with his fifty-plus homers a season, he would yell exultingly, "I can knock the penis off any ball that ever was pitched." It would come out in a card game, on the golf course, in a railroad dining car, or just in general conversation. Furthermore, it didn't sound offensive; he was so supremely confident, and it was the Ruthian way of saying he was master of all pitchers, even the greatest. They would get their share of strikeouts, but sooner or later, he would knock their best pitch out of the park.

Once when we were taxicab companions between a Chicago railroad station and our hotel, Ruth made conversation by remarking, "When we get to the Cooper Carlton, there will be a stack of mail for me as big as my penis." Another time when Babe was leaving the clubhouse shower, he pointed dolefully to the big belly he had gradually acquired and said, "The worst of this is that I no longer can see my penis when I stand up."

When Col. Til Huston, half-owner of the Yankees, signed Ruth to a five-year contract (three full seasons, and an option on the next two) for $50,000 a year early in 1922, he spoke sharply to Ruth: "We are tying up a lot of money in you, Babe, far more than any player ever has received, and we feel you should give us something in return, not only hitting home runs, but in your conduct. We know you've often been drinking and whoring all hours of the night, and paying no attention to training rules. As we are giving you a quarter of a million for the next five years, we want you to act with more responsibility. You can drink beer and enjoy cards *and* be in your room by eleven o'clock, the same as the other players. It still gives you a lot of time to have a good time."

"Colonel, I'll promise to go easier on drinking, and get to bed earlier," Ruth promised. "But, not for you, fifty thousand dollars, or two hundred fifty thousand dollars will I give up women. They're too much fun." Later in telling the story Col. Huston grinned and said, "What can you do with a fellow like that?"

When Ruth was the big gun in the Yankees' "Murderer's Row," the New York writers often covered up for Ruth in his escapades. Such an incident took place in Baton Rouge, Louisiana, in March 1921, Babe's second year with the club. That spring the Yankees trained in Shreveport, and their neighbors, the Brooklyn Dodgers, trained in New Orleans. We had a pair of weekend exhibition series in each of the training cities.

We were on the Southern Pacific Express from Shreveport to New Orleans when the train stopped at Baton Rouge to take on water. The Yankee party had three Pullman cars, the first two for regular players, the third shared by newspapermen, Yankee rookies, and second-string pitchers. Most of the other writers were typing, reading magazines, or just staring out of the windows. I was in a card game. Suddenly the front door of our car opened violently and a panting Babe Ruth came rushing through. He was being pursued by a dark-haired, dark-eyed woman carrying a knife pointed at Babe's back. Ruth was about five feet ahead of her, and the irate woman failed to gain on him as they rushed pell-mell through the Pullman. Babe got off at the rear end of the train and ran up the platform the full length of the train. Gradually Babe, no slouch as a base runner, increased his lead to about twenty feet and scampered back on the first car just as the engineer started his train on its way to New Orleans.

I still wonder why we newspapermen acted as we did. There were eleven of us sitting there and no one said a word. We just went on typing, reading magazines, and playing cards. Perhaps Bill Slocum of the *Morning American* put it best when he said whimsically, "Well, if she had carved up the Babe, we really would have had a hell of a story." Later I was told the woman was the wife of a Louisiana legislator.

Later in the season the training camp adventure had a sequel in Detroit. This time Ruth came rushing out of a Detroit hotel with a man carrying a revolver at his heels. Ruth rushed into a taxicab standing at the curb, slammed the door, and ordered the driver to take off. After the cab had gone about twenty feet, Babe left by the other door and, by bending low, dodged his way unseen through traffic to the other side of the street, finally ducking into a stationery store. In the meantime the man with the gun followed the vacant taxicab. Again, there wasn't a word of this escapade in the New York papers.

Years later when I wrote of these incidents in a winter "Hot Stove" column for the St. Petersburg *Times*, a man who said he was a retired captain of the Detroit police department telephoned me to say he enjoyed my story of reminiscences on Ruth. "I know that the things you wrote about happened," he said, "for I had my own experience with Ruth about that time. There was a house in my precinct that was regarded with some suspicion. I decided to investigate and rang the bell of the house.

"To my great surprise, one of the outstanding judges in our city answered the bell. He wasn't a little fellow, such as a police magistrate, but one of our most distinguished jurists. The house was well lighted, and as I talked to the judge in the vestibule, Babe Ruth, with a nude girl riding on his shoulder, came down a flight of stairs. Both were singing loudly and joyously something like, 'Oh, what a gal! Oh, what a pal!' 'You wouldn't deprive the Babe of some of his fun, would you?' the Judge continued with a laugh.

"I agreed to let the fun go on as long as Ruth was in town, but insisted no more fun after the Yankees concluded their series," the ex-policeman added.

Just what kind of girls did Babe select as his favorite playmates? Mostly prostitutes, who in the 1910s and 1920s spoke of themselves as sporting girls. Ruth had telephone numbers of girls in all the big cities, and he knew the red-light districts of the smallest towns. Some of his visitors were semipros, bored women who came to him out of curiosity, and some were amateurs.

While we were in Shreveport, a high-school senior asked Jimmy Sinnott of the *Mail* whether he could arrange a date for herself with Ruth. Jimmy declined, and asked, "Why does a nice kid like you want to get mixed up with a guy like Ruth?"

"Oh, it would give me some standing in my class and my sorority if I could tell them I had gone to bed with the national hero."

Ruth had two wives. Helen was a pretty little brunette from the province of New Brunswick and had been Babe's breakfast waitress in a Boston restaurant. Claire, also brown-haired, was more sophisticated and she was Ruth's wife for the last nineteen years of the slugger's life. I know Babe loved both of them, but by nature he was not a man to tie up with one woman.

Helen was only seventeen when Babe married her as a young pitching star with Boston. He called her Hon, and for several years at least he showed her real affection. For a while she tried to keep pace with her big husband, but later she said to me, "I guess I just don't keep up with the competition." She filed divorce proceedings against Babe, but a Catholic priest from Erie, Pennsylvania, a mutual friend of both Babe and Helen, induced her to drop the case. Eventually she became a victim of alcohol and drugs. She died a tragic death in 1929 when she was fatally burned in a farmhouse that Babe owned outside of Boston.

Helen's death led to Ruth's marriage to Claire Hodgson on April 17, 1929, right after the opening of the season. Babe had known Claire several years before. She was a beautiful woman with style and the knowledge of how to wear her clothes. She had breeding and education. Her father was a professor at the University of Georgia, and her first cousin was Johnny Mize, a slugging first baseman with the New York Giants, the Yankees, and the St. Louis Cards.

He behaved much better while at home, of course, than when the

Yankees were on the road. Claire knew just what type of man she was taking on; they had their battles, and she could give as well as she received. She did tame Babe to a degree; she was a good hostess and gave the Ruth home a gentler atmosphere than it had in earlier days. Claire improved Babe's table manners and grammar and eventually succeeded Christy Walsh as Ruth's business manager.

Ruth loved young boys, especially those who reminded him of himself at St. Mary's. Whenever I left the ballpark late, I could see Ruth at the exit with dozens of boys surrounding him, asking for his autograph on scorecards, notebooks, or just scraps of paper. Once I stopped for a moment and asked Babe, "Don't you get tired of these kids pestering you every day?"

"If they don't come around to pester me, then I'll have something to worry about," replied the Babe.

He was especially interested in the lame, the crippled, and kids injured in accidents or suffering from serious if not fatal diseases. He visited untold numbers of boys in hospitals, private homes, even six-story walk-up tenements. He always gave them the greeting "Hello kid, now you get well." Usually he closed by saying, "I'll hit a homer for you tomorrow."

He usually followed up on his promise, and often the boys were better after his visit. I myself saw one of Ruth's miracles that sounds like something from the New Testament.

In a Yankee–Cincinnati Reds exhibition game at Phillips Field, Tampa, I saw a big black shining car drive on the playing field and park just outside the right-field foul line. In the press box we speculated it must belong to some dignitary. After the game when I joined my wife, Mary pointed to the black car and said, "Leo Durocher [then a Yankee infield rookie] just told me to tell you to look inside the car and you would have a whale of a story."

In the front seat was a man in a state of wild excitement, tears running down his cheeks, and on the back seat was a boy of about ten, standing up and grinning. "This is the first time in two years that my boy has stood up," said the man. "You see him standing, don't you? I'm so happy I can scarcely speak! It's two years since my boy could stand up!"

Two years earlier this man's son had lost his ability to walk and even to stand up. Confined mostly to his room, he became a Babe Ruth fan, even a worshipper. The boy acquired all the pictures of Ruth that were available. He read anything that he could get on his hero and pasted all the clippings in scrapbooks. When it was announced that Ruth would play in Phillips Field, Tampa, the father got permission to park his car at the edge of right field so his son would be as close as possible to his idol. At the end of the game, Ruth had to run past the car to reach the

Yankee bus taking the team back to St. Petersburg. He may have no-ticed the boy slouched on the back seat earlier, but he waved his hand through the open window and said, "Hello kid!" In his joy the boy stood up to return the greeting. Durocher, who was running behind Ruth, later confirmed the man's story. Bill Slocum, who was Ruth's ghost-writer for the Christy Walsh syndicate, was angry with Ruth for turning down a small favor. Bill said that Ruth's love for youngsters was a sham and a put-on. "You're smart enough," he told Ruth face-to-face, "to know that your visits to sick and maimed kids square you with the club and the public for some of the rotten things you've done and for all the trouble you have caused Miller Huggins." Slocum had a right to be sore at the time, as he frequently had covered up for Babe, even lied for him. But, I believe Ruth did care for the boys he visited.

In one sense, of course, everything Babe did was an act. In addition to being the greatest home-run hitter, he also was the game's foremost showman. He sizzled with charisma. He was worshipped by the multi-tudes, and boys followed him in droves wherever he went. He may have been dumb in some things, but he knew he was good as an athlete and as the center of attraction. He gloried in it and he acted according-ly.

Though I was close to Ruth for years and played cards and golf with him, I asked few favors of him. One I well remember. During the depth of the Depression, New York City decided to save a little money by cutting out high-school baseball. A baseball fan and family friend asked for my help in staging a big rally at one of the schools, and asked if I could bring Ruth and Gehrig to support his campaign. Gehrig, a graduate of New York's High School of Commerce, quickly accepted. Without questioning Christy Walsh, Ruth's syndicate boss, I asked Ruth to come along. "If Lou is there, I'll be with him," said Ruth. "Anyhow, I think it is a lousy thing for the schools to wipe out base-ball." I also enlisted the services of John Heydler, president of the Na-tional League.

At the high school where the the rally was held, Gehrig, John Hey-dler, and I spoke briefly, and then there was a general call for Ruth. "Babe! Babe! We want to hear Babe Ruth," shouted the boys. In case of such an emergency, I had written out a few lines for Ruth, and when he got on his feet he remembered them well: "It would be a crime to kill high-school baseball in New York. Your schools gave us Lou Gehrig, Frankie Frisch and Waite Hoyt. You kids all love baseball, and it is our national game. What will the rest of the country think if baseball is killed in the city of Yankee Stadium, the Polo Grounds, the Yanks, Giants and Dodgers, and Babe Ruth?" Babe received a tremendous ap-plause. He was also pleased with the headline of a New York paper: "BABE RUTH MAKES A PLEA FOR THE CITY'S HIGH SCHOOL BASE-BALL." I regret to report that despite the rally New York high-school

Babe Ruth, 1924.

baseball was discontinued for several years. Happily the game was later restored to high-school scholastic programs, and it flourishes today.

In 1973, when Hank Aaron was closing in on Babe Ruth's lifetime total of 714 home runs, he was much vexed by racists who threatened bodily harm to Hank if he persisted in his efforts to wipe Ruth's home-run record out of the book. Hammering Hank, rightfully annoyed, said plaintively, "Babe Ruth never had to contend with anything like that when he was establishing his record." Hank Aaron was wrong in thinking that Ruth had no race problem. Many players, including fellow members of his old Red Sox team, thought that Ruth was part Negro. When he was pitching and batting, nothing would enrage him more than to have some coach or rookie, hiding in the obscurity of the bench, yell "nigger" at him.

Even Ty Cobb, his great fellow star of that period, joined the baiters. Once when Ruth and Cobb were fellow guests at Dover Hall, a big league hunting lodge near Brunswick, Georgia, both stars were assigned sleeping space in the same cottage. Cobb would not permit his luggage to be brought to the cottage, saying, "I never have slept under the same roof with a nigger, and I'm not going to start here in my own native state of Georgia."

Ruth did have a Negroid nose and mouth, but when he took his shower his body from the neck down was as white as the body of Ty Cobb or any other Aryan ball player. Bob Considine had a picture of Ruth and his German-born father tending bar at their Baltimore saloon, and they looked strikingly alike, more like brothers than father and son.

When Aaron was creeping near Ruth's record, Claire Ruth said to me, "Even if Aaron does pass Babe's seven hundred fourteen home-run total, Babe still will be the home-run champion. Hank has been in so many more games than Babe and has had over two thousand more times at bat. Furthermore, Babe spent his early years as a pitcher and these things should be considered." However, my reply was: "Claire, once Aaron hits his seven hundred fifteenth home run, he'll be the home-run champion. But those who remember Ruth's day will always see Ruth as the champ of the home-run division."

I take nothing from Hank Aaron. He has been magnificent, both on the playing field and in the way he has conducted himself since he swept to the top of most baseball records.

When he was a young .300 hitter with the Milwaukee Braves, Milwaukee writers talked of Hank as a shy player who could sleep any time of the day and in any position. "If he sits down for even a minute or so, he is soon sound asleep," Bob Wolf of the Milwaukee *Journal* once told me. This ability to relax completely, thus recharging himself, made possible Aaron's longevity, his comparative freedom from injury,

Babe Ruth's home-run swing in 10 frames.   New York *Daily News* Photo

and his ultimately successful onslaught on some of baseball's most select records. We no longer see the sleepy, shy, almost overlooked star,
but a man fully conscious of the world he has conquered—a superstar
who shines only a little less brightly in my eyes than the number one
Babe Ruth.

Baseball scholars, historians, and statisticians will long study the
figures of Ruth and Aaron. Including the four seasons that he worked
solely as a pitcher, Ruth participated in only 2,503 games; he appeared
at bat officially 8,399 times, approximately 3,700 less than Aaron. His
714 home runs gave him a home run for every 3.4 games and for every
11.7 times at bat.

Aaron has played in a record 3,298 games, was officially at bat 12,364
times, and finished his career with 755 homers. He has averaged 1
home run in every 4.8 games. In the ratio of home runs to times at bat,
Aaron's ratio is considerably higher than Ruth's, 1 homer in every 15.7
times at bat.

Ruth had four seasons in which he hit 50 or more home runs. In contrast, Aaron has never enjoyed a 50-home-run season. His highest was
47 with the 1971 Atlanta Braves. Ruth won ten American League
home-run titles to Hank's four in the National League. From 1962 on,
Aaron also played in the extended 162-game seasons. All of Ruth's
home-run firing came in 154-game seasons. Though Hank banged
away at a 35-to-45 home-run pace each season, he never threatened
Hack Wilson's 54 in 1930, highest in the National League.

Ruth closed his career with a short, unhappy stay with the Boston
Braves in 1935, when he started the season as the club's vice-president,
assistant manager, and right fielder. But Judge Fuchs, president-
owner, soon ran out of money and wanted Babe to invest further in his
club. Manager Bill McKechnie had a tail-end ball club on his hands, a
situation unknown to Ruth. And worst of all, Babe was hitting only
.181, with six homers in twenty-eight National League games. He did
close with a flourish, a three-home-run day in Pittsburgh, including the
first ball driven over the right-field fence of old Forbes Field.

Ruth became a daily golfer and brooded over the fact that no major
league club gave him a managerial offer. He was sorely disappointed
when the Yankees twice passed him over for the manager's job. But he
muffed a chance to manage the Detroit Tigers. Frank Navin, the Detroit owner, had Ruth under serious consideration and wired him in
1934 before Babe went to the West Coast to join Christy Walsh in their
yearly exhibition jaunt. Ruth wired Navin he would stop in later, so
Navin gave the job to Mickey Cochrane, who promptly won the 1934
and 1935 American League pennants.

Larry MacPhail, when he had the Brooklyn club in 1938, offered
Babe a job as coach of the Dodgers. The next year Leo Durocher, the

Ruth, the day he had a double-eagle at the Jungle Club, St. Petersburg, 1936.
Left, Charley Segar, then of the New York *Mirror*. Right, Fred Lieb.

brash kid infielder who hung on Ruth's heels in 1928 and 1929, was
Brooklyn manager. But this turned out to be no break for Babe. Leo
said Babe couldn't get his signals, and Babe was not rehired for 1939.

Babe Ruth died of throat cancer on August 16, 1948. The Yankees
were on the road; Bob Considine was in Europe; and I was the only
New York newspaperman named by Claire Ruth to serve as an honor-
ary pallbearer at the big funeral held at St. Patrick's Cathedral in New
York. Other pallbearers were Connie Mack, the venerable Philadelphia
Athletics president, Waite Hoyt, Joe Dugan, and Whitey Witt.

Thousands of New York fans who had known the thrill of Babe's
homers, or merely worshipped Ruth through newspaper accounts, filed
past the body, which lay in state at Yankee Stadium for a full day and a
half. Ruth was given the highest rites of the Catholic Church, with four
priests, including Cardinal Spellman, officiating. The cathedral was

full to overflowing, thousands of fans standing in the rain outside the cathedral during the long service.

Despite the rain, the day was hot and humid, and after the honorary pallbearers took a last look at the body of America's foremost athlete, one of the ex-Yankees, Joe Dugan, whispered, "I surely would like to have a big glass of beer." "So would the Babe," whispered Waite Hoyt.

14

LOU GEHRIG: THE IRON HORSE

Ludwig Heinrich Gehrig was the name his parents gave him. Mom and Pop, as Lou always called them, were German to the core.

Lou first came into my ken when he was a high schooler. A young writer who covered school sports for the *Evening Telegram* described him to me: "There's a big boy up at the High School of Commerce who hits the ball a mile . . . pitches and plays first base . . . his long-distance clouts are setting records."

Not long afterwards, Lou broke into the sports columns of all the New York newspapers by smashing a ball out of Wrigley Field, home of the Chicago Cubs, in an inter-city scholastic game against Lane Tech High School of Chicago. For a schoolboy this was a startling performance.

Lou Gehrig also played football for Commerce, so well, in fact, that he was given a football scholarship to Columbia University. Later John McGraw recognized Lou's potential as a baseball player, and the New York Giants expressed their interest in signing him up.

Lou later told me, "I went to Mr. McGraw's office after my graduation from high school. McGraw wanted me to sign a contract, but of course I was a minor. He told me the Giants knew how well I had done in high school, and now he himself wanted to see how I would do against professional pitching. Then he told me that the Giants would offer me a contract to play with Hartford in the Eastern League."

Lou told Mr. McGraw he had a scholarship from Columbia and expected to play football and baseball for them. According to Lou's account to me, McGraw then said, "Oh, you can do both. You'll play in Hartford under the name of Henry Lewis. Nobody will know that Lewis of Hartford is the same guy as Lou Gehrig of Columbia. A lot of ball players do that and have still kept their college eligibility." Apparently for the Gehrigs it was enough that the practice was common. So Lou signed the contract and played twelve games for Hartford, batting .261 and putting one double and two triples into his box scores.

Then an angry Andy Coakley, Columbia's baseball coach and a former big league pitcher, came to Hartford and indignantly demanded, "What are you doing in that uniform? Don't you realize you're throwing away four years of as good a college education as you can get anywhere in this country?" Coakley told him, "You come back to New York with me. You're a very foolish boy. I don't know whether you have killed a scholarship, but I'll do my best to have our athletic board go easy with you."

The board permitted Lou to keep the scholarship but suspended him from all Columbia athletics for his freshman year, 1921-1922. However, he did play in all of Columbia's football games in the fall of 1922 and in all its baseball games in the spring of 1923. It was an eventful year for Gehrig. At baseball he was a sensation, pitching well and driving home runs over trees to shatter the windows of Morningside Heights. People began to compare his home runs with the massive homers of Babe Ruth at new Yankee Stadium.

Soon Lou received a visit from the other New York club. Paul Kritchell, head scout of the Yankees, came with a substantial offer from the Yankee colonels, Jake Ruppert and Til Houston. There was an important meeting at the Gehrig apartment between Kritchell and Pop, Mom, and Lou Gehrig, then twenty years old. Kritchell brought them first to a decision that when Lou turned professional, it would be with the Yankees. The discussion then turned to whether he should report immediately or continue his work at Columbia for two more years and report after his graduation in 1925. Of four Gehrig children Lou was the only one who survived infancy, and Mom Gehrig, who had dreams of her big boy becoming an architect, voted for college. Kritchell argued immediate signing and reporting, and Pop was neutral.

Lou finally decided to report immediately. As he told it to me, "No matter what I do now, ultimately I am going to be a ballplayer. I've now had two years of college, thanks to my scholarship and the sacrifices of my parents. But we are a poor family; we need money, and now it is my turn to earn money, real money, and make everything easier all around." So Lou and his father signed for a substantial bonus.

Oddly, the Yankees sent him to Hartford where McGraw had sent him two years earlier. But this time, the new Hartford first baseman was Lou Gehrig, not "Henry Lewis." He was a hitting fool right from

Lou Gehrig, extraordinary pitcher and batter at Columbia University, 1923.

the start, finding Eastern League (then Class AA) pitching as easy as the college pitching had been at Columbia. In fifty-nine games with Hartford he hit .369, and his power was explosive: 13 two-base hits, 8 triples, and 24 home runs.

Recalled by the Yankees at the close of the Eastern League season, Lou hit .420 in thirteen games as a Yankee pinch hitter and first baseman. Everyone was beginning to realize the Yankees had come up with another real find. Wally Pipp, the team's regular first baseman, ran into the stands in the last week of the regular season and badly bruised three ribs. Judging from the doctor's report, there seemed to be no chance of his playing in the Yankees-Giants World Series the following week. Manager Huggins immediately announced that he would play young Gehrig at first base if the club could get him declared eligible. Under World Series rules, only players with a contending club on September 1 are eligible for championship play. Col. Ruppert applied to Commissioner Landis for permission to play Gehrig, citing a case of three years before, when in 1920 the Brooklyn Dodgers permitted Cleveland to play rookie Joe Sewell at shortstop after the regular shortstop, Ray Chapman, had suffered a fatal injury when hit on the head by Yankee Carl Mays.

Landis said he would permit Gehrig to play if John McGraw, the Giants manager, gave his consent. Mac refused, saying, "The rules are quite specific on that point. If a regular player gets injured after September first, it is all part of the hazards of baseball." McGraw's refusal to let Gehrig play left it up to the Yankees' club physician and trainer to work on Pipp and ready him for the Series. Trussed and taped like an Egyptian mummy, Pipp went through the full six games, playing well, considering his condition, and helped the Yankees win their first world championship.

Lou felt McGraw's refusal to let him play stemmed from the events of 1921 when he sent Lou to Hartford, only to have Andy Coakley bring him back to Columbia. As long as both McGraw and Gehrig were alive there was no love between them. McGraw accused Lou of letting him down, and Lou in turn felt it was McGraw who let him down. Lou said, "In 1921 McGraw was a sophisticated, experienced baseball man, and I was a dumb, innocent kid. Yet he was willing to let me throw away a scholarship as though it was a bundle of trash."

The Yankees sent Lou back to Hartford for the full season of 1924 and he hit .369, again with a full bag of extra-base blows; 40 doubles, 13 triples, and 37 home runs. Back with the Yankees for ten games in the fall, he hit a fancy .500. From then on he never wore any uniform other than that of the New York Yankees.

On the 1925 training trip Miller Huggins told me, "I just have to get this kid Gehrig in my lineup. I think he has the potential to be a great hitter, perhaps one of the greatest." In some of the early spring games Huggins played Gehrig in right field, with Ruth shifting to first base. It wasn't exactly a success. On June 1, 1925, Miller used Lou as a pinch hitter. The next day, first baseman Wally Pipp reported he had a severe headache and Huggins told Gehrig, "Get out your first baseman's mitt. You're my first baseman today." Pipp never regained the position, and Lou was off on the greatest playing streak of all baseball, 2,130 consecutive games, lasting until early 1939.

By an odd coincidence, the day before Gehrig's streak started, Huggins broke the currently longest consecutive-game streak by benching his regular shortstop, Everett "Deacon" Scott, who had played 1,307 consecutive games for the Red Sox and Yankees. The Yankees of 1925 were not winning. Scott had slipped perceptibly that year, and so Huggins tried a youngster, Peewee Wanninger, at shortstop.

Gehrig's long playing streak won him the title of baseball's Iron Horse. Lou's record, which I think will stand as long as baseball is played, wasn't easy to come by. There were several occasions when this streak could have ended: a fractured little finger, a charleyhorse, spike wounds, and a recurring pain in the back. On the road, while he had these back torments and shoulder pains, Manager Joe McCarthy

Murderers Row," 1925 version. Left to right, Earle Combs, Bob Meusel, Lou Gehrig, Babe Ruth.   PBA Photo

would announce him as his shortstop and place him in the leadoff position in his batting order. But as soon as Lou had completed his time at bat, Frankie Crosetti would take over his regular shortstop position. Grit, courage, and intense determination enabled Gehrig to stand at his post through the years.

Excluding the 1923 World Series when Gehrig was an ineligible bench sitter, Lou played on his first championship team as a regular in 1926, hitting .313. That October he took part in his first World Series as the Yankees lost to the St. Louis Cardinals four games to three, and batted a satisfying .348. In his early years he never was as poor or as clumsy a first baseman as some have regarded him. However, knowing that this was not his strong point, he did practice constantly to make himself a better fielding first baseman. He never became as good in the field as the graceful George Sisler or Bill Terry, but few played the bag any better than Lou Gehrig.

Prior to 1926 I had known Gehrig as I knew many of the Yankee players—that is, as an acquaintance on a first-name basis. But that year a true friendship developed and ripened until Lou became the best friend I ever had among ballplayers. (In the movie *Pride of the Yankees*, the sports writer, played by Walter Brennan, was supposed to be me.) Perhaps our friendship started with Mom Gehrig, Lou's 220-pound mother. By that time I was an established writer and frequently passed up morning practice at the Yankees' training park in St. Petersburg to take advantage of the nearby Spa Beach. Half a dozen writers' wives, including mine, would be there, three or four other writers, and Mom Gehrig. We spoofed a lot and I kidded Mom in German. Mary and Mom hit it off from the start. Mary was never bothered, as some of the other women were, at Mom's occasional crudities. So when I wasn't around, Mom would huddle next to Mary.

As far as Lou was concerned, anyone who did something nice for Mom Gehrig did something nice for him. Lou began taking me into his confidence and talking a lot with Mary and me. In New York our families visited each other, the Gehrigs often inviting us to their home in New Rochelle where Mom served some of her plentiful and delightful meals. We also became better acquainted with Pop Gehrig, a former copper worker who had become caretaker of a New York tenement house. Pop suffered from attacks of epilepsy and usually let Mom go to the ball games by herself. At their home he was usually quiet, but every now and then he would enter the conversation and express himself forcefully.

What struck me as somewhat odd for Americans in the late 1920s was that Mom and Lou would converse almost entirely in Mom's native tongue, German. On his return from a road trip they would warmly embrace and kiss each other happily, and then Lou would talk fast and tell her his adventures while Mom at the same time wanted to tell everything that had happened in New Rochelle.

In 1927 Lou blossomed into a superstar. He batted .375, scored 159 runs, drove in 175, and had 52 doubles, 17 triples, and 47 home runs. Furthermore, if Mom hadn't fallen ill in September, requiring a dangerous operation, Lou would have been even better. For a time Gehrig and Ruth were running neck and neck for home-run honors. But Babe closed with a terrific September and recorded the old home run record of 60. I still recall arguments in the Yankee Stadium press box—Ford Frick, Bill Slocum, and Marsh Hunt rooting for the Babe, and Arthur Mann, Will Wedge, and I for Larropin' Lou.

I particularly rooted for Gehrig to bat in 200 runs. But by mid-September he had almost all of the 175 runs batted in that he ended with. All his thoughts were on Mom. As soon as he finished the game he would rush to the hospital and stay with her until her bedtime. Lou just stopped hitting for that closing fortnight. "I'm so worried about

Mom that I can't see straight," he told me. "If I lost her I don't know what I would do."

The Yankees that year were voted the greatest team of all time, and they crushed the Pirates four straight in the World Series. But Lou's mother still was on the critical list and he only knew half of what was going on. Ruth hit the only two home runs of the Series; Lou collected two doubles and two triples and drove in five runs. His mother wasn't taken off the critical list until late in the Series. Shortly after the last game was over, he smiled again as he said proudly, "Mom is out of danger. She is much better and is itching to get home."

Lou had another great season in 1928 when the Yankees made it three straight pennants for Ruppert, and Lou almost duplicated his 1927 batting average — off one point, to .374. This World Series Lou was unworried and swung away, free and easy. As the Bronx Bombers rolled over the Cardinals in four straight, Gehrig's contribution was a smashing .545 batting average, including 4 home runs, 1 double and 1 single, and 9 runs batted in.

As the years rolled on, Lou continued at his vigorous pace as he batted over .300 for twelve consecutive seasons, scored over 115 runs for

Gehrig performed in many ways besides at bat.   The *Daily News*

fourteen seasons, drove in 107 runs or more in thirteen consecutive seasons, and collected home runs by the dozens, helping to bring in precious and profitable pennants and World Championships for Jake Ruppert as long as he lived.

Gehrig frequently joined Babe Ruth on lucrative post-season barnstorming trips engineered by Christy Walsh. Despite Ruth's vulgarities, Gehrig liked the Babe (until they had a falling-out in 1934). Ruth was often at the Gehrig home along with Bob Meusel, Tony Lazzeri, and Joe Dugan, all of whom came to be known as Mom's boys. Ruth gave Mom a Mexican hairless dog, which she promptly named Jidge (a corruption of Babe's first name, George), his nickname for close associates in the clubhouse and card games.

It was commonly said at the time that Gehrig lived in Ruth's shadow. Such talk never bothered Lou. "It's a pretty big shadow," he said. "It gives me lots of room to spread myself." None of Ruth's vulgarities and animal-like crudities rubbed off on Gehrig. Rarely did he use a cussword in his daily conversation. Nor did he attend the sex parties Ruth often gave in his hotel room when the team was on the road. Some writers have suggested that Lou was a "virgin" then, but this I know not to be so, for he shyly admitted to me an occasional sexual adventure.

In 1931 when I organized a barnstorming tour sponsored by the Japanese newspaper *Yomouri Shimbun*, our hosts particularly wanted Babe Ruth and Lou Gehrig to come.

The year 1931 was an especially good one for Gehrig. He led the club in runs scored, 163, and most hits, 211; he tied Ruth for most homers, 46. He also broke his own American League runs-batted-in record, advancing it from 175 to 184.

I was able to sign Lou, but Ruth was beyond my reach; he was completely tied up with Christy Walsh for a post-season tour. The two Yankee stars had finished the season tied for the home-run title, so Walsh began to build up his tour as the one that would decide the home-run championship, and he put tremendous pressure on Lou to leave my team and join the Ruth-Walsh circus in its junket around the U.S.A. Lou stood by his earlier word and pleased me very much by saying, "I would much rather be in your company. And it's a new country, and I always like to see new things."

On our two-week boat ride across the Pacific Ocean to Japan, Lou Gehrig often would disappear for several hours. "Have you seen Lou?" Lefty O'Doul would ask me. Or, Rabbit Maranville would say, "Lou Gehrig has done that disappearing act again; I've looked all over the ship and can't find him."

I knew exactly where Lou was, as my wife Mary had told me that she was off for another rendezvous with him. They were meeting inside a lifeboat on the top deck. Had some of the players or their wives known where Lou and Mary were, there might have been some arching of the eyebrows. But I knew Mary was as safe with Lou as with Billy Graham or the Pope. People just naturally opened their hearts and minds to Mary and, without urging, told their innermost secrets. She was a good listener and often passed out some good advice. It was Lou who had found the lifeboat as a place to share with Mary some of his secrets and inner thoughts. And one visit led to another. He told Mary of his early hardships, his hopes, fears, ideals, expectations, and something of his love life. He really wanted to get married. Even though he was shy, he had known lots of girls, but whenever he started to get serious with one, Mom Gehrig filed her objections. He loved his mother dearly and could not think of marrying a girl unless he obtained his mother's okay.

At least twice he had brought prospective wives over to our house, asking us what we thought of them. Lou's girls were always attractive, with both brains and humor. Then one time, he had been smitten with a girl and was thinking of proposing. On learning this, Mom journeyed to the young lady's hometown, looked around, made some investigations, and filed an adverse report, which Lou accepted.

On one of their lifeboat meetings, Mary said, "Lou, you know I'm fond of your mother and wouldn't do anything to hurt her. But, I also am fond of you. You're an honest, decent fellow, a very desirable bachelor, and at twenty-eight you should be married like most of your comrades on the Yankees. If you wait around for a girl that will suit Mom, you'll still be unmarried at fifty. When you again meet a young lady to whom you are attracted and she seems to be a possible Mrs. Lou Gehrig, you hold your ground. Mom will offer her usual objections, but stand firm and she will eventually come to your side. If your marriage produces children, Mom would be the happiest grandmother in the world."

Lou started the Japanese trip as a great adventure; he was playing well and making many Japanese friends when two bones in his right hand were broken by a little Japanese pitcher from Keio University. Lou was heartbroken to have to sit on the sidelines for the last eleven games of our schedule.

On the boat trip to Japan Gehrig had frequently been in the company of an attractive, sophisticated divorcee. One morning after we had arrived, he called my room at the Imperial Hotel and asked whether I could come up to his room for a few hours. I had things to do and tried to reduce the time involved, but Lou said it was important—the young lady he had spent some time with on the boat was about to call on him and he wanted me to baby-sit for him.

"You know the game some of these girls try to pull off on a man who is in the public eye," he said. "If you can spare this time I would like you to stay in the room until she leaves. I would want you as a witness that nothing happened." Nothing happened.

Some of the players on the Yankees had let it be rumored that Gehrig was stingy and left poor tips. That was probably true in his early years with the Yankees when he worked on a $6,000 contract. It wasn't true on this trip, and he certainly wasn't stingy when it came to buying things for Mom and Pop. He received $5,000 for making the trip, but spent $7,200 for gifts for his mother and father, mostly for Mom. There were rolls of silks, ivory, kimonos, and oriental jewelry. Through Lefty O'Doul's influence with the customs authorities in San Francisco, Lou got several trunks of this material through customs for a mere trifle. Being a national hero sometimes had its advantages!

As a result of our close association on the Japanese trip, Lou became an even closer friend to Mary and me than ever before. So it was natural that we would hear early of his latest sweetheart, a businesswoman from Chicago, Eleanor Twitchell. He had met her three years before, but at first neither Lou nor Eleanor had been impressed with the other. They met again in 1932 through mutual friends in Chicago and soon concluded they were meant for each other. It was a real romance.

Gehrig had a terrific 1932 World Series when the Yankees downed the Cubs four straight. It was the Series in which Babe Ruth hit his called home run off Root, but Lou was nevertheless the batting star of the Series. Charlie Grimm, the manager–first baseman of the Cubs, himself an outstanding player, said in discussing Gehrig after the Series, "I didn't think a player could be that good."

Charlie didn't exaggerate. In those four games Gehrig was a ball team all by himself. He had nine hits, including three home runs and a double. He scored nine runs and drove in eight. All Chicago, including Eleanor Twitchell, thrilled at this outstanding performance, and the next thing we heard, Lou and Eleanor were engaged.

Back home in New Rochelle, Mom Gehrig was not impressed. From 1926 she had travelled everywhere with her son. For home games she never was absent from her Yankee Stadium seat near the New York dugout. She was almost as well known at Yankee Stadium as her distinguished son and she didn't want to be displaced. That always stuck in her craw. Eleanor was a girl in her late twenties, attractive, well-groomed, sophisticated, and competent at holding a good job for a woman in the Depression years. But Mom did her best to talk Lou out of the engagement. She met with no success. "Mom is the most wonderful woman in the world," Lou told us. "She broke up some of my earlier romances and she isn't going to break up this one."

The wedding, slated for the evening of the last Saturday game of the season, was at the Long Island home of friends of Eleanor. They were racing people, as was Eleanor's father. Lou invited me and my wife and daughter to the wedding reception. The only Yankees there were Bill and Vi Dickey. Fred Linderman, brewmaster at the Ruppert Brewery, and Mrs. Linderman were the only others with a baseball connection.

At the Saturday game Lou sent a clubhouse boy to ask me to come down to the railing near the Yankee bench. When I went, Lou seemed disturbed and said, "I want you and Mary to bring Mom to the wedding reception tonight. She says she won't go. You almost pass the house on the way to the ferry, so please pick her up." Then he told me he and Eleanor had been married the previous day. There had been an ugly argument between Mom and Eleanor over some drapes, and Eleanor said something about calling off the wedding. Lou didn't like that kind of talk, so he took Eleanor over to the New Rochelle City Hall where they met the mayor of New Rochelle, and when they left they were Mr. and Mrs. Lou Gehrig.

I knew where Mom always sat in the grandstand. She was there by herself, and I said, "Lou has asked me to pick you up this evening and bring you to the reception."

"I won't go!" she snapped.

I told her, "I know how close you and Lou have been. Now he has taken an important step in his life and he wants his mother at his side."

"Freddy, I won't go," she persisted. "If I went there I would only raise hell."

Nevertheless, when I arrived at 5:40 she was on the porch, all ready for the Long Island trip. At the reception they ushered her to a big chair in the living room and she never left that seat.

It was a pleasant celebration. There was lots of champagne floating around but no drunkenness. Lou was happy and Eleanor was charming. On the ferry back to New Rochelle I fell asleep and was suddenly awakened by someone pulling at my shoulder. Mom whispered in my ear, "Freddy, wasn't I a good girl? I kept my Dutch mouth shut."

It would be nice to report that things thereafter were harmonious between Mom and her daughter-in-law. But from the start there were clashes whenever the elder and younger Gehrigs got together. Mom, Pop, and Lou always conversed in German and since Eleanor spoke no German, this annoyed her. Mom told me, "Eleanor always thinks we are talking about her but, goodness, there are things to talk about that a son has in common with his parents—but Eleanor just won't understand."

That first year of their marriage (1934) was one of Lou's greatest years. He was a Triple Crown winner with highest batting average (.360), most home runs (49), and most RBIs (165). Eleanor was proud of that. "You know how managers are afraid of too many brides on the

club. Young husbands usually have off seasons. Well, I guess Lou's Ellie didn't hurt his ball playing any in our first year of married life."

The Yankees won World Championships in 1936, 1937, 1938, and
1939. Gehrig had a big hand in winning the 1936 and 1937 Series from
their old New York City foes, the Giants. In 1938 he had an off year for
Lou Gehrig, though it still would have been a big year for the average
ballplayer. His batting average was .295. His first year under .300 since
1925. His home runs dropped to 29 and his RBIs to 111. In the four-
game World Series cleanup against the Cubs he hit only four singles
and did not drive in a single run.

In the closing weeks of the 1938 season Gehrig's fielding was sluggish. People were asking, "What is wrong with Lou? He is only thirty-
six and should have at least two or three more good years. Has that long
string of consecutive games (now 2,122) worn down the Iron Horse?"

Mary and I continued to have a close association with the younger
Gehrigs but were now seeing little of Mom and Pop. Early in 1939,
Mary received a letter from Eleanor asking us to rent a small house for
them in St. Petersburg near ours. Lou hadn't been too well, she wrote,
didn't have the old starch. The doctor in New Rochelle was treating
him for a sluggish gall bladder. They wanted to come down a month
before the club started training so that Lou could fish or just sit in the
sun.

We found a place two blocks from us in late January. Lou looked
well and still had his distinctive hearty laugh. They came over the first
evening they were in town.

Knowing Mary and I had used the Ouija board frequently, one of
them suggested sitting down to it. Shortly after an exchange of greet-
ings, the entity whom Mary and I at that time had contact with spelled
out a message for Eleanor: "You soon will be called upon to face the
most difficult problem of your life." We were all somewhat startled.
Since Mary and I had been in the habit of arguing with this entity
named Mark Antony, much as though he were a real person, I said,
"Mark, that is not fair! You scare Eleanor and then you stop. Why don't
you let us in on what this big problem is? We are all interested."

Eleanor asked, "Is it about the adoption of a baby?" and Mark said,
"No." Then Eleanor explained, "We have been married for six years
and have no child. We did talk some of adopting one." Lou then broke
in and said, "Mom wouldn't have any of that. She said she didn't want
a grandson if it wasn't a Gehrig." But Mark would say no more.

After lounging around St. Petersburg for a month and doing a little
fishing, Lou appeared stiff and sluggish at the training camp. However,
it wasn't until the exhibition games, mostly with the Cardinals, that we
saw how far off he was in his performance. In one big scoring game
when Lou, after failing four times, came up for his fifth time at bat

with two out, the bases filled, and St. Louis leading, 7–6, a single by Gehrig would have won the game for New York. He took a mighty swing at the ball and popped an easy fly to the second baseman.

Lou really was down after that game. "What in hell is wrong with me? Or what am I doing wrong? I just need more work, lots of work." I replied, "No, you need to relax and let go. Everybody knows you can hit. The hits will come in the regular season, and that is the time they count."

Gehrig tried desperately to work himself into condition. It was almost an obsession. He was the first to report in the morning and the last to leave in the afternoon, but the sluggishness continued.

On the Yankees' trip North they played a game in Norfolk and Gehrig hit three home runs. I was happy and told Mary, "Well, Lou has finally found himself." However, it was his last day of glory.

The Yankees played their first League games at home with Washington and the Red Sox. Lou played in eight games, hit four singles for a poor average of .143 and drove in one run. There was an open date and then the first western trip. On the idle Monday, Lou called up his manager, Joe McCarthy, and said, "When we open in Detroit you better put Babe Dahlgren at first base. I feel I'm not helping the club."

Lou later told me how he came to this decision. "There was a fairly routine play late in the game in which the batter hit a ground ball to me. I picked it up and made an easy toss for the putout to pitcher Lefty Gomez, covering the bag. Then both Gomez and Joe Gordon slapped me on the back as they said, 'Good play, Lou. Great play, Lou.'

"That hurt like the devil that two of my fellow players would slap me on the back and say, 'Great play, Lou,' when I make a play that any high-school kid would handle with ease. I knew I must be through."

Mary and I drove North around the same time the Yankees started on their first western trip. The day after we got back I called up Eleanor, who asked us to come up to their home that afternoon. "Something is coming up and I would like to have friends with me." When we got to Larchmont, she said, "Lou is in the Mayo Clinic in Rochester, Minnesota, for a thorough examination. He called me this morning and said he would call back later in the day when the Mayo doctors had given him their verdict."

A half hour later the phone rang and it was long distance from Rochester. Eleanor excused herself to take it in the bedroom.

When she emerged she said, "I guess I need a drink, a real stiff drink. You know what that Dutchman just told me? 'Don't worry, Ellie, I have a fifty-fifty chance to live' — just as though he were asking about the weather in Westchester County. Something is really wrong with him, and I think his spinal cord is affected."

I knew it was a hell of a story that any New York paper would pay me a good bonus for, but I made no mention of the Gehrig disability to anyone until the Yankees made the official statement two days later. Both Eleanor and I consulted our own physicians, explaining Lou's condition and the diagnosis of the Mayo physicians. They quickly told us it was no fifty-fifty chance; it was more like one in a hundred. He suffered from amyotrophic lateral sclerosis, a disease the medical world is still quite helpless to treat.

At first the affliction didn't show too much in Lou's appearance. He remained with the Yankees as nonplaying captain-coach right to the end of their four straight wins over the Cincinnati Reds in the 1939 World Series.

On July 4 of that year, the Yankees held a special Lou Gehrig Day in which the former Iron Horse made a tremendous speech. "I have a wonderful wife, I have a wonderful mother and father, and wonderful friends and teammates. I have been privileged to play many years with the famous Yankees, the greatest team of all times. All in all, I can say on this day that I consider myself the luckiest man on the face of the earth."

At the same gathering, before 65,000 at Yankee Stadium, Babe Ruth lovingly put his arms around Lou's shoulders. It ended a five-year feud which had started on their 1934 trip to Japan with Connie Mack.

In the winter following the 1939 World Series, there was a distinct change for the worse in the famous athlete. It was pitiful seeing him try to light a cigarette, unsteadily groping for his mouth with a lighted match. Bill Dickey, his favorite bridge partner, told of cards falling from his hands as he studied them to make a bid. He was unable to shuffle the cards.

Eleanor confessed she had an inkling something was indeed wrong with her handsome husband at the 1939 St. Petersburg training camp, something unrelated to conditioning. "When we were out for walks and crossed streets, I noticed his foot came down with an unnatural clump as we stepped off the curb." The spring and the control in his legs apparently was pretty well gone.

In 1940 Mayor Fiorello LaGuardia appointed Gehrig as special assistant to work with New York kids who were in trouble with the law. His Honor explained, "I am sure Lou can help many boys, but I also was thinking of Lou helping himself. I was thinking that in studying the boys' problems he could, for the time being, forget himself, and that would be helpful."

However, by late 1940 he had steadily degenerated until he no longer could go to his office in New York's City Hall. He gave up bridge, for he no longer could hold his cards. It was a terrible ordeal for Eleanor, seeing her handsome husband fading away daily. For Mom Gehrig to see her pride and joy—the only one of four Gehrig children who sur-

Lou Gehrig: the best friend I ever had among ballplayers.   Cosmo-Sileo Co.

vived babyhood—at death's door at the age of thirty-seven was almost
enough to drive her out of her mind. Yet even sharing a common tragedy, Mom and Eleanor could not bury the hatchet. The hostility between the two women remained unabated long after his death.

Lou Gehrig died in June 1941 in Riverdale, a residential section of
New York City, a city which Lou had served so well as a star high-
school athlete, home-run slugger at Columbia, and co-star with Babe
Ruth. They were original "prides of the Yankees."

What remained of his once powerful body was cremated. An urn
containing his ashes lies in a cemetery in Westchester County, where
Mom cooked her gargantuan meals for Lou and his friends in New Rochelle; where Lou and Eleanor spent the happy early years of their
marriage; where Larropin' Lou made his home during those years
when he reached the heights of stardom, winning the Most Valuable
Player prizes of the American League in 1927, 1931, 1934 and 1936.

15

OLD PETE:
GROVER CLEVELAND
ALEXANDER

"Pete," later to become "Old Pete" to baseball writers, broke in with the Phillies with a smashing 28–13 record in 1911, the year I began my baseball writing career in New York. But it was only in the last month of his life that I came to know him intimately and to share some of the bittersweet memories of one of that fabulous trio of pitchers often linked together in the top rank: Walter Johnson, Christy Mathewson, and Grover Cleveland Alexander.

In 1950 the Phillies won their first pennant since 1915, the year Pete was 31–10 with Pat Moran's champions. Someone connected with the Phillies' organization invited Alex the Great to the Phillies–Yankees World Series. And then that person left him to his own resources, though very possibly Pete took the tickets and just never cooperated with any plans for taking care of him between games. In any case, when the Series shifted to Yankee Stadium for the third game, Alexander had a good seat in the press stand, with an empty seat beside him. Bill Cunningham, the ace Boston sports writer of that era, called my attention to him, saying, "Grover Alexander is sitting up there all by himself. Why don't you take the empty seat next to him? A big star like Alex should get a little attention."

I was working for *The Sporting News* at the Series, but I could sit with Alex and still score the game. When I introduced myself he remembered me, "Yes, you wrote for the New York papers; you said

185

some nice things about me, even when I didn't deserve it." I think he.
may have been referring to articles I wrote praising his pitching talents
and successes in his mid-career, when some writers were hopping all
over him in a moralistic way for his problem drinking.

Old Pete had been voted numerous honors in baseball. He had been
one of the select group of superstars inducted into the Hall of Fame at
the shrine's dedication eleven years earlier, 1939. From that induction
ceremony Grover took away a replica of the tablet that now hangs in
Cooperstown. "You know I can't eat tablets or nicely framed awards.
Neither can my wife. But they don't think of things like that." No pen-
sions . . . an improvident person . . . I was face-to-face with
a human tragedy.

Grover went on. "I lasted long in the big leagues—twenty seasons—
and won more games than any other National League pitcher except
Christy Mathewson. We are tied at three hundred seventy-three victories. But I should have had more. I don't feel sorry for myself, or excuse my drinking. I guess I just had two strikes on me when I came
into the world. My father back in Nebraska was a hard drinker before
me, and so was my grandfather before him. Sure, I tried to stop—I just
couldn't. But I'd still go on winning games until I was forty-two.
That's when I was suspended by Bill McKechnie in August 1929.

"The next year, St. Louis traded me back to Philadelphia, my first
big league club. The Phillies, as usual in those days, had a bad club,
and at forty-three I didn't have much stuff left on the ball. Burt Shotton
was the manager, and he used me in nine games as a starter or in relief.
By the time they released me in mid-season, I hadn't been able to pick
up my three hundred seventy-fourth win. I was none and three and
was still tied with Matty. I pitched a little for Dallas after that, and then
I grew a beard and qualified to pitch for a House of David team. I still
could get batters out, and it did bring in groceries for our table."

When Alexander died exactly one month after our reminiscing in
Yankee Stadium, *The Sporting News* asked me to write the obituary.
They gave me plenty of space and before writing a word I laid out his
whole career before me: his thirty or more victories for the Phillies
three years running, 1915–17; his sixteen shutouts in 1915; his twenty-
seven games won for the 1920 Cubs; his two victories and great relief
job (striking out Tony Lazzeri with the bases full) in the Cardinals' first
World Series victory in 1926. I knew all about the bouts with alcohol,
the nervous twitchings of the St. Vitus's dance from which he sometimes suffered , and all the streaks of gray he put in the hair of his managers. But his human failings seemed insignificant in comparison with
his marvelous ability to get batters out late in his career with less than
sensational "stuff." I cherished the warm note Mrs. Alexander wrote
me afterwards.

Grover Cleveland Alexander, 1915.   C. M. Conlon, New York *Evening Telegram*

Way back when the spring training season of 1930 rolled around, I had decided there was a story in the 1929 season that I had missed: the story behind Alexander's suspension. Why had Bill McKechnie, a kindly, compassionate man, taken such action—sending Alexander back to St. Louis and standing by without protest as Sam Breadon suspended him instead of giving him a shot at breaking his tie with Mathewson? (At the time of his suspension, Grover's record for 1929 was 9–8.) I decided to ask the Deacon, as McKechnie was called.

I had known Bill for a long time, ever since I was a kid scorer for the Highlanders. For a while in 1913 Bill played second base for Frank Chance's weak seventh-place club. I had few opportunities to record hits for the Deacon in my official scorer's book, for he hit only .134 in his forty-four American League games in 1913. Yet Bill was the only player manager Chance chose to socialize with, and when he didn't play, Bill always sat next to Chance on the bench. "Why do you pick that .134 hitter for your constant companion?" asked this curious reporter.

Chance, a little sluggish in his hearing, from frequent beanings, growled back, "Because he's the only son-of-a-sea-cook on this club who knows what it's all about. Among this bunch of meatheads, his brain shines like a gold mine!" He was the first to appreciate McKechnie's managerial potential, which put the Deacon into the Hall of Fame by virtue of pennants in three cities.

Anyway, on one of these visits I asked Bill about Alexander's indefinite suspension of 1929, and why he didn't give Grover a chance to pass Mathewson's record.

"Fred, I am as sorry about that as I possibly could be. I was partly to blame. I never should have left him alone over a Philadelphia weekend in August 1929. There was some staff trouble, and Alexander went haywire.

"Pete got so bad that the club sent him to a sanitarium to dry out and prepare for the final two months of the season. The Cardinals still had an outside pennant chance. When Alexander was discharged from the sanitarium, I was pleased at his appearance. His eyes were clear, his hands were steady, and his face had a good ruddy color, not a gin- or whiskey-red. I had been his manager before, on the Cardinal National League champions of 1928, and asked him, 'If I pitch you in our first game in Pittsburgh, do you think your arm is ready?' 'Sure, Bill, I not only can pitch, but I can win for you.' Alexander was as good as his word and pleased me mightily with a low-hit 3–0 shutout.

"Our next stop was Philadelphia, where Alex had cronies from his early days, and some of them had a poor influence on him. But he pitched another winning game in Philadelphia and was behaving himself. At that time we had no Sunday ball in Philly. It was an open date, and on Monday we were playing the Giants in New York.

Manager Bill McKechnie and Alexander, 1929.   Acme Newspictures

"I guess here is where I made my big mistake. Instead of keeping Alexander under my nose after the Saturday game, I told him, 'I know you have many friends here, and that you like to be with them. I am going to trust you. You can have a few beers, but no gin. I am going to pitch you in the opening game of the series in New York. I want you to have a good night's sleep, and I want you to be at the Ansonia [our hotel in New York] on Sunday night.'

"On Sunday night there was no Alex. On Monday morning there was no Alex. I asked Jimmy Wilson, our catcher, whether he could find him. Wilson knew several hangouts in New York where Alex slept off his drunks. Jimmy found him and told him to report to me at my room in the Ansonia.

"By sheer happenstance, from my hotel window I could see a telephone in a drugstore across the street. And, as I stood by my window I saw Wilson and Alex enter the drugstore. Almost immediately my phone rang. It was Grover. He mumbled some incoherent things into the mouthpiece to explain why he hadn't been at the hotel and asserted he could pitch that afternoon. I told him I wanted to see him as soon as he could get over there.

"Alex had only to cross the street, but he allowed some fifteen minutes to elapse before he knocked at my door. He was a sight. His eyes were watery and bloodshot; he looked as though he hadn't slept since Friday; his clothes looked as though someone had rolled him in the gutter; and two minutes after he arrived the room reeked of bad gin. When Alexander was on a real bender, he not only drank quantities of gin, but rubbed it into his skin. I was pretty well disgusted with him; I told him to get transportation back to St. Louis and report personally to our club president, Sam Breadon. It was Sam who had put him in the sanitarium, and I thought it was up to the top man to decide Alexander's punishment.

"Sam scolded him, told him he had again let down the club. We thought as soon as he sobered up, we could lift the suspension and have him for our September home games. Instead, Alexander kicked over the traces entirely, and Breadon had no alternative but to suspend him for the remainder of the season. I wish it could have been otherwise.

"The way he pitched in Pittsburgh and Philadelphia in early August, he easily could have won another eight or ten games to add to his three hundred seventy-three victories."

Hard drinking in his later years held down Old Pete's seasonal victories. Had he been made of different stuff—had he not been an alcoholic—the name of Grover Cleveland Alexander would today stand well above Mathewson in total victories and near Walter Johnson's 416.

16

MY BIGGEST BASEBALL
THRILL

One of the questions most often asked me is: "What was the great-est thrill you ever experienced in big league baseball?" Question-ers usually expect me to cite some great Ruthian performance, maybe his sixtieth home run in 1927, or the two World Series games he played in St. Louis, in each of which he hit three home runs. But my biggest thrill came in a World Series game between the Cubs and my boyhood favorites, the Philadelphia Athletics, in old Shibe Park on Columbus Day, 1929, a few days before the stock market crash of that year.

The afternoon started out a disaster for the Philadelphia fans, and as late as the middle of the seventh inning the Cubs led, 8–0. The Athlet-ics were leading in the Series, two games to one, and it looked as if the Cubs were about to tie it up, 2–2. The Cubs, led by Joe McCarthy, had battered down three Athletics pitchers, ancient spitballer Jack Quinn, left-hander Rube Walberg, and veteran reliever Ed Rommel, for eight runs, while the sturdy Cub right-hander, Charley Root, had held the A's to three scattered singles and no runs.

When Al Simmons started the Athletics' seventh inning with a pow-erful homer to the roof of the left-field stands, it seemed like just a drop in the bucket in the midst of a drought. It merely deprived Root of a shutout. However, when Jimmie Foxx, Bing Miller, and Jimmy Dykes followed with sharp singles, Foxx scoring, the apathetic Philadelphia crowd began to sit up and take notice.

Before light-hitting shortstop Joe Boley went to bat, manager Mack told him, "I think the big fellow out there is losing his stuff. If the first

Joe McCarthy, Manager of the Chicago Cubs, and Fred Lieb at the Polo Grounds, 1927.

ball comes anywhere near the plate, I want you to swing at it." Boley followed instructions and lined the first pitch for a single to left to drive in Miller with the third A's run. Now the score was 8–3. By this time, the strongly pro-Athletics crowd was yelling like wild Comanches.

There was a momentary lull in the firing as Root induced pinch hitter George Burns to pop up to Chicago shortstop Woody English. But when leadoff man Max Bishop came up, there was a quick resumption of the artillery barrage. Max lined a crisp single to center, scoring Dykes. That cut the Cub lead in half, 8–4, and there was only one out. Phillies fans were jumping.

By this time, there was consternation on the Cubs bench. Manager Joe McCarthy came to the same conclusion as had Mack earlier, that Root had lost his stuff. He yanked Charley and put in Art Nehf, a veteran left-hander who had done some strong World Series pitching for John McGraw and the Giants on their great teams in the early 1920s.

The first batter that Nehf faced was center fielder Mule Haas. He hit one with the kick of a mule, a screeching line drive far into center field. Center fielder Hack Wilson misjudged it, took a few steps forward, and then changed directions too late. The ball went well over Hack's head and rolled to deepest center field for an inside-the-park homer. Boley

Fred Lieb and Connie Mack at
Shibe Park, Philadelphia, during
the 1929 Cubs-A's World Series.

and Bishop had trotted in ahead of Haas, and the A's now trailed Chicago by only one run.

The stands thundered with screaming and shouting, and the Athletics players were jumping up and down, slapping each other on the
back and rear. Jimmy Dykes grabbed a vacant spot on the bench and
sat down, not noticing who was sitting next to him—Connie Mack.
With a yell of pure joy, Dykes slapped his neighbor so vigorously that
slim Connie was knocked off the bench and sent sprawling among a
bunch of scattered bats on the dugout floor.

Jimmy sobered up immediately and helped his boss to his feet, saying most apologetically, "Oh, I am so sorry, Mr. Mack! I didn't know it
was you!"

"It's all right, Jimmy. Perfectly all right," interposed Mack, "especially on an occasion like this one."

The A's had a few good licks left. McCarthy left Nehf in after the
homer, but when Art walked Mickey Cochrane, the Cubs chieftain
pulled him out and substituted Sheriff Blake, an experienced right-
hander. Nothing made any difference. The A's bats remained red hot,
and hard singles by Simmons and Foxx brought in Cochrane with the
tying run.

The harassed McCarthy now called in his strong Pat Malone to try

Hack Wilson. PBA Photo

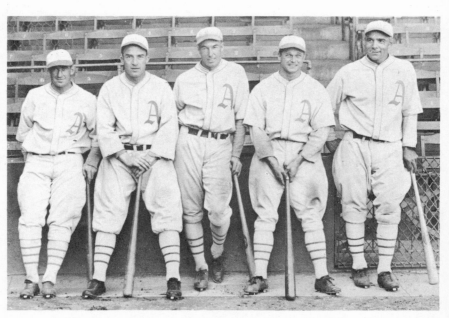

Stars of Mack's great teams of 1929–31, left to right: Mickey Cochrane, Al Simmons, Mule Haas, Jimmy Foxx, Bing Miller.   *Herald Tribune* Photo—Acme

to put out the fire. Pat's first pitch plunked Miller in the ribs for a hit batter, which again filled the bases. Dykes, the next batsman, swung with all his might and sent a high line drive to left field, down the foul line, but a few feet within fair territory. Riggs Stephenson jumped for the ball, but it bounded off his fingertips for a double, bringing in Simmons and Foxx with runs that made the score 10–8, Athletics leading. The crowd went hysterical.

An amusing sidelight about Jimmy Dykes's last hit, the one that drove in the two winning runs, is that he went to bat with but one purpose—to hit a sacrifice fly and bring in one more run. "We had scored so many runs I had lost track of the score," he said. "I thought we still were trailing, eight to seven. Simmons was on third with only one out, so I decided that my job was to bring him in with a long fly. I intentionally uppercut at the ball to give it lift, and I swung for distance. To my surprise I did even better, whacking the ball out of Stephenson's reach for a double. And then to find that not just the tying run, but the two go-ahead runs came in!"

With his team now two runs ahead, Connie Mack took no pitching chances. He called in his best, Robert Moses Grove, to hold the lead. Old Mose did it magnificently. Only six Cubs faced Grove in the eighth and ninth innings, and Lefty struck out four of them. Seldom has a pitched ball arrived at the plate so swiftly and overpoweringly as in these two innings. The final score remained 10–8.

After the game I tried to see Mack at the Athletics' clubhouse, but strangely the sixty-seven-year-old tactician was not there in a moment of magnificent victory and no one knew where he was. I had a hunch Connie might be in his hideaway, a room with a couch in the tower of Shibe Park. As I started up the stairs, I was surprised to meet Rud Rennie of the New York *Herald-Tribune* coming down. "I think you better not go up there, Fred," Rennie advised. "The old gentleman is pretty well fatigued. He just murmured to me, 'I guess that seventh inning was a little too much for me.' I think he may have had a slight stroke, either in that seventh inning or after the game. He's in no shape for talking." I took Rud's advice and turned back.

Whether it was a slight stroke or just a reaction to that terrific ten-run seventh inning, I never did determine, but I incline to the stroke theory. However, Mr. Mack continued to manage the club until 1950—his fiftieth year (at age eighty-eight) as director-general of the old Athletics. In his last years Connie was not only the "beloved" Connie Mack but the "venerable" one—truly a great manager and a lovely person. I really loved the old fellow with his stiff white collars of the 1900s.

17

EXPEDITION TO NIPPON

In 1931 ex-player Herb Hunter and I, as Judge Landis' representative, headed a baseball mission to Japan. It was both an artistic and a financial success. We invaded the islands with one of the greatest teams ever assembled.

Seven of the fourteen men who made up our playing personnel subsequently were voted to the Cooperstown Hall of Fame, including three-quarters of our infield: first baseman Lou Gehrig of the Yankees; second baseman Frank Frisch of the Cardinals; and shortstop Rabbit Maranville, then playing a second time for the Boston Braves. The Philadelphia Athletics contributed three Hall of Famers: Mickey Cochrane, a super-catcher often ranked as the number one of all time; Al Simmons, the hard-hitting left fielder; and Robert Moses "Lefty" Grove, superb left-handed pitcher. Our seventh Hall of Famer was George Kelly, former crack first baseman of McGraw's Giants. Kelly was taken along as an extra infielder but as a result of an early injury to our regular, Iron Horse Gehrig, George played most of our games at first base.

The non–Hall of Famers also were players of distinction and skill: our left-fielder, Frank "Lefty" O'Doul, twice National League batting champion; Willie Kamm, a slick-fielding third baseman for the White Sox and Cleveland; our second string catcher, Harold "Muddy" Ruel, a 150-pound iron man who caught the great Walter Johnson in Washington; Larry French, a fine young left-hander then of the Pittsburgh Pirates; Tom Oliver of the Red Sox, who could go back for flies over his head like Tris Speaker and Joe DiMaggio; pitcher Bruce Cunningham of the Boston Braves, our only right-handed pitcher; and Ralph Shinners, substitute outfielder who had played with Frisch and Kelly on the New York Giants.

The way I got to head such a prestigious baseball expedition was a combination of good luck and good friends. Herb Hunter, who had played on four big league clubs—the New York Giants, Cubs, Red Sox, and Cardinals, participating in only twenty-four games—had led a big league team to Japan in 1922, bringing along such stars as Waite Hoyt, Herb Pennock, Casey Stengel, Luke Sewell, and lesser lights. Hunter had also taken Ty Cobb, Bob Shawkey, and umpire Ernie Quigley on a goodwill tour of the Flowery Kingdom. Hunter was a baseball man and promoter with vast enthusiasm, but he lacked business know-how and the ability to handle money. Herb was in Judge Landis's doghouse because of an unsettled debt to Ty Cobb and because Landis was convinced that he had deliberately permitted his club to lose a game in Korea in 1922.

Waite Hoyt, who was the pitcher that day, told me later that Landis was wrong about the game's being thrown. Landis, however, based his suspicion on a report which perhaps came from George Moriarty, an American League umpire assigned to the trip. Moriarty and Hunter were known not to get along well.

At any rate, after Hunter had lined up the 1931 trip with Japanese authorities in Tokyo, Judge Landis refused to sanction the expedition and prohibited all players from signing for it with Hunter.

In desperation Hunter turned to me. He knew that I had a friendly relationship with both the National League president, John Heydler and Commissioner Landis, so he told me he would split any profits from the trip fifty-fifty if I could get the necessary official sanction. Heydler was easy; he thought such trips had educational value and were good for international relations as well as for baseball. Landis was much more difficult. At first his position was that I "could pick up Herb's Japanese contracts," but he didn't want Hunter to make the trip. I pleaded that it would break Herb's heart if he was left behind. After the Judge had had another talk with Heydler, the upshot was that he gave a rather reluctant permission with certain stipulations: Hunter was not to handle any money, he was not to play in a single game, and I was to sign the players to personal contracts. The Judge told me that I would be his personal representative and official head of the party. I could discipline players if they got too far out of line, especially when it came to drinking and wenching. To be so chopped down was tough for Hunter to accept, but he fell into line and each ended up netting a tidy sum from the enterprise.

Our trip was long before planes whizzed across the Pacific in twelve hours. In 1931 it took a full two weeks by steamer to get to Japan, including a day's stopover in Hawaii and a loss of eighteen hours crossing time zones.

We sailed on one of the Japanese luxury liners of the day, and fellow

"We invaded Japan with one of the greatest teams ever assembled." Left to right, back row: Larry French, Mickey Cochrane, Frank O'Doul, Fred Lieb, Lefty Grove, Herb Hunter, Bruce Cunningham, Tom Oliver, George Kelly, Lou Gehrig. Front row: Willie Kamm, Rabbit Maranville, Frank Frisch, Muddy Ruel, Al Simmons, Ralph Shinners, Doc Knolls (trainer).

passengers included the Japanese naval delegation returning from an international conference in London, the arms limitation conference that produced the so-called Five-Five-Three Compromise (The three great naval powers of the world, Britain, the United States, and Japan, agreed to a five-five-three ratio in the size of their navies, Japan accepting the lesser figure). The chief of the Japanese delegation was a short, bald-headed admiral who, when freed from the bickering for battleships, cruisers, destroyers and submarines, acted like a kid out of school for his summer holidays. He and his lower-ranking officers found huge enjoyment in talking with Gehrig, Cochrane, Frisch, and Ruel, whom the officers knew were idols of the American fans.

The distinguished admiral's great favorite, however, was little Rabbit Maranville, who had served in the American Navy in World War I. They both were approximately the same height, around 5 feet 4½ inches. The Rabbit's name for the admiral was Icky, and once when the distinguished chief of the Imperial Japanese Mission was taking a daytime snooze, Maranville obtained a bottle of ink and drew a face on the admiral's bald head.

On paper, it looked as though our team would crush all opponents, not only in Japan but even in the United States itself. A representative of a Japanese sports association approached me with the suggestion that we give the Japanese teams a handicap advantage of twenty runs per game.

I was a little aghast! "I don't think our players would take kindly to such a suggestion," I replied. "While it is true our players are taller and heavier than yours, in baseball a team of good little men often can defeat a team of taller but heavier and slower players. Also, I have a feeling your countrymen, on the whole, would not like the suggestion. They would think we were belittling your players."

So we played without handicaps. Including our one victory in Honolulu on the stop over from San Francisco, we won all of our eighteen games.

In 1931 there was no professional ball in Japan, and we played against collegians, most of them from "The Big Six" universities such as Keio, Waseda, and Imperial in the Tokyo-Yokohama district. Later we played the Nippon All-Stars, made up on the order of our All-American football teams, only this All-Star team was selected from all Nippon teams for the past ten years.

Oddly, the college teams played us much closer than the supposedly superior Nippon All-Stars. While we defeated the All-Stars by such convincing scores as 20–3, 22–4, 19–1, some of the pitchers on the college teams had real success against our batters. We defeated a little 140-pound left-hander from Keio by only a 2–0 score, and the little guy pitched the in-shoot to Gehrig that broke two small bones in the Iron Horse's right hand, ending Lou's play for the trip. It was a strange quirk of fate that Gehrig, who played 2,130 consecutive games for Col. Ruppert through fifteen seasons, should be side-lined by an injury after playing only seven games for me.

Even though baseball was strictly a college and middle-school amateur sport in 1931, it already was the Japanese national game. More kids played baseball in Japan than in the United States. Golf and tennis were still played largely by aristocrats and the wealthy, and basketball and soccer ranked far behind baseball in the public interest.

One Sunday morning, friends took us to visit the big Buddha at Nara. To get there we took an eighteen-mile automobile ride along the shoreline from Yokohama. The route ran through literally hundreds of baseball games played along the sandy shore. The diamonds were so closely placed together that the right fielder in one game played alongside the third baseman in another. The route to Nara was busy with hundreds of young men on bicycles in baseball uniforms. As two teams would finish a game, two more would be ready to go.

One time we returned to Tokyo on a sleeper, arriving at the big Center City Depot at 6:00 A.M. On fields to both sides of the stations ball games were in full swing—young men in their late teens or early twenties playing ball games before reporting for work in nearby offices!

All seats except for the grass seats at Meidji Shrine Stadium were sold out for our first two Saturday and Sunday games. The beautiful stadium was built on the side of a hill, and spectators for lower-priced seats sat on the grassy hillside. The seating capacity was 65,000 and you couldn't have squeezed another Japanese boy in anywhere. We played seven games there and later played six in a ball park situated halfway between Kobe, a seaport, and Osaka, a large industrial city. The grandstand there was an immense single-decked wooden horseshoe, something like New York's Polo Grounds before the 1911 fire. Here we were told there were 75,000 at each of our first two weekend games. In our seventeen games in Japan, we drew 450,000, and that was forty-six years ago!

Sotaro Suzuki, the representative of the *Yomouiri Shimbun*, the Tokyo newspaper that sponsored our trip, was with us throughout our itinerary in Japan. We began a lifelong friendship which still continues. Suzuki has written many Japanese baseball books and generally is credited as being the "Father of Japanese professional baseball." In 1975 he was given a citation by Emperor Hirohito for his contribution to Japanese culture.

When I congratulated Suzuki on the high honor his emperor had bestowed on him, he replied: "Your great American team of 1931 and the later team led by Connie Mack and Babe Ruth in 1934 made such an impression on our people that it paved the way for professional baseball in Japan. It showed the Japanese people how baseball was played at the highest level and filled our players with the desire to give the Americans equal competition."

As an indication of how much the Japanese have learned since 1931, when the New York Mets, National League champions of 1973, sent a team to Japan in 1974, the Mets played four games with a Nipponese champion club before the New Yorkers won their first game. There were two tie games and two Japanese victories. It wasn't until Joe Torre, the slugging first baseman, was traded by St. Louis to New York a few days after the close of the 1974 season and Joe was able to join the Mets in Japan that the New Yorkers really caught fire and eventually wound up ahead, 7–5, with two tie games.

Among the heroes of our 1931 American team was little Rabbit Maranville, shortstop and field manager. Though we had two players who later became famous playing managers, Mickey Cochrane and Frankie Frisch, the Rabbit outranked them in seniority, for he had managed the Cubs in 1925. The shortest man on our squad by far, the Rab was the size of an average Japanese man. Naturally, they identified with Ma-

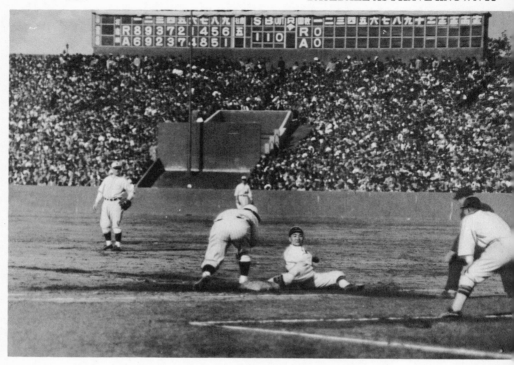

Gehrig taking a pick-off throw at first base. Frank Frisch is standing at second base. Japan, 1931.

ranville. Like Casey Stengel, he was a natural comic and mimic, full of fun and antics. He kidded constantly with the Japanese fans and they loved it.

Grove and George Kelly, both 6 feet 4 inches, also appealed to the Japanese, just because of their height. Lefty and George had to tie themselves into pretzels to get into the sleeping berths on Japanese railway cars. The Japanese knew all about Grove's 31–4 record for Connie Mack's 1931 Athletics. He early distinguished himself with a typically overpowering strikeout performance, and everywhere we went, the crowds expected Grove to pitch, even though it was somebody else's turn. "G'vove, G'vove, G'vove!" was the cry, and frequently we gave in, letting Grove pitch the last inning or two. Lefty led all the other players in demands for autographs. He finally had to have a rubber stamp made.

The nearest we came to losing was in a game with Waseda University. They had a good right-handed pitcher, fairly large for a Japanese—5 feet 10 inches and 180 pounds. Lou Gehrig later recommended him to

Ed Barrow, Yankee general manager, saying "The Waseda man could pitch as well as any pitcher the Yankee organization has in Newark or Kansas City." Our pitcher was Larry French, the sturdy ex–University of California left-hander.

Larry almost started the war ten years before Pearl Harbor. It's a long story, beginning when he took pictures in the rain the day before a game and caught a heavy cold. But as one of only three pitchers with us, he had to take his turn. After six innings the score was a surprising 1–1. The Japanese fans could scarcely believe it; neither could I. Then in the seventh inning, with the bases full, one of their stronger batters drove a ball well over the head of Tom Oliver, our center fielder, for a triple, cleaning the bases. Rabbit took out an unhappy Larry French. In case of an emergency we had counted on using Lou Gehrig, who had pitched some at Columbia, to work a few innings. So we had Lou take the pitcher's box.

The score now was 5–1, but the big Japanese pitcher who had held the Americans to four hits in seven innings lost his stuff and cunning in the eighth. Suddenly it rained doubles and triples all over the place and in no time the Americans had scored seven runs, taking the lead by 8–5. Manager Maranville then called on Grove to hold the lead. He struck out the side in order in both the eighth and ninth innings, using only nineteen pitches to do it. There were few foul strikes; Big Mose just pitched his superb fastball and the collegians didn't know whether it was coming or going.

Larry French, meanwhile, was still storming on the bench, disgusted at having been knocked out of the box, and now unfortunately he started to use profanity and racial slurs: "The yellow so and so's, the yellow blankety blanks." I did my best to shush him up, directing his attention to a distinguished Japanese official we had sitting at the end of the bench. In addition to being a Waseda graduate, the Baron, as we called him, was also a graduate of Harvard and each autumn exhibited his prize chrysanthemums at the Cambridge, Massachusetts flower show. He was the third-ranking golfer in Japan and held a position in the Japanese cabinet similar to that of the chancellor of the exchequer in Britain. The Baron spoke English as well as any of us, but he took French's tirade like a thoroughbred and never let his eyes stray from the field.

The Baron was game enough to invite us all to a house party on Armistice Day. It also was Rabbit Maranville's fortieth birthday. At the Baron's house there was lots of music, dancing, champagne, Japanese lobsters, steaks, and American and Japanese delicacies. There were also a score of the Baron's aristocratic friends present. But the big event of the evening, to me at least, was bringing in Rabbit's birthday present. Lou Gehrig and Mary had seen Maranville admiring a large white ivory elephant, about the size of a fox terrier, on display in a shop across the street from our hotel. They learned that Rabbit had asked the price of the elephant, but when the shopkeeper said it was 300 yen (approximately $150 in our money), the Rabbit had decided it was a little above his means.

Shortly before midnight, one of the Baron's servants smote a big gong forty times, one for each of the Rabbit's forty eventful years. Then two other servants appeared carrying a large chest. Rabbit was told to unwrap it. Inside the chest was a smaller chest, also well wrapped, and inside was a still smaller one and then one even smaller. It still was a pretty good sized box when Rabbit finally unwrapped the white ivory elephant. Like a small boy, he gave a yell of joy. Then when he tried to express his gratitude, the tears rolled down his tanned cheeks. It was something to see this grizzled veteran of the big league trails, quite a playboy in his time, cry as he tried to express thanks to his comrades.

In addition to being given a reception at the United States Embassy, our party was honored by an invitation to have tea with the Japanese prime minister, at that time Reijiro Wakatauki, He received us graciously in the prime minister's residence, displayed some knowledge of baseball and was familiar with names such as Gehrig, Cochrane, Simmons, and Grove.

Before the tea was served, a messenger came in and told Mr. Wakatauki that something urgent needed his attention. He excused himself and was absent for about ten minutes. When he left the room, I regret to say that some of us acted as real Ugly Americans. Three or four players filled their pockets with the prime minister's Havana cigars; others snitched pens from the premier's desk; some of the ladies took small vases from the shelves. Even my Mary, who was as honest as a Florida summer day is long, could not resist the temptation and secreted a vase in her bag. "After all, we don't have tea with a prime minister of an important nation every day," she explained lamely. My daughter still displays the vase in her home.

At the end of our visit a photographer took a picture of our group with our host. The prime minister and I were in the center, shaking hands, while the players and their wives were circled around us. Just before the picture was snapped, Mrs. Frank O'Doul worked her way to the front so that she was standing right behind our clasped hands. She was wearing a black dress with big blotches of white all over it. In 1931 such a pattern was considered way-out. Later Mrs. O'Doul explained, "I wanted to show some of the Shanty Irish in San Francisco what company I was now traveling in."

As for her husband, Frank O'Doul brought back a lot of honors himself. On the ship out he won all the deck games—fastest runner around the ship, highest jumper, and broadest jumper. He also took the other players at cards and in shooting dice. On land he established himself as the best golfer in the party, and in his early baseball games of the trip he hit .600, far above anyone else.

O'Doul also brought back two broken ribs, the result of an "accident" in the eighth game. In the big leagues, players of rival teams often like to jaw at one another, sometimes quite uncomplimentary. Our players also tried to kid some of the Japanese college players, most of whom knew a little English; but with one exception the Japanese, whether they understood or not, remained mute. The one exception was the second baseman on the Waseda team, whom Rabbit nicknamed Nosey. He talked back and even had a few fresh things to say to the Americans.

As O'Doul left the bench to go to bat, he said, "I'm going to bunt and force Nosey to cover first base. We'll have some fun." It was painful fun for O'Doul. He bunted down the first-base line; the Waseda first baseman fielded the ball, and Nosey ran over to cover the first-base bag. Frank ran full speed down the line to the bag and ran smack into Nosey, bouncing away some ten feet into foul territory. When O'Doul got up, his face showed that he was in considerable pain. He suffered two broken ribs, while the Japanese second baseman held the ball for a putout and returned smilingly to his second-base position. He said something to O'Doul which we did not understand, but his Japanese teammates did, and they smiled big toothy smiles.

They taped up O'Doul's side at a Tokyo hospital that night and he was through with baseball and golf for the remainder of his stay. As Gehrig had been injured in the previous game, we had to get by with a twelve-player squad for our last ten days.

Despite the incident and the disappointment, O'Doul made many friends on the trip. After 1931 he made a dozen trips back to Japan, both before and after World War II, and often he was called the Baseball Ambassador to Nippon.

One of the most amusing incidents to happen on our trip, though it wasn't funny for the victim, was in connection with a 450-foot home run by Mickey Cochrane, our great catcher, which knocked out three front teeth of a bleacher fan. The fun was how the Japanese handled the situation.

It happened in Sendai, the northernmost city we visited on our trip. When we arrived, a high wind was blowing, and as game time approached, the wind increased in intensity to almost a gale. In my years of attending ball games I have never seen a game attempted under such conditions. It was worse than a windy day or night in Candlestick Park in San Francisco. In Candlestick a gust of wind will often blow the pitcher from the pitcher's rubber, but this Sendai wind blew steadily throughout the game.

Fred Lieb receives a gold medal from the Boy Scouts of Japan in Tokyo, November 1931.

Cochrane hit his home run into the wind. The ball wasn't hit high, but rode into the wind about fifteen feet above the level of the ground and finally came to rest in an uncovered bleacher full of fans. Ordinarily it would take a cannon to hit a home run into this bleacher, an estimated 450 feet away, and a monstrous swat against a small gale. Since I could follow the flight of the ball all the way, I would think any bleacherite could have done so also and ducked or scrambled aside when he saw the ball headed in his direction. But this unwary fan was hit right in the mouth; his lips were bloodied and three teeth were knocked out. At the time there seemed a little disturbance in the bleacher, but the game was held up for only a few minutes.

Now, about twenty minutes later, arrived First Aid, Japanese style. A pint-sized (to our occidental eyes) ambulance drove on the playing field and stopped behind home plate. A little doctor about five feet tall stepped out, followed by two pint-sized nurses dressed in gray and white. With the doctor leading the way, they marched single file across the entire field from home plate to pitcher's box, second base, and out to the distant bleacher. Arriving at the scene of the accident, they learned that the victim was already in the promoter's office and had received emergency treatment. The man who tried to catch the ball with his mouth received 100 yen from the management and apparently felt that he had put in a good day.

18

GRANNY AND DAMON
AND HEYWOOD AND ME

Among the many memorable happenstances in my carrer as a baseball writer was breaking in with Grantland Rice, Damon Runyon, and Heywood Broun in the Polo Grounds press box in 1911. What marvelous writers each became in his own distinctive way! And they were delightful, friendly, and interesting individuals.

Rice of the New York *Mail* had just come up from the South, where he had been writing for a decade. He was the poet of the press box, the only sports writer I can recall who ever published volumes of poetry about American sports. Not only was he the greatest sports writer on the American scene, but he was the most beloved. I never heard anyone criticize or speak unkindly of Granny. Had anyone done so in our presence, we would have knocked him down.

Granny did me an early good turn. After Frank Munsey acquired the New York *Press*, editors within the Munsey management chain frequently turned to our sports staff for advice on sports articles. One day the editor of *Railroad Man's Magazine* came to me with a list of a dozen different sports grips, for which he wanted a descriptive and explanatory text: the batting grip of Hans Wagner, the golfing grips of England's famed Harry Vardon and Ted Ray, the tennis grips of U.S. champ R. Lindley Murray and the fabulous French star Suzanne Lenglen, the grips for driving a four-in-hand carriage, and the grip for fly casting. He gave me the list and asked me to knock out 2,500 words on the subject.

I was over my head. I showed the list to a couple of my associates in the Polo Grounds press box and was at once told, "Ask Grant Rice."

The New York Baseball Writers at the 1912 Giants-Red Sox World Series.

Left to right, standing: Wheeler—*Herald*, Foster—*Telegram*; seated: Crane—*Journal*, Lieb—*Press*, Runyon—*American*, Bulger—*Evening World*, Mercer—*Globe*, Rice—*Mail*, Trumbull—*Evening Sun*; foreground: Stevens' nephew, Harry Stevens.

When I approached Rice, he invited me to his Riverside Drive apartment and after introducing me to his charming wife, he looked at the list and said "grips" would make an interesting article because of their basic importance. He showed me his grip on driver, mashie, and putter, explaining how Vardon and Ray held them. Then he shifted to Wagner's grip on a baseball bat and demonstrated how the Dutchman uncocked his wrists at the point of impact. (Rice had played shortstop at Vanderbilt University.) Before I left, Rice had either shown me the grips or given me the names and addresses of men who could help me. I never forgot this early kindness.

Rice covered baseball regularly only in his first year in New York, but he always covered the World Series, first for the *Mail* and later for the *Tribune*. His syndicated column, "Sportlight," frequently dealt with baseball highlights. While I was president of the Baseball Writers Association of America (1922–24) I introduced annual awards for the best-written baseball piece of the year. It was a delight to present the first award to Grantland Rice for his terrific story of the first game of the 1922 World Series.

Much later Harry Stevens, famous caterer at the Polo Grounds, passed on to me one of the most gratifying compliments I have received for my writing. He quoted Grant Rice as saying: "Freddy Lieb can write a story on the official fielding averages and make it sound as interesting as a World Series game."

My last view of Granny was just before the final game of the Boston Braves–Cleveland Indians World Series in 1948. I encountered him in the lobby of the Hotel Cleveland, only a few blocks from Municipal Stadium. He was alone and appeared confused and bewildered. Apparently he had missed connections with his closest pals among the baseball writers, Red Smith and Frankie Graham. When I greeted him, he said, "Freddy, will you please let me go with you to the ball park. I don't know present-day Cleveland and I get lost going through all those passages." I could see he had lost his bearings, and I was happy to be his reliance. He leaned rather heavily on my arm, and when I steered him safely through the press gate and to his seat in the press box, he was profuse in his gratitude. "Thank you, thank you, Freddy! I couldn't have got here without your help." I left him with tears in my eyes, thinking that I was the one who should have thanked him for the chance to do a small service to a great sports writer and a genuine southern gentleman. Though he lived six more years, I never saw him again.

Some people thought Damon Runyon was an iconoclast, one who liked to demolish tin gods and hallowed traditions. That wasn't the Runyon I knew. He had a sharp sense of humor, liked fun, and was willing to go wherever it led him. He didn't smile or laugh much, but when he peered out at the world through glasses that made him look studious, there was a suggestion he was smugly amused at the foolishnesses he saw. I thought he liked most of all to stand quietly in the background watching and half laughing at the people who passed his vision. But destructive or bitter—never.

Runyon came to the New York *American* in 1911 after a decade of writing for papers in Denver and San Francisco. He did not write baseball consistently after 1911, and I think he felt more at home by the prizefight ring than by the baseball diamond. In fact he "owned" and managed a few boxers. In a way I could never be, Damon was quite comfortable with the characters who infested the fight business—men who owned "pieces" of fighters, promoters, trainers, touts, and general hangers-on. He was also deeply interested in the racetrack. Both ring and racetrack provided him with those marvelous characters who darted or slunk in and out of his bizarre stories that earned him a distinctive niche in American literature.

To Damon there were no good guys and bad guys, no gracious ladies who promoted church fairs, no tawdry streetwalkers. They were all guys and dolls, and you judged them, if at all, by their inner qualities, not their outward circumstances. He was an observer, not a judge or moral censor. There was nothing in him of the reformer or crusader or champion of good causes. He did not care for athletes regarded to be "clean as a whistle" or for appeals for pure amateurism in the sport world. Yet he was an inherently honest and totally decent person. I remember well his chiding me once for a bad habit of knocking people I had fallen into. "Freddy," he said to me earnestly, "Why do you do it?" It brought me up short, and I think it marked the start of a new philosophy toward people in my life.

When I knew Runyon he drank no alcoholic beverages, not even beer. That was fine by me, for my digestive system couldn't handle more than two drinks an evening and I had to learn to make each of them last a long time. But when Runyon gathered with other sports writers to talk—chewing fat, he always called it—he would drink quarts and maybe gallons of coffee while the others were putting away beer, rye highballs, and sloe gin. Some of these sessions lasted until four o'clock in the morning, and Runyon was usually the last to leave.

He didn't feel virtuous about not drinking; he was in fact ashamed of it. "I just can't drink, and now I'm smart enough to know it," he once told me. "I used to drink, hard. I frequently got stinking drunk. And when I was drinking I was real mean.

"I'll tell you why I stopped. It was in a saloon in Denver. There was a big guy at the bar, talking loudly, and I took a dislike to him. I moved over to his group and tried to interrupt his conversation. The big guy didn't hit me—he just extended his long arm, put a big paw on the left side of my face, and kept me at arm's length. When he said, 'Shut up, you little twerp,' I began swinging, but I was just churning up the stale air and making a laughing stock of myself. The man conversed with his friends as though nothing was happening.

"When I recovered from that souse and reviewed what had happened to me, I said to myself, 'Runyon, I don't mind you picking on little guys, even those as big as you are, when you're drunk. But when you take on a guy who is two feet taller and outweighs you by eighty pounds, it's time for you to stop drinking.' And so I stopped."

I believe Damon did fall off the wagon two or three times afterward for short periods, but in the years I saw him he never drank anything but coffee. He had a dread that he would follow in the footsteps of his father, whom he worshipped—a hard-drinking newspaperman, printer, and proofreader, who was usually broke because of his drinking.

When I brought out my first book, *Sight Unseen: A Journalist Visits the Occult,* I sent an autographed copy to Damon. The book was on metaphysics, the psychic world, Hindu lore and philosophy, and Ouija board conversations. Damon was confined to his New York hotel with throat trouble, which soon was to be diagnosed as cancer. He reviewed *Sight Unseen* in his general news column which still ran in the *American,* beginning with something like this: "When I was in New York's low forties, writing of my guys and dolls, Freddy Lieb was ten blocks north—in the fifties—cavorting around with bearded Hindus, psychics, mediums, and other strange folk."

I should have introduced Damon to all those "strange folk." They would have made a marvelous cast of characters for a Runyon book or movie script, and he might have immortalized one or two of them as he did Nathan Detroit and Miss Adelaide in *Guys and Dolls.*

Compared to smart dressing Damon Runyon, Heywood Broun was a slouch. He had a fancy name, Matthew Heywood Campbell Broun, and he went to Harvard. A big 6-foot 3-inch nonathletic-looking man, he wore clothes that looked as though they were hung on him; they invariably needed pressing. His flat broad-brimmed hat had at least a month's supply of New York's grime on it. He liked to eat, and he ate often and well. When he broke in as a baseball writer for the New York *Morning Telegraph* and then moved to the New York *Tribune* in 1912, he weighed about 225 pounds. By the time he became the *Trib*'s drama critic in 1916, his weight had zoomed to 250. To me, though, he was a delightful, fun-loving companion.

Before Sunday baseball was legalized, Heywood occasionally came to our home for Sunday dinner. I can still hear him complimenting Mary on her cooking and me on having enough sense to marry a good cook. And of course the *Press* and the *Tribune* were close neighbors, so we often shared the same double seat on the now long-demolished

Sixth Avenue El that transported us from the Polo Grounds to what used to be called Newspaper Row. Looking back, I suppose we were some sort of odd couple—Heywood, the big brow from Harvard and I the high school boy from South Philadelphia. But I never sensed—or was made aware of—any intellectual gap between us. Our forty-five-minute ride together permitted lots of conversation. I remembered he invariably carried with him his copy of *The Masses* or some other "radical" literature, but he and I discussed baseball, who played well, and who wrote well.

Politically, I was a Progressive Republican, a devout follower of Teddy Roosevelt. Broun shared my liking for the onetime Rough Rider and he told me, "If your politics are those of Roosevelt and Gifford Pinchot, then we are reasonably close." Although we never discussed a newspaper reporters' union, in 1933 Heywood became the father and the strongest pillar of the Newspaper Guild, which substantially upped the pay of editors and reporters from New York to San Francisco.

During the period of the war of the big leagues with the upstart Federal League, 1914–15, Heywood and I covered a "peace meeting" held near Times Square. When the dinner recess was called, Broun invited me to dine with him at the Harvard Club. One of his old Harvard professors stopped at our table and chatted familiarly for several minutes. As the professor started to move away, he stopped and said, "I forgot to ask, what are you doing now, Broun?"

Heywood replied, "I'm writing baseball for the *Tribune*."

The professor's face dropped. "Bah! Have you fallen to that?"

Heywood beamed at me. "Methinks the professor doesn't think much of our business."

No doubt the professor felt better when Broun became the *Trib*'s drama critic in 1916.

Heywood loved to play with words, find fun in them. Among his verbal delights were two New York Giants pitchers of the 1915 era, Rube Schauer and Ferdie Schupp. With the pitching off and the Giants low in the standing, McGraw often used both in the same game. Usually Schauer would get the first call and then Schupp would finish up. So Broun worked into his *Tribune* story a line that was repeated for years in the Polo Grounds press box, "It never Schauers, but it Schupps."

Heywood was a man of few inhibitions. When he felt an urge to do something he did it. One late afternoon on our subway ride home together we were talking baseball, when a Buttinski type, sitting on Heywood's right, tried to make a threesome. Broun withered him with a look and told him he was not invited into our private conversation.

A moment later when Heywood got up to leave the train, I saw him rolling up the newspapers he was carrying into a solid club. As the train doors closed, Broun reached through an open window and smacked Mr. Buttinski a resounding whack on the top of his head.

Once I introduced Heywood to a quick-witted, smartly dressed girl from the Philadelphia News Bureau. Heywood showed up at our apartment for his date in his usual attire—unpressed suit, unshined shoes, and his flat hat looking as though it had been rescued from a trash barrel. That evening the four of us ate one of Mary's bounteous dinners, and when we all done and relaxed in lazy conversation, Heywood spotted some asparagus stalks still in the serving dish. He stretched his oversized frame, plucked out the stalks with one large paw, got them all successfully in his mouth, and downed them. "Mary, you do cook good asparagus!" he commented, with sauce dripping down his chin.

Broun hoped to see more of the girl, but whenever I mentioned him to her after that, she would put her hand to her mouth as though stuffing it with asparagus.

Broun fell in and out of love easily. Once, just after he turned from sports to the stage, he became infatuated with a blonde Russian beauty starring in a Muscovite repertory company playing in Greenwich Village. He wrote and spoke glowingly of her talents, beauty, intelligence, and It—a word about as much abused in those days as "charisma" is today. Then one day he caught the enchanting Lydia Lapopka in the lap, so to speak, of her Russian director.

This time Heywood let go all inhibitions. He walked east on one street, knocking over every garbage and trash can he passed. Then he walked west on the street giving it the same treatment. Just as he was getting really warmed up to the sport he ran into the hands of the law. Heywood spent the night in the hoosegow before friends bailed him out the next morning.

Evenutally Heywood found true love in Ruth Hale, then head of the New York women's rights organization, the Lucy Stone League. They shared the same political philosophy and became comrades in various crusades. Ruth Hale was also a baseball fan. She sat in the Polo Grounds press box and once told me, after Heywood was covering drama, "You're my favorite baseball writer." Naturally I respected her acumen.

Heywood and Ruth were married and begat Heywood Hale (Woody) Broun, who became a successful baseball writer and is now seen on CBS at every important horse race. Woody accepted his illustrious father's citation when Heywood was voted into Cooperstown's galaxy of sports writers in 1971. His acceptance speech was adjudged by those who remembered his parents, as being "up to the standard of the best of the Brouns."

When I first came to New York, afternoon games started at 4 P.M. in order to include what was called the Wall Street crowd. We writers had the starting time set back to 3:30 and later to 3:00. Except on opening day, however, we were not very punctual. Of the thirteen writers assigned to the Polo Grounds on any particular day, no more than ten of us were in our press seats to see the opening pitch.

The laggards were delayed by a golf game, a stalled subway train, or stopping off at the corner saloon for a few beers. Bill Chipman, who worked for practically every New York morning and afternoon newspaper in his fifteen-year sojourn in Manhattan, was likely to drift in at any time from the third inning to the sixth, saying, "Will one of you guys fill me in on the first five innings?"

Men on the afternoon papers had to be in their press seats at the Polo Grounds, Yankee Stadium, and Ebbets Field a half hour before their morning associates. They were there to write or dictate a one-hundred word lead and the opening lineups, which the Western Union telegraph operators in the adjoining seats would send to the newspapers in lower Manhattan. During the course of the game, we dictated, play by play, the unfolding of the day's baseball activities. Most of the operators were fans and were well posted on the players. Some of them were as adept at sending the stories as the men dictating the play.

Some of the writers, especially the afternoon men, arrived a half hour early for talks with the managers and players. There was practically no interviewing after games. At the Polo Grounds, manager John McGraw of the Giants discouraged his players from talking to reporters ever. "What did that fellow say to you?" he would ask an athlete after seeing him in an interview. "Next time, tell him you're out here to practice, not to talk." McGraw appointed a big former cop to guard the clubhouse, which was located above the center-field bleachers. On the door, a big sign said NO ADMITTANCE. If a writer expressed a wish to see McGraw, Mathewson, or a lesser player, Mike would point to the sign and say, "That means you."

It was easier for a writer to talk to a player on the road than it was when the club was at home. You could chat with him in a Pullman car or get him away from his card game on nights after games. In New York it was possible to see some of the players—Giants, Yankees, and out-of-towners—at a saloon on the corner of West 155th Street and Eighth Avenue. On hot summer nights players gathered there for a few cold beers before going home to their dinners.

In my early days with the *Press* and *Morning Sun,* I scored the game, made notes on outstanding plays, sent the Associated Press lead and box score by messenger to their office downtown, and then went home for a leisurely dinner. Most of the other baseball writers also lived within easy walking distance from the Polo Grounds. Later I took the subway down to the newspaper offices, usually reporting around 7:45, and two hours later handed my copy to my sports editor. There was no

New York baseball writers at the Yankees' training camp in St. Petersburg, 1928. Left to right: Fred Lieb—*Post*, Jim Harrison—*Times*, Bill Slocum—*American*, Jimmy Kahn—*Sun*, Rud Rennie—*Herald-Tribune*, Ford Frick—*Journal*, Charley Segar—*Mirror*, Willie Hennigan—*Morning World*, Mark Roth, Yankees' road secretary.   Thorne Photo

need for hurry, as our first edition did not come out until 1 A.M. The last edition, which hit the streets at 6 A.M. and was delivered to local subscribers, rarely had to be made over for a sports item.

Even before radio and TV, such big circulation tabloids as the *Daily News* and *Daily Mirror* changed journalism deadlines. They had papers on the street as early as 8 P.M. To meet that kind of competition, papers such as the New York *Times*, *Herald-Tribune*, and *Morning World* got papers on the streets at the time the theaters opened. The writers naturally were affected. No more going home for dinner. Now they were wiring, and later phoning, full coverage of the game from the ball parks.

In 1930 when there still were six evening papers in New York—the *Telegram*, *Post*, *Journal*, *Evening Sun*, and *Evening World*, and the *Eagle* in Brooklyn—the newspapers decided to cut expenses by having only one play-by-play wire out of the New York ball parks. A City News Association wire, manned by a City News reporter, then began to send the same story to the six afternoon papers. The names of the in-

New York baseball writers in St. Petersburg, 1931. Left to right, standing: Jim Dawson—*Times,* Rud Rennie—*Herald-Tribune,* Buck O'Neill—*Journal,* Bill Slocum—*American,* Harry Schumacher—*News,* Dan Daniel—*World-Telegram,* Bert Gumpert, Bronx *Home News.* In foreground: Fred Lieb—*Post,* Al Lang—St. Petersburg's "Mr. Baseball", Frank Graham—*Sun,* Charley Segar—*Mirror.* Thorne Photo

dividual sports writers were taken off the front pages, and it made boring reading for fans who had always bought three papers to get the individual views of Frank Graham (*Evening Sun*), Dan Daniel (*Telegram*), and Fred Lieb (*Post*). Of course we did retain second-day signed stories and features of the game.

When radio, TV, and air travel came in, most clubs played their games at night and it doomed the Sports Extras of the afternoon papers. Second-day rehash of yesterday's game was out and so was the NO ADMITTANCE sign on the clubhouse. Writers had to think up new angles for features, so they freely quoted manager and players. Soon the morning men gave less and less attention to the game they were covering and more space to the personal lives, habits, and whims of the players.

In my first four years as a baseball writer, I did no traveling except when the Giants were playing in a World Series. The afternoon papers had men on the road, but the writers for the morning papers covered the games in New York. Afternoon writers who traveled with the teams picked up extra money by covering the Giants and Yankees on the road. Sid Mercer once sent stories to five morning papers in addition to his own *Evening Globe.*

However, as baseball became more popular, the morning papers began sending writers on road trips. Jacob Ruppert and Til Huston bought the Yankees in the winter of 1914–1915, and the *Press* felt there was enough interest in the new Yankees to send me, their number one baseball man, to Savannah for the team's 1915 training trip.

It was customary then for the ball clubs to pay the full expenses of writers—railroad and Pullman fares, hotel and dining-room bills. As far as I can recall, all New York newspapers accepted this courtesy. They were, after all, giving the ball clubs free advertising.

The arrangement had some disadvantages. On one training trip, Willie Hennigan of the *Morning World* wrote something that displeased Squire Ebbets, president of the old Brooklyn Dodgers, and Ebbets recalled Willie to Brooklyn. When the *Daily News* entered the New York field in 1920, they did not take courtesies from ball clubs. Some years later the New York *Times* adopted the same policy. For years the St. Louis *Post-Dispatch,* working on the same policy, even forbade its men from serving as official scorers. Today most of the major papers pay the expenses of their own men.

During my days as a roving reporter, the club road secretaries were our "shepherds." They looked after us, told us when and where our trains would leave, took care of our baggage, assigned us to our rooms, and often "poured" a tipsy reporter into his Pullman berth.

I wonder whether any crop of new baseball writers ever came up to the majors with such widely diverse talents as those of the "Class of 1911": Rice, Runyon, Broun, and Lieb. Rice "graduated" to a column covering football and golf primarily and to the editorship of a leading golf magazine. Runyon and Broun moved on to their own specialties in fiction and social commentary. Only I "went the route." I admired them for their accomplishments; but never for a moment was I jealous of them. I preferred baseball—it had become part of my life.

19

The Sporting News
AND THE SPINKS

Late in January 1961, I received a long distance call from St. Louis at my home in St. Petersburg. "Freddy, who is going to be elected to the Hall of Fame at that meeting of the Veterans Committee next Sunday?" boomed the loud voice of J. G. Taylor Spink, publisher of *The Sporting News.*

"You know, Taylor, I'm not a member of that committee." I replied. "How would I know what is in the minds of those twelve men?" (I was not appointed to the Hall of Fame Veterans Committee until 1965.)

"Oh, you know all about such things—what candidates they're considering and who is most likely to be named," Taylor persisted.

Giving it a little thought, I said, "I think Billy Hamilton may make it this time. For the second choice it may be Max Carey or John Montgomery Ward."

"Ward is out," snapped Taylor, "and who the hell is Billy Hamilton?"

"Hamilton was a great hitter, base runner, and outfielder for Philadelphia and Boston when we were wee kids," I explained. "Ward has his backers, and so has Max Carey. Besides, Max has been waging quite a campaign to get in the Hall of Fame."

"Well, if you were voting, who would you vote for?" he asked.

"Hamilton and Carey," I told him.

"Now, Freddy, I'll tell you what I want you to do. Get at it immediately, because this is for our next issue. I want you to write a first-page story that Hamilton and Carey have been chosen and then write separate stories on them. Write it, not as if they *will* be elected, but as if we know they *have* been chosen and the committee on Sunday will only

219

make it official. (*The Sporting News* went to press then on Tuesday, was on the streets in Chicago on Thursday, and in New York on Friday.)

"If the committee doesn't elect these men, we're going to look pretty bad," I cautioned.

"We'll have to take that chance," he said; but I thought it was a daring, if not foolish, chance.

I followed instructions, though with a feeling of trepidation. I knew all the men on the committee—executives, former star players, and older writers. They were strong-minded men who might resent having *The Sporting News* do their committee work.

On the Sunday afternoon of the meeting, Taylor called me on the phone. "We won!" he shouted. "Just had word from New York that Hamilton and Carey were voted into the Hall of Fame. I'll buy you a dinner the next time you're in St. Louis!"

I never knew exactly how the 1961 Veterans Committee felt about our scooping them. No one ever mentioned it to me, and I certainly did not raise the question. The incident just shows what a fearless, daring person John George Taylor Spink really was. "The alphabetical Mr. Spink," Red Smith once called him. Taylor wanted the news, and whenever possible he wanted it first.

Taylor Spink was certainly one of the outstanding men I met in seven decades of association with baseball. Judge Landis, who generally was considered to be an agnostic, if not an atheist, once remarked to me, "How could God make such a man?" But, Spink might have asked the same thing about Landis. However God felt about it, they had a mutual dislike for each other. Landis's gripe against Spink was that he exacted pay from the many minor leagues that once dotted the country for reporting their results. In an era before TV baseball, when there were fifty to sixty minor leagues and *The Sporting News* was devoted wholly to baseball, "The News" printed *all* box scores, from the majors down to class D. Of course box scores from Rocky Mount, North Carolina; Carthage, Missouri; or Pocatello, Idaho, had news value only to scouts and those few baseball buffs who followed their local boys through the minor leagues.

But there were two sides to the question. Spink was doing those presidents of little minor leagues a service. Someone had to pay for the paper, the editing and printing, and I think J. G. T. S. reasonably felt he needed this subsidy money to operate.

The ill feeling between the two men probably really stemmed from Taylor's strong support of Ban Johnson during Landis's feuds in the 1920s with the first American League president. Taylor Spink almost worshipped old Ban Johnson, even named his only son, Charles C. Johnson Spink. Taylor was loyal to Johnson, the old tsar who used to run baseball, and in his support he stepped on the toes of the new tsar, Landis.

Taylor was famous for enormous telephone bills—he would call up people at any hour of the twenty-four, for his unflagging energy for work, often from 7:45 A.M. to 10:30 P.M., for his knowledge of baseball and all sports people, for his ambiguities, changeability, temper, outbursts, and his colorful profanity.

I first met Taylor Spink during the week's rain that interrupted the 1911 World Series. Occasionally after that he would ask me to send him a few paragraphs on some New York player. *The Sporting News* also picked up and reprinted pieces I had written in New York, and they once ran a baseball fiction story which I had done for *Short Stories* magazine.

While I was free-lancing in New York in the summer of 1935, Taylor phoned to ask me to come to St. Louis for a talk. He said he wanted me on the St. Louis staff, and I was to replace one of two men he then had working for him. I was not wild about working in St. Louis, and felt uncomfortable about replacing either of his two hard-working, loyal employees. But Taylor was persuasive, so I stayed with him during the rest of the 1935 season and covered the 1935 Cubs-Tigers World Series for *The Sporting News*. From then on for nearly a quarter of a century I took care of most of the All-Star games and World Series for Taylor's sports weekly.

After I had spent several summers in St. Louis, Taylor asked me to come to St. Louis full time in 1943. I accepted, but retained my house and legal address in St. Petersburg. I did the weekly letters on the Cardinals and old Browns, wrote features on baseball happenings and on wartime players, helped with editorials and Taylor's weekly radio chat, and did the obituaries on deceased baseball gladiators. I also made extensive contributions to early Spink *Baseball Guides* and *Baseball Registers*.

After I returned to St. Petersburg in 1948 to write books and baseball articles, I continued to contribute features to *The Sporting News*. I felt I could do the same work in St. Petersburg as I did in St. Louis and get in an occasional game of golf as well. I continued to write the obituaries of deceased Hall of Famers. You could always judge a player's worth by the space given to his obit in *The Sporting News*, and Taylor gave me the big ones. I covered the passing of the real greats, Nap Lajoie, Hans Wagner, Bobby Wallace, Walter Johnson, Paul Waner, Grover Cleveland Alexander, Mickey Cochrane, and dozens of others. I wrote so many of these "last rites" that Bob Broeg, the gifted baseball writer and sports editor of the St. Louis *Post-Dispatch*, dubbed me the "baseball undertaker."

In the 1950s a quintet of us writers and editors had a little group that

J. G. Taylor Spink Award
1972
Frederick G. Lieb
1888 ~

A slender, dignified, soft-spoken man who in his mid-80's still wrote a Hot Stove League column for the St. Petersburg Times, he long held forth as an historian whose vast contributions include nine books, most of them the anecdotal story of the rise and fall of Major League franchises.

A Philadelphian, covered the game in New York from 1911 until the mid-30's, continuing on The Sporting News and free lance. An expert with his nose in every phase for more than 60 years. Holder of the No. 1 Baseball Writers' Honorary membership card, chaired New York Chapter's first annual dinner in 1924.

Essentially a meticulous reporter, with memory long and clear, he could turn a phrase, exemplified by description of brand new Yankee Stadium in 1923 as "The House that Ruth Built". Reporting many of Babe's 714 homers, Lieb influenced the 1920 rules change, crediting a home run even if only one base is necessary to score the winning run, breaking diehards' insistence that none could be scored after the game-winning run crossed the plate.

Baseball Writers' Association of America

Jack Lang
Secretary

Joe Heiling
President

Cooperstown, New York
August 6, 1973

we called The Boys of 1888, consisting of Taylor Spink and Sid Keener of St. Louis, Tom Swope of Cincinnati, Irving Vaughan of Chicago, and me. All were born in the far distant year of 1888. Taylor was the first to go, slipping out in 1962. He was followed by Swope and Vaughan, leaving only Keener and me.

When Taylor left us, every one remarked what big shoes his son C. C. Johnson Spink would have to fill. Some shook their heads as if to say, "The young man can't do it." But they were in for a big surprise, for Johnson not only filled his dad's shoes, but he made *The Sporting News* bigger and better than ever, an all-sports newspaper that far exceeds the old baseball weekly in circulation and advertising.

Johnson, like his father, is a strong, firm executive with daring, imagination and a kind of inner wisdom which allows him to do the right thing at the right time, such as change *The Sporting News* from an all-baseball weekly to one that also reports football, basketball, hockey, golf, and tennis.

Johnson doesn't swear and rant as his father did. His editorial office and his print shop operate with less tension than when Taylor ran the ship. He also seems to have more faith in his subordinates than his father did. While Johnson as president, publisher, and editor always has the last word on policy or what gets into the paper, he has greater confidence in his managing editor, Lowell Reidenbaugh, than Taylor had in men who held the same title. Both Lowell Reidenbaugh and Oscar Kahan, assistant managing editor, were aspiring young newspapermen when I was on the St. Louis staff. They have grown with experience and responsibility, and they get out a fine newspaper.

J. G. Taylor Spink in 1957.

When I was in Chicago shortly after New Year, 1977, as a witness for Bowie Kuhn in his $3,500,000 legal hassle with Oakland's Charley Finley, former American League president Joe Cronin, another pro-Kuhn witness, told me, "I've just been talking to my wife, on long distance, and she just read a TV flash that *The Sporting News* was sold to a Los Angeles concern. Isn't that strange?"

Indeed, it was strange. Also, the news was true and it almost knocked me for a loop. *The Sporting News* had been in the Spinks family since 1886, and Johnson was the fourth Spink to serve as its editor-publisher. Now *The Sporting News*, including *The Sporting Goods Dealer*, its record books and guides, had been sold to the Los Angeles *Times-Mirror*, for an estimated sum of between $15,000,000 and $20,000,000.

Johnson Spink, a loyal member of the Spink clan, later explained it in a personal conversation, "You know that Edith and I are childless. I now am in my latter fifties and if I should die there would be no real Spink heirs to run the publications. If I died, the heirs could employ someone to run our publications who might mess up things.

"In my deal with the Los Angeles *Times-Mirror*, I will remain as editor-publisher until I am 65, and will personally direct the paper's policy. After my retirement, I will continue to serve as an adviser. However, when I reach the end of my earth journey, it will be with the knowledge that an able, experiencd publishing firm will take over, continue *The Sporting News* and *The Sporting Goods Dealer* under the Spink traditions and advance them into new fields whereby they will acquire even greater distinction."

20

AT OUR HOME IN ST. PETERSBURG

Mary and I made our home, from 1935 until 1970, at 136 Seventh Avenue, N.E., in St. Petersburg. This was also my writing headquarters, even my official address while I was in St. Louis writing for *The Sporting News,* in the mid '40s. Some of our neighbors in the late 1960s used to say we had entertained almost everybody in baseball's *Who's Who* sometime or other, which was exaggeration; but from our guests we could certainly have fielded a pretty good team of all-stars, complete with owners, managers, umpires, a league president or two, and a corps of sports writers.

Sometimes illustrious personages were attracted to our door because they wanted some baseball information from me, but in many cases the lure was Mary. Mary was an attractive person. There are some—and I am foremost among them—who think she was lovely. The loveliness stemmed less, perhaps, from her physical beauty than from the warmth and radiance and integrity that one saw in her face. Mary had an innate goodness uncorrupted by her upbringing or by her experience of life. By her nature she was open to other people, uncritical, and accepting of them as they were.

Mary and I were blessed with a devoted, intelligent, talented, and pretty daughter, Marie Theresa Lieb Pearsall, who was born in New York in 1912, my second year as a big league writer in Gotham. I nicknamed her Binky when she was two weeks old. She remains Binky today to my family and early friends, but to her husband, R. Leslie Pearsall, a born Canadian, she is Marie.

While I followed all sports, and my wife studied modern and ancient religions, Binky was always fascinated by the theater. She attended Boston College of Oratory, and later was graduated from the American Academy of Dramatic Arts in New York. After a year in Hollywood do-

ing bit parts, Binky returned to New York and took drama courses at
Columbia and a course on direction under the eminent Lee Strasberg.
Though she played leading roles in neighborhood plays, she spent
much of her adult life directing plays in suburban northern New Jersey
and, for the last twenty years in Houston. Binky's daughter, Mary Ann
"Mimi" Pearsall Holloway, felt the same lure of the theater as did her
mother. She too lives in Houston with her actor husband David Holloway, and appears in plays directed by her mother.

In early adulthood, while attending an ill mother, Mary developed
the habit of reading the Bible regularly, a habit which grew to reading
the literature of other religions, of Eastern mysticism, and of metaphysics generally. Early in life she practiced what now is termed transcen-
dental meditation, but with it she could be very much down-to-earth.
Of course I knew Mary better than any one else in my life, but she was
the one person I regard as having charisma in its original sense of pos-
sessing a spiritual gift.

She was the kind of person one felt one could confide in. She made
everyone who came inside her door feel comfortable and important.
Not least among her attractions was her ability to cook. The men who
visited us may have liked talking baseball with me, but they and their
wives would have been just as happy had I not been there, if Mary was
cooking a meal.

Mary had an acute sense of the supernatural, perhaps acquired from
her Irish mother. She had experiences of telepathy and precognition of
events. A student of psychology, parapsychology and the occult, and
oriental mysticism, she became adept at yoga and read palms and the
character of our guests from their signatures. In reading palms she said
it seemed as though another person, perhaps a Hindu, was telling her
just what to say.

One January back in 1920 on an old Clyde Line steamer sailing from
New York to Jacksonville, Mary read palms of fellow passengers just to
pass the time. After reading several others, including Brooklyn right-
hander, Al Mamaux, she came to another Dodger pitcher, Clarence
Mitchell, the last of the left-handed spitballers. I knew Mitchell hardly
at all and had told Mary very little about him. Mary said to him, looking at his palm, "You are a farm boy, raised on a farm. I see dogs all
around you, hunting dogs and some very fast running dogs. I can see
them running all around you now."

"Yes, I had some racing dogs in Nebraska," said Mitchell. "We ran
them over our ranches—you folks in the East call them farms—and
they raced in a straight line, not in circles." (In 1920 there was no dog
racing in Florida or anywhere else in the East. Until that moment I had
not the slightest idea that Mitchell raced dogs.)

Returning to Mitchell's hand, Mary said, "You've had lots of love

At home in 1937. Left to right: Marie (Binky) Lieb Pearsall, Fred Lieb, Mary Ann Lieb.

affairs both in and out of marriage. Even now I can see an angry man with a club chasing you right up to the gangplank of this steamer."

Mitchell jerked loose his hand and said, "How could you know about that? A jealous husband chased me right on to the boat, but he had a gun, not a club."

It was Mary's palm reading that drew Col. Jacob Ruppert, president-owner of the Yankees, to our home. Jake had had his palm read by her in St. Petersburg at both of the hotels we stopped in, the Princess Martha and Don Cesar, while I was covering the Yankees' training season. Each year the Colonel had been anxious to know whether Mary saw a pennant ahead. And she was quite lucky in foretelling the 1932 flag and the World Championship over the Cubs that followed.

"After that," she had said, "you will be close but you won't make it to the World Series." Sometimes during the barren years he would almost demand a pennant, saying, "Mary, look again. You must see something good for the club!" But she would only reply, "I just don't see a pennant this year."

So when we bought the house on Seventh Avenue, Ruppert came to have his palm read and enjoy the way Mary cooked her spaghetti!

During one of these sessions, Ruppert dropped his usual stern exterior. He confided why he had never married: "When I was thirty, and perhaps forty, I did not want a wife. It was too much fun being single. Then when I really wanted a wife, I was afraid to get married. I was afraid of what would eventually happen. I was afraid that I would kill her. I would be certain that she had married me for my money and that sooner or later she would take on a younger lover. And then I would have no alternative but to kill her."

Another time, Mary read the palm of Fred Wattenberg, Ruppert's great pal. Early in 1938 Wattenberg died, and whenever Mary and I brought out the Ouija board for the next two months, we would get Fred Wattenberg on it, insisting that he still was alive. "I am as much alive as any of you," he would spell out on the board. He asked Mary and me to tell his daughter and Ruppert that he was still alive. Later he would reprove us saying, "You always pretended you were my friends, but you won't do this for me."

I knew if I told Wattenberg's daughter, then a young woman about twenty-one, that her father still was alive, she would have considered me nuts. But I did mention it to Ruppert at the Princess Martha. I told him, "Colonel, he insists he wants to speak to you, he says he has something important to tell you."

Ruppert did not reply with the skepticism that I expected. He said, "All right, I will arrange it with my secretary, Al Brennan, on a day we can come to your house." Before I left, I fixed up a date with Brennan. The morning of the engagement, Brennan called up and said, "The Colonel will have to postpone that visit. He has a heavy cold and is so hoarse he can scarcely speak."

I told Wattenberg on the Ouija board that Ruppert could not come to the house as expected. I then asked him what was the important message he wanted to give to Jake.

He spelled out on the board, "I wanted to tell him that within a year he would join me over here."

Ruppert did not get over the cold for the remainder of the team's stay in St. Petersburg. He was a sick man all through the championship year of 1938, saw only two games during the league season, and did not attend the World Series which the Yankees won against the Cubs in four straight.

Ruppert died in New York in late January 1939, almost exactly a year from the time Wattenberg left us in 1938.

Mary, her cooking and friendliness, and the Ouija board did not draw all of our baseball callers. One morning the doorbell rang, and there stood old Connie Mack on our front porch.

"Fred, I want to ask you to do me a favor," said the veteran manager. "Some of my friends said that while I still am alive I should have my voice recorded—something for posterity. Could you take me to wherever I could have this done?"

This was in the very early days of television, before we had any TV in St. Petersburg. So I took him to Station WSUN, the city-owned radio station then located on the end of our municipal pier. We visited Major Robinson, an English-born veteran of World War I, who was the station's manager and leading news commentator. Robinson had one of his subordinates make recordings of Mack's voice telling something about his nine American League pennants and five World Series championships. Ultimately Robinson gave one tape to me, kept the master tape for the station, and delivered four copies to Connie.

Another time when I answered the doorbell I found myself looking at a rather bulky man with a tan cap on his head. Much to my surprise it was Babe Ruth. "I got into an argument at the Jungle Club last night about my pitching," said Babe. "I told them I could pitch just as well as I can hit. A guy said, 'Of course, we all know what a slugger you are, but as a pitcher you were just a thrower.' I said, 'Nuts to that. One year I had an earned run average better than Walter Johnson, and that was when Walter was in his prime.' The guy said, 'Horse manure.' I don't know the exact year or the exact figures, but I know you have them here. Write them down on your typewriter and sign it. The guy said if I did that he would believe."

Babe was entirely right. I looked up the records, and in 1916, pitching for the Boston Red Sox, he had an outstanding earned run average of only 1.75, while winning 23 games and losing 12. In that same year Johnson's earned run average was 1.88, 13 points higher than Ruth's. The hard-worked Johnson won 25 games and lost 20. As a matter of fact, Ruth led the league that year in both earned runs and in winning percentage.

When I gave Ruth the signed statement he was pleased: "Thanks, Freddy, that should satisfy that dumb kluck."

Miller Huggins and his housekeeper-sister Myrtle had a house not far from ours and first came to number 136 on a social visit. Later Myrtle and Mary became warm friends, and Myrtle used to speak of my wife as her best friend in St. Petersburg.

One morning after Miller's death in 1929 Myrtle Huggins came to our door, holding a magazine in her hand. When I let her in, she stood there crying and pointing to an article. "Is this really true, Fred?" The article told of Huggins's troubles with his players, but the paragraph that brought Myrtle to tears told of Babe Ruth and Bob Meusel dangling their little manager from the rear of a Philadelphia–St. Louis Express. According to the story, Babe held the mite manager with his right hand and Meusel with his left.

Myrtle said, "Miller never kept anything from me, even some of the toughest arguments he had with Ruth, Meusel, Mays, and Bush; but he never told me anything like this. I can't believe it happened."

I told Myrtle, "This is the first I ever heard of such a thing happening. I did not make all the Yankee western trips, but I made a good many of them, and I doubt if such a thing happened. If it did, I am sure Miller would have suspended both players indefinitely." I did see the story printed in another sports magazine a bit later, but without any convincing proof.

Myrtle made her last visit to our house in the late summer of 1942. We had been away on our customary summer trip. A woman who was occupying our house while we were absent said Myrtle came onto the porch shouting, "Mary! Mary!" The woman told her, "Mary isn't back yet, but I expect her next week." Myrtle said, "I'm afraid that isn't enough time." That night she died from taking doses of cyanide potassium poison.

John Heydler, National League president for half a year in 1909 and from 1918–1934, and his wife Nancy were our longtime friends. In New York we frequently had dinner with the Heydlers at their home in Garden City, Long Island, and they called on us at our Nepperhan Heights home. Shortly after his retirement from the National League presidency, Heydler asked me whether I could get him winter quarters in St. Petersburg. I did and the Heydlers spent most of the winter there. John and I golfed frequently as the ladies shopped.

Around this time things were going rather badly for the old National in contests with the American League. The Yankee juggernaut was riding roughshod over the National League champs in World Series, and the American League was winning most of the early All-Star games. The situation gave Tom Meany, a gifted writer and usually a friendly, good-natured person, a topic for an acidulous article for the *Saturday Evening Post:* "National, the New Minor League." The slur on the National League was right there on the cover in big print.

Heydler discussed the article while we had dinner. He expressed his deep hurt over the piece and the humiliation of his venerable league. Tears rolled down his cheeks as he spoke of his chagrin that Meany should write such an article and that the *Saturday Evening Post* would publish it. Though deep down, if pressed to confess it, I have American League sympathies in interleague play, I felt a true sympathy for Heydler, for he did care so much for his organization. I felt the article unfair, in the sense that it was overstated and occasionally resorted to sarcasm. I have often wished that John Heydler could have lived another decade or two to see the National League hold its own in

The convention of major and minor leagues in St. Petersburg, December, 1950. Left to right: Fuller Warren, governor of Florida; Fred Lieb, host chairman; Al Long (standing); Happy Chandler, Commissioner of Baseball; George Trautman, president, National Association of Minor Leagues; Charles Hirth, president, Southern League; Ray Knight and E. C. Robison, host committeemen.

Fred Lieb receives from Ralph Kiner the Stick of Type Award of the St. Petersburg *Times,* January 1975. St. Petersburg *Times*—Tony Lopez

World Series and mangle the American League in All-Star play, winning thirteen out of the last fourteen, through 1976.

It was John Heydler who, in 1930, first proposed the use of the designated hitter. He called it a ten-man team. The irony is that he was laughed at to the point of scorn by the American League, which then adopted the practice in 1973 and is now its advocate.

One of our most enjoyable relationships over a period of years was with the family of Tommy Leach—Tommy the Wee, as he was referred to by writers when he played third base and center field for the Pittsburgh Pirates in the first fifteen years of this century. Only 5 feet 5½ inches, Tommy was the National League home-run leader in 1902 with a paltry six—all of the inside-the-park variety—the fewest ever to win the crown. I knew Tommy from way back, but we became much better acquainted when I was player-chairman of the St. Petersburg Annual March of Dimes Old-Timers' Game. Tommy Leach Yeager, his grandson, had been stricken by polio.

Our first game, in 1959, was preceded by a parade of old-time players riding in old-time automobiles. On hand were Leach, Al Lopez, Fred Merkle, Zach Taylor, Rip Sewell, Dazzy Vance, Jimmy Foxx, Eddie Roush, Wes Ferrell, Johnny Allen, Fred Hutchinson, Johnny Vander Meer, Heinie Groh, and Spud Chandler. At the very head of the parade rode little Tommy Leach Yeager in a small two-seated sports car of ancient vintage. He was the hit of the parade. Young Tommy's mother, Margaret Leach Yeager, who was assistant publisher of the *Haines City Herald,* soon became the warm friend of Mary and me. In the following years there were many visits of three generations of Leaches to our house. Young Tommy eventually recovered from polio and today is a pilot for one of the major airlines.

Back in 1920 I met Eddie Roush and his wife Essie for the first time when the Yankees visited Miami to play Roush's team, the Cincinnati Reds. Later the St. Pete Old-Timers' Game and its organization brought Eddie and Essie back each year into our circle of friends.

It would be very easy for me to get sentimental about the friendships that baseball and Mary brought to our home in St. Petersburg. St. Petersburg itself has been most generous to me. I cannot think of a better place for a baseball writer to make his home. Even now that Mary is no longer with me, I return there eagerly when October arrives and the baseball season comes to its annual conclusion. And where else should one be when the first rookie pitchers start tossing the ball to rookie catchers at winter's end?

21

THE OLD PERFESSER

As I entered the St. Petersburg Hilton to attend the 1974 Governor's Dinner—an annual Florida celebration of the baseball training season—from the opposite direction came that fantastic character Charles Dillon "Casey" Stengel. Ol' Case greeted me warmly and held my hand, for we had known each other some sixty years. To Casey I was one of the "old guard," for I was among those who knew him when he was a prankish, fun-loving outfielder for the Brooklyn Dodgers before World War I.

In a baseball sense, Ol' Case is an immortal. Physically, though, he proved mortal after all, and if there had been a Florida Governor's Dinner in 1976 there would have been no Casey Stengel to liven things up. In September of 1975 he left us—an entire nation mourned, knowing it had lost an extraordinary citizen.

I believe that with the exception of Babe Ruth, Casey Stengel was the most widely known and best loved man in baseball before he finally put away his uniform. And it was at an advanced age that he captured the fancy of the multitudes, both male and female. Superstars like Babe Ruth, Ty Cobb, Christy Mathewson, Walter Johnson, George Sisler, Rogers Hornsby, Ted Williams, Joe DiMaggio, Willie Mays, and Hank Aaron achieved national recognition in their early twenties. Freddy Lynn, the new wonder boy of the Red Sox, made it in his freshman year, 1975.

No such immediate fame came to Casey. He was a good, but by no means great, outfielder and hitter. His managers used to yank him out of the lineup whenever a left-hander came in to pitch for the opposition. As a ballplayer he was known to be a clown, a mimic, a comedian. He had funny cracks to fit any occasion, he could twist his face into all kinds of grimaces, and he could tell a story just by moving his eyes.

In Stengel's early years, in the minors and with the 1911–12 Dodgers, he was known as Dutch Stengel. Dutch had "Charles Stengel, K.C." stenciled on his luggage and some fellow players began calling the young outfielder K.C. It eventually got changed to "Casey" and went on to become one of the best-known nicknames in the history of baseball.

In the earlier years of his managerial career—the 1930s and 1940s— people still thought of him as a clown. The Brooklyn Dodgers even paid him a full season's salary not to manage the Flatbush team in 1936. In 1943 Dick Egan, a Boston sportswriter who often dipped his pen in acid, wrote that the man who did the most for Boston Braves baseball that year was the taxicab driver who ran down Casey Stengel, putting Ol' Case in the hospital while someone else managed the team.

As a matter of record, in eight seasons of big league managing in this phase of his career, Stengel's high-water mark was fifth place—once. Five times he finished sixth. In the minors Casey did better, winning a pennant with the Oaks in 1948. This was his managerial record when half-owner Del Webb and general manager George Weiss put Casey in charge of the New York Yankees for the 1949 season.

Casey wasn't hired to take over a rundown franchise. The Yankees were an ambitious, viable team, and the players had enjoyed the rich taste of a world championship. Over twenty-eight years, under Miller Huggins, Joe McCarthy, and Bucky Harris, they had won fourteen American League flags and nine blue ribbons. Harris had been there only two years. In 1947 he won an easy A.L. pennant and a difficult four-to-three World Series from Brooklyn. In 1948 he had his club in the race until the last Saturday of the season and played to home attendances of approximately 2,500,000, still the record for any New York team.

Bucky didn't get the heave-ho for not winning in 1948, as some writers pontificated, but because he couldn't get along with George Weiss, the brainy general manager. George especially was annoyed whenever he would telephone Bucky's room and find the manager "out," most often at dog races. So Bucky was "out" and the former managerial clown, Stengel, was "in."

New Yorkers reacted to Stengel's appointment without enthusiasm. A friend and student of baseball asked me, "Is this serious? Are they really going to put in a clown to run the Yankee operation? He surely did nothing with the Brooklyn Dodgers and Boston Braves to warrant getting the job." This was typical, too, of the way most baseball writers felt in the winter of 1948–49. Most of us liked Casey: he was a good guy, lots of fun at baseball get-togethers. But was he the man who could carry on the Yankees' pennant-winning tradition?

In the early spring of 1949 at St. Petersburg, then the Yankees' training spot, Casey was serious and almost all business. Knowing that his

Casey Stengel, surrounded by old friends and rivals during taping of PBS-TV show "The Way It Was" in Hollywood, June 1974. Left to right, back row: Clem Labine, Duke Snider, and Sal "the Barber" Maglie of the Dodgers; Mickey Mantle and Don "No-Hit" Larson of the Yankees. Front row: Yankees' broadcasters Mel Allen and Curt Gowdy.   UPI

engagement was not being hailed as a brilliant choice, he remarked to a few of us writers, "Because I can make people laugh, some of them think I'm a damn fool. But as a player, coach and manager I have been around baseball for some thirty-five years. I've watched such successful managers as John McGraw and Uncle Robbie [Wilbert Robinson] work. I've learned a lot and picked up a few ideas of my own."

Stengel was then approaching his sixtieth birthday. By that age, many good managers have called it a career. But Stengel tackled his New York post with almost youthful enthusiasm. He knew that he was taking over a strong bunch of players, including the great Joe DiMaggio, and that with George Weiss in the front office he always could depend on players being sent up, if needed, from the vast and productive Yankee farm system.

Casey's 1949 season was a gigantic success. He showed his wizardry early. DiMaggio, still bothered with a spur on his right heel, was out for weeks with a dangerous infection—and that gave Casey the chance to jockey his outfielders. His platooning of right-handed hitters Bauer and Lindell with left-handed batters Mapes and Woodling became famous. He used no fewer than seven first basemen in his first season in

New York: Tommy Henrich, Dick Kryhoski, Billy Johnson, John Phillips, Fenton Mole, Joe Collins and, late in the season, Johnny Mize.

One day when I visited the Yankee bench I commented on the number of players Stengel was using nearly every day. Casey pointed to the row of pinstriped players who rode the bench with him, "None of those guys boards here; they all work. That's why they give us twenty-five players—to let the manager play games with them."

Despite injuries to key players and sore-armed pitchers, Stengel played games with his twenty-five players so well that when the final weekend of the season rolled around, Stengel's Yankees trailed Joe McCarthy's Boston Red Sox by only one game. The schedule makers of the winter before must have consulted a soothsayer, for they had billed the two contenders for single games at Yankee Stadium on that final Saturday and Sunday. McCarthy needed only one game to win his ninth major league flag; Stengel had to sweep the series to win his first.

Everything was going Marse Joe's way when Boston took an early 4–0 lead in the Saturday game. But the Yankees, goaded on by Stengel, pecked away, tying the score at 4–4, until outfielder-pitcher Johnny Lindell won it 5–4 with a home run in the eighth. That put the leaders into a first-place deadlock. The Sunday game was another spine-tingler. Before 68,000 fans, Vic Raschi of the Yanks and Ellis Kinder of the Red Sox dueled evenly for seven innings. But the Yanks had scratched one run in the first inning, and Joe McCarthy removed Kinder for a futile pinch-hitter in the Boston half of the eighth. In the bottom of the eighth the Yanks climbed all over Mel Parnell and Tex Hughson for four big runs. Though Raschi was knocked out of the box by a brave Red Sox rally in the ninth, the Yanks held on to win gloriously, 5–3.

In the following World Series with the Brooklyn Dodgers, led that year by Burt Shotton, the two teams traded 1–0 wins in the first two games. With the score 1–1 after eight innings of the third game, the pitchers on both teams were in charge with only four runs scored so far by both teams. Then the bats started swinging. Managerial brains began operating in supercharged fashion in both dugouts, both offensively and defensively. In the first half of the ninth, with the aid of two walks and three singles—one a two-run pinch single by Johnny Mize—Stengel's Yanks put three big runs on the scoreboard. Then it was Casey who did the suffering in the Brooklyn half of the inning: with two out, both Luis Olmo and Roy Campanella bombed homers off Stengel's crack left-handed relief pitcher, Joe Page. However, Page had enough left to strike out pinch-hitter Bruce Edwards, giving the Yanks a 4–3 win.

After this, both teams came out of their batting slumps, but the Stengelmen's hits were longer and more timely, as the Yankees closed out

the Series with 6–4 and 10–6 victories before moaning, jeering, Ebbets
Field fans.

"That victory was sweet, very sweet," said Stengel after the season,
"but I've got to win some more before I convince some people that I'm
a real manager."

In 1950 Stengel repeated the feat. Most of the season he ran second
to Detroit, managed by Red Rolfe, former Yankee third baseman. But
Casey coaxed a little something extra out of his players in September,
and at the wire New York was three games ahead. The Phillies, known
that year as the Whiz Kids, skipped their way to picking up Philadelphia's second National League flag. The 1950 World Series was
short and sweet—four games to none—as clean a sweep as Miller Huggins and Joe McCarthy ever gave the Yankees.

The year 1951 was the season of "the little miracle of Coogan's
Bluff," the Giants having come from 14½ games behind in mid-August
to tie the league-leading Dodgers on the last day of the regular season.
Then of course they crushed the Dodgers in a three-game play-off on
Bobby Thomson's historic ninth-inning homer in the third game. As
Stengel's Yankees had won their third American League flag, the stage
was set for the sixth New York subway World Series. Many thought the
Giants' momentum would carry them through to a world championship. But Stengel had other ideas and despite injuries to his young superstar Mickey Mantle, he defeated his rivals, four games to two. Casey
remarked happily, "Now I am tied with Mr. McGraw, at three world
championships."

It took a lot of doing for Stengel to make it four straight, especially
with Whitey Ford in military service. Walter O'Malley, the new Brooklyn president, had vowed this would be the year Casey's world championship charge would be stopped. "This year," he said, with some
truth, "Brooklyn has the best team it ever has put on the field, and we
just have to win this one."

But what Casey wanted badly enough, Casey usually got. Knowing
his baseball records perfectly, he was aware that Joe McCarthy had the
record of four consecutive World Series winners in 1936–39. "I sure
would like to share that record with Joe," Casey told me, and later he
said he had murmured it to himself over and over again before the first
game.

The 1952 Yankees-Dodgers set-to was an explosive, hard-hitting Series, with the Yankees hitting ten home runs and Brooklyn eight. It was
the only Series in which Stengel's Yankees had been behind, two
games to three. Furthermore, the final two games had to be won in the
enemy's park, a small one in which homers came easily.

Casey saw his team tie it by winning the sixth game in Ebbets Field,
with Raschi and Reynolds gaining a 3–2 verdict over Billy Loes and

Preacher Roe. Even more agonizing for O'Malley was the 4–2 Yankee win in the seventh and final game. It is rare that a pop fly sticks in one's memory, but this one is as vivid to me as if it happened yesterday. And when Casey reminisced of big moments in his career, he always gave this pop fly a full Stengel treatment.

Stengel used all three of his somewhat weary top pitching trio, Lopat, Reynolds, and Raschi, in this decisive game to still the Dodger bats of Snider, Campanella, Robinson, Furillo, Pafko, and Hodges, not to forget Reese and Cox. But it was Yankee left-hander Bob Kuzava who emerged as the game's hero. Lopat pitched the first three innings and then out came Reynolds. Allie left for Ralph Houk, a pinch-hitter, and then with the Yankees two runs ahead, Stengel called on Raschi to protect the lead through the last three innings.

Vic quickly got into trouble by filling the bases with only one out on two walks and Cox's single. Stengel called in left-handed Bob Kuzava, 8–8 for the season. "Has Stengel gone mad?" was the general reaction in the press box. The Brooklyn lineup was loaded with right-handed hitters, and the Dodgers were usually death to southpaws. But grim-faced Casey leaned forward from the dugout as he signaled the deliveries he wanted Kuzava to pitch.

The first man to face Kuzava was the left-handed-hitting Duke Snider, the one Dodger who did not relish southpaws. The count was three balls and two strikes on the Duke—and the tension tremendous—when he lifted a high infield fly, caught by third baseman Gil McDougald.

Now the Brooklyn fans pleaded with Jackie Robinson to break up the game. Jackie also hung in there until the count was three balls and two strikes. On the next pitch Jackie swung hard, but got only a piece of the ball and popped an infield fly over the pitcher's box. All three Dodgers on the bases were running full tilt, but the Yankees were acting stage-struck. First baseman Joe Collins, nearest to the ball, made no move from his position, and Kuzava seemed paralyzed on the mound. Yogi Berra stood at home plate. It looked as though the ball would drop safely on the ground when second baseman Billy Martin, alive to the situation, came charging in at full speed and, with a last-moment forward thrust, caught the ball at the level of his shins, retiring the side and nullifying the runs of two Dodgers who had dashed home.

Kuzava, saved by Martin's picturesque catch of a pop fly, then had the stuff to retire the Dodgers without a score in the eighth and ninth innings, and Stengel had his fourth straight blue ribbon.

Compared to 1952, winning five straight in 1953 was easy. In the league races Stengel's Yankees won over Cleveland by a comfortable eight games, and the Dodgers won their pennant over Milwaukee by thirteen games. This fourth Yankees-Dodgers Series saw a continua-

Billy Martin charges in to catch Jackie Robinson's pop fly to close out the Dogders in the 1952 Yankees-Dodgers World Series. In background, Phil Rizzuto (left) and Ralph Pinelli (right).

tion of the heavy cannonading of 1952, with the Bombers hitting nine homers and the so-called Bums hitting eight.

The tension in 1953 lessened, especially as the Yanks opened with 9–5 and 4–2 victories at Yankee Stadium. The feeling prevailed, even among National Leaguers, that this would be another win for Stengel. True, the hearts of Brooklyn fans leaped when their Bums tied the Series at two-all by winning the third and fourth games, 3–2 and 7–3.

"We'll win it," a stony-faced Casey said at the start of the fifth game, and his men responded by slugging the Dodgers with five runs in the third off Podres and an 11–7 win. It was a game raw with power, as Mickey Mantle, Gene Woodling, Billy Martin, and Gil McDougald smote homers for the Yankees, while Billy Cox and Junior Gilliam hit for four bases for the O'Malley team.

The Yankees closed it with a 4–3 decision in their own park, scoring the winning run in the ninth, to give Casey a record of five straight world championships, a mark which (as the phrase goes) may withstand the ravages of time. For this last one, Stengel gave Billy Martin major credit, saying, "Everybody contributed, but Billy was wonderful, really magnificent. We couldn't have won without him." Martin hit .500 and tied the record of most hits in a Series, 12. He also scored 5 runs and drove in 8. In his extra-base collection were 2 homers, 2 tri-ples and a double.

In 1954 there was an interruption in Casey's pennant progress. He drove the Yankees to 104 wins—enough to have won 80 percent of the old 154-game pennant races. But this time the Cleveland Indians, man-aged by Al Lopez, swept by Casey to set a new American League rec-ord of 111 wins. The Indians then lost the 1954 World Series to the New York Giants. "All I can say," said Stengel, "is that it's a helluva state if a manager can win a hundred and four games and not win a pennant. As for the Giants, they're not a great team, and we would have murdered them."

Even though Casey and his Yankees were stopped for one year, they were right back in the pennant fight in 1955 and continued to capture the flag until 1959. Stengel was not so successful in his later World Se-ries play—losing to the Dodgers in 1955, to Milwaukee in 1957, and to the Pirates in 1960—but staging memorable come-from-behind victo-ries over Brooklyn in 1956 and Milwaukee in 1958.

The 1960 defeat to the Pirates on Bill Mazeroski's ninth inning home run in the seventh game was especially bitter to Stengel. Studying the World Series figures, one wonders how New York could have lost. As a team the Yankees had hit an impressive .338, highest for any World Se-ries team, winner or loser. The Pirates hit only .256. The Yanks out-scored the victors, 55 runs to 27, outhit them 91 to 60, out-homered them 10 to 4. But still Pittsburgh won, four games to three.

"We got beat on the damndest, craziest bouncer I've seen in my long career in baseball," Stengel explained after the game was over, perhaps forgetting the McNeely bouncer over Lindstrom's head in 1924. "Maybe God can do something about such a play; man cannot."

In the eighth inning, with the Yankees leading 7–4, pinch hitter Gino Cimoli opened the Pirates' half with an infield single. Bill Virdon, later manager for both the Pirates and Yankees, hit a sharp grounder to shortstop Tony Kubek that looked like a ready-made double play. But the ball took a crazy jump, hitting Kubek in his Adam's apple. Tony went down as though he had been shot; a sharp blow on one's Adam's apple causes excruciating pain. Instead of the Yankees having two out and nobody on, there were now two Pirates on base and nobody out. With this help from fate and a three-run homer by catcher Hal Smith, the Pirates scored five runs. In the top of the ninth inning the Yankees struggled back to a 9–9 tie, but Mazeroski's clout off Ralph Terry in Pittsburgh's ninth made the Buccaneers the winners.

On July 30, 1960, Ol' Case reached his seventieth birthday, and shortly after the Series rumors were circulated from the Yankee front office that the colorful Stengel was about to call it a career and would soon announce his retirement. Gossip reported that Topping and

Webb had a compulsory seventy-year retirement policy in some of their other business enterprises and would install the rule in their baseball investment. This would put both Stengel and his immediate boss, general manager George Weiss, on the sidelines.

In fact, Topping called a news conference to announce Casey's retirement and the club's generous parting gift to its ten-pennant manager. It went very badly. "You are retiring of your own volition, aren't you, Mr. Stengel?" asked Topping,. There was a moment of silence in which you could have heard a pin drop. Then Stengel, raising his voice, electrified the session by saying crisply, "Boys, I'm not retiring; I've just been fired." On this low note was ended Stengel's magnificent career with the Yanks.

Among the informed talk I heard later was that the two owners had been dissatisfied with Stengel's management of the club in the Series, thinking he should have gotten more out of that team batting average of .338. There also was some feeling that Stengel erred in starting the Series with pitcher Art Ditmar, who was quickly knocked out, and saving Whitey Ford, his prize left-hander, for the third game. Ford pitched two shutout victories. The contention was that if Ford had started the Series, he would have been available for a seventh game, if necessary. This hindsight argument is weakened by the 15-9 Ditmar season record against Ford's 12–9—an off year for Whitey.

Some fans agreed that Casey's managing in his last World Series was not exactly amazing. However, most of them stuck with Stengel, and as Casey himself might have said, "Look up the record." Ten American League championships and seven victorious World Series in twelve years made him the wizard of baseball managers. That's where he earned the title of the "Old Professor," which in Stengelese was always pronounced "Perfesser."

Baseball scholars for years will look at that record as almost supernatural. Connie Mack, the fine old gentleman who managed the Philadelphia Athletics, won nine American League flags and five World Series in exactly fifty years in active command. John McGraw, the legendary "Little Napoleon" of the New York Giants, won ten National League pennants and three World Series in thirty years. And a third son of Erin, Joe McCarthy, won nine major league flags and seven world championships in the twenty-one years in which he led teams—always contenders—in Chicago, New York, and Boston. It makes Casey's twelve-year record in the second phase of his managerial career look miraculous. Even his ten-and-seven out of twenty, with those bad Brooklyn and Boston teams thrown in, is a bit better than Marse Joe's record, compiled with nothing but top-quality teams to manage. (Nobody should count the early Mets in Stengel's record.)

Stengel once told me the reason he could handle young ballplayers,

some of whom may be inclined to act a little wild, is that he was quite a
flaky kid himself. Young ballplayers, especially if they are a bit lively,
are beset with many temptations. When Casey was a kid outfielder in
Brooklyn, 1912–17, he had his share of them. That's why he knew how
to manage some of the youngsters who now and then imbibed one or
two too many.

Maybe Stengel was remembering that he wasn't always the merry
Casey, quick with the quip and a knowing twinkle in his eyes. He
might have remembered an incident early in his career, in 1915. I never
printed it while Casey was alive, and have now written of it only sixty
years later in the St. Petersburg *Times.*

The story was told to me by George Underwood, a fellow writer of
mine who covered the Dodgers for the New York *Press.* The Dodgers
trained in Daytona Beach, and as the hotel there was not large enough
to take care of the entire club, players were quartered in private board-
inghouses all over the resort. This meant there was little after-hours
discipline. At the time, Daytona Beach and Daytona on the mainland
were separate municipalities connected by a trestle bridge. Underwood, after making a call at the Western Union office and attending a
movie in Daytona, was driving back to the beach around midnight via
the old trestle bridge. About fifty yards out on the bridge, he caught
sight of a figure on the walkway and as he came closer, he recognized
Casey Stengel, Dodger outfielder.

Underwood stopped his car and asked, "Casey, what in hell are you
doing on this bridge this time of the night? If Uncle Robbie [the
Brooklyn manager] hears of it, he'll slap a good fine on you."

"George," said Casey, "I was trying to get up the guts to jump off
into the deep water."

"Whatever gave you such a crazy idea?" asked Underwood.

"Well, I'm not hitting," said the despondent Stengel. "Besides, Uncle Robbie doesn't like me. And I've got the clap."

Underwood persuaded him to get into the car instead of jumping,
and so perhaps saved Casey for posterity.

Though Casey escaped death and a fine, he remained in Robinson's
doghouse. Bothered by his VD problem, Stengel let his batting average
drop from .316 in 1914 to a puny .237 in 1915. However, he snapped
back to .279 in 1916 when he helped bat the Dodgers into the National
League championship, their first since 1900. In the 1916 World Series,
won by the Red Sox four games to one, Casey batted .358, but he hit
only against right-handers. Whenever a left-hander pitched, manager
Robinson inserted Jimmy Johnston in the lineup.

"They said I couldn't hit left-handers," Casey later observed. "Both
Robbie and McGraw pulled me out as soon as an opposing left-hander
appeared. How was I expected to hit them when I never faced one?"

Young writers have claimed that Stengel originated the business of having right-handed and left-handed batting lineups, "platooning" as it is called. But Stengel saw the use of this strategy in his own playing days; platooning was used by such managers as George Stallings, John McGraw, and Tris Speaker when Casey was still a young player.

Stengel never hit it off too well with his first big league boss, Charley Ebbets. On the Brooklyn team of Stengel's days there was a foursome the Brooklyn writers dubbed "the four rascals," or the "four hell-raisers." And of course Stengel was one of them.

Ebbets Field wasn't far from Coney Island, then the fun spot of greater New York. It was natural for Brooklyn players to jump on a trolley for Coney Island after they finished their Saturday game. (At that time there was no Sunday ball in Brooklyn.) Being essentially a team of beer drinkers, sometimes the "rascals" had fights that brought them to the attention of the police.

Every so often, Ebbets would hold a Monday morning court session in his Brooklyn offices. He usually started with Stengel. One morning's indictment: "You've been drinking and fighting again. We kept tab on you, and you downed eight beers inside of an hour."

"No, Mr. Ebbets, I only had two beers," said Casey, holding up two fingers, and with an innocent look on his face.

"What started the fight?" asked Ebbets.

"It was them other guys," explained Stengel. "Some of those toughs want to add to their reputation so they try to say they licked a lot of Dodgers," volunteered Casey, his imagination taking over.

"Did they lick you?" asked the club owner.

"No, they didn't," replied Stengel. "We wouldn't have permitted that, for your sake as well as ours. What would people say if a bunch of bums beat up some of your best players?"

At this point Ebbets, as always, lost his anger and caved in. "Of course, you had to stand up for the integrity of the club. Case dismissed."

For some time after the Coney Island fight, Giants players and Polo Grounds bleacherites would tease Casey by holding up two fingers and yelling, "It was only two beers, Mr. Ebbets."

Stengel had numerous salary disputes with Squire Ebbets. Whereas some present-day ballplayers hold out for an extra twenty grand, the differences between Ebbets and Stengel were as little as $500 or even $250. One spring the Brooklyn contract offer was $4,500, and Casey's demand was $5,000. Ebbets agreed to split the difference and pay Stengel $4,750. The outfielder still insisted he wanted $5,000.

"I've been fair with you," said Ebbets. "I've agreed to split the difference, and now you haggle with me for two hundred fifty dollars."

"It's not me haggling for two hundred fifty dollars, it's you," shot back Casey.

After fussing with Stengel for five full seasons, in early 1918 Ebbets

shipped Casey and second baseman George Cutshaw to Barney Dreyfuss Pittsburgh Pirates for pitchers Burleigh Grimes and Al Mamaux
and shortstop Chuck Ward. It was a good deal for Brooklyn. As for
Casey, it started him on a merry-go-round which put him in four clubs
in the next two years. After playing only thirty-nine games with the Pirates in 1918, he decided to trade a Dreyfus uniform for one of Uncle
Sam's. Stengel became probably the most comical gob in the U.S.
Navy.

At the end of World War I, Stengel returned to Pittsburgh but soon
was traded to the Phillies, owned then by the thrifty William Baker. In
1921, when Casey had a sore leg, Baker peddled him to the New York
Giants for cash and players, the bundle representing $75,000. The
move to the Giants was a good experience for Stengel, who had a
chance to share in world championship spoils in 1921, '22, '23, and to

Casey Stengel as a Giant in 1923.

get close to John J. McGraw, then the smartest manager in the National League. Sitting on the bench with McGraw laid the foundation for Casey's managerial career.

Stengel's last two seasons with the Giants were among his best. Playing center field on the left-handed batting shift, he contributed batting averages of .368 and .339. He batted .400 in the 1922 World Series against the Yanks and .417 in 1923. Including his early .364 with Brooklyn in 1916, it gave him a .393 average for three Series. Such figures show that he didn't go to bat with a toothpick in his hands.

The Giants lost the 1923 Series to the Yankees, four games to two; but it should have gone into the record book as Yankees 4, Casey Stengel 2. The irrepressible Stengel was directly responsible for both of the Giants victories. In the first game, played in Yankee Stadium, the score was 4–4 with two out in the ninth when the mighty Casey stepped to the plate. This Casey didn't strike out, as in Ernest Thayer's poem, but hit off Joe Bush to deepest left center.

It was a hectic inside-the-park homer, and Casey contributed every ounce of drama it contained. As he ran around the bases, his left shoe came loose. On the last lap, between third base and home, as Bob Meusel's strong relay was coming to the plate, Stengel, trying to run and keep the shoe on, lurched from side to side like a drunken man. Finally, he made a headfirst dive for the plate, arriving only a fraction of a second before Meusel's throw. All the air had been knocked out of Casey's lungs in his final slide and he lay there exhausted. Other Giants helped him to his feet and assisted him to the bench. His homer had won the game, 5–4.

Herb Pennock tied up the Series for the Yankees in the second game, and it was Art Nehf, crack Giants left-hander, against Sad Sam Jones in the third. Both men pitched brilliantly. There was only one run scored, that being Stengel's seventh-inning home run into the right field bleachers. The Yankees had been riding Stengel on his first-game home run and now, as he trotted around the bases, Casey had his right thumb at the tip of his nose and wiggled the other fingers at the Yankees' dugout and at their royal box in which sat owner Col. Jake Ruppert.

Ruppert took offense and insisted to Commissioner Landis that Stengel be punished for "insulting my players, our fans and me." The Judge laughed it off, remarking, "Casey Stengel just can't keep from being Casey Stengel," but he did fine the outfielder fifty dollars. By the fourth game Casey had run out of homers and the Yankees swept the last three games 8–4, 8–1 and 6–4.

Stengel's reward for his heroics in the 1923 World Series came a month later when, along with shortstop Dave Bancroft and outfielder Billy Cunningham, he was traded to the second division Boston Braves for outfielder Billy Southworth.

Casey had one fair year with Boston, but when he could show only one hit for his first twelve times at bat in 1925, he was demoted to the Braves' farm team in Worcester, where he was to become outfielder, manager, and president. Ultimately president Stengel fired outfielder Stengel.

It seemed that when Stengel reached thirty-five, big league baseball had seen the last of the zany outfielder who laughed at and talked back to bleacher or grandstand patrons. Once in Pittsburgh, when accepting the cheers of the crowd, he doffed his cap and a bird flew out. Stories as to where the bird came from, and what kind it was, conflict.

But Stengel was not one to be kept down or away for long. Soon he reappeared, first as a coach and then as a manager. In 1932 he returned to the scene of "the Four Rascals" as a coach under Brooklyn's Max Carey. When Max was fired, Stengel was engaged as manager, but not until after he had cleared it with Carey. Casey managed in Brooklyn in 1934 and 1935, but in 1936 the Dodgers board of directors agreed to pay Casey a year's salary not to manage the club. That is, they "bought up" his contract, which had another year to go.

After sitting out 1936, Stengel got another chance to manage, from Bob Quinn of the old Boston Braves, and Casey held forth in Boston, 1938–43, with a string of sixth placers or lower.

One of these years, while the Braves were training in Bradenton, Florida, Taylor Spink asked me to go there and do a story for *The Sporting News* on the Braves' training, adding, "If there is nothing new on the Braves, 'Ol Case is always good for a story." So, I called on Stengel to get the latest on his team. I wish I had the talent to reproduce our interview in Casey's own Stengelese and describe his gestures.

"We look better on paper than we really are," said Stengel. "Fellows who should be pitching well by now have sore arms, and my team is riddled with injuries. And one of the damnedest things you ever heard of happened to one of my young outfielders who can also play first base, George Metkovich. A catfish chawed off a hunk of his foot."

What happened is that Metkovich was catfishing in the Manatee River, and he hauled in a real big one. He was holding down the "cat" at the bottom of the boat with one foot, trying to extricate the hook, when the fish struck back, ramming one of its stingers through the composition sole of George's shoe and into the player's foot. When Metkovich tried to pull the stinger from his foot, it broke off and lodged there. The rookie required hospitalization and it was several weeks before he could play. Afterward Metkovich bore the nickname Catfish.

By the time Stengel got over the effects of being run down by a taxicab in 1943, Bob Coleman was named manager of the Boston Braves, and it was back to the minors for 'Ol Case—Milwaukee, Kansas City,

King George of England
greets Casey Stengel,
1924

King George V of England greets Casey Stengel in 1924 during a European tour by members of the New York Giants and Chicago White Sox.

and Oakland—all now big league towns. He won the 1948 Pacific Coast League pennant with the Oaks, attracted Del Webb's attention, and was on his way to the greatest managerial record of all time.

Stengel not only was a left-handed hitter, thrower, and manager, but he also was a left-handed dentist. During some of the fanning sessions with reporters, he used to give imitations of his early days as a dental student—how he yanked teeth left-handed while working on charity and low-pay patients. Even though in later life he talked mostly Stengelese, a language without grammar, syntax, punctuation or continuity of thought, he was an educated man as well as a bright and ingenious one. He was graduated in the top half of his class from the Kansas City High School, and attended dental college in Kansas City for three years. He needed only another term to graduate with the title Dr. Charles Dillon Stengel.

In fact, at some point in Casey's early baseball days, his German-born father wrote "Charley" a man-to-man letter which went something like this: "Dear Charley: I think you should give some thought to your future. I know you love to play baseball, but you've got to think about the money end of it. Some day you'll be married and have children, and I think you would do much better if you go back to school and finish your dental education. You will have a much more secure future if you go on with your dentistry, get your degree, and set up an office here in Kansas City."

At the time, Christy Mathewson, at $6,000, was the highest-paid National League player except for Honus Wagner. Hal Chase, manager and first-base superstar of the Yankees, received $5,500. Few big leaguers drew anything above $4,000, and Casey started with the Dodgers for about $2,700. Little would Papa Stengel, knowing such facts, have suspected that even before his son Charley had his successful managerial career with the Yankees, ballplayers already considered him a millionaire. Up to 1949 Casey had never made any real big money, but by carefully investing his baseball earnings, he had amassed considerable wealth. For one thing, he and a few baseball friends had gotten in on an oil well that proved a bonanza.

George Weiss and Casey Stengel were out of baseball in 1961, after their chilly departure from the Yankees following the 1960 World Series. But the expansion of the National League to a ten-club circuit in 1962, bringing back a New York team to replace the Giants and adding Houston, opened a new chapter to their careers as top baseball men. When the wealthy Payson family provided the backing for the new New York team, the illustrious baseball brain, George Weiss, was announced as president–general manager. George's first move was to appoint Casey Stengel, then seventy-two, as first manager of the new Mets, named after the Metropolitans, New York's team in the old-time

Casey Stengel, then manager of the Boston Braves (1940), in a characteristic jaw-boning posture with umpire Beans Reardon. Buddy Hassett is listening in.

major league known as the American Association back in the 1880s.

With the collection of overage veterans, humpty dumpties, misfits, and alleged ballplayers Stengel had playing for him in 1962, Casey enjoyed managing as much as when he led the highly competent Yankees to their great successes. He had become a man who could adjust to any situation. It was great fun for him to regale an audience with talk of his first baseman, Marvelous Marv Throneberry. Casey would get down on the floor on all fours as he imitated the antics of Marvelous Marv playing his position.

In the first year of the new Mets, the team had an atrocious percentage of .250, winning only 40 games and losing 120. Instead of expressing wonder how a club that had some good players could lose 120 games, Stengel observed, "Sometimes when I go back in my mind to our play of 1962, I just wonder how we ever got to win forty games."

However, if Stengel's new Mets were tailenders on the ball field, they were wonders at the refurbished Polo Grounds box office. In their first year they drew only about 100,000 fewer fans than the Yankees, who were world champions under Ralph Houk. From 1963 to 1975 the Mets consistently outdrew their famous neighbors at Yankee Stadium. Beginning with 1964, Stengel and his Mets had a playpen of their own, Shea Stadium, near Flushing on Long Island. National League fans, without a New York team since 1957, flocked to the turnstiles to see Stengel and his amusing upstarts.

After the disastrous first season of 1962, Casey increased the Mets' percentage slightly to 51–111 in 1963 and 53–109 in 1964. Then they slipped back again to 50–112 in 1965. "This baseball is a funny game," he observed. "Just as I start telling people, 'We're making slow but sure improvement,' bop, we slide back again." But to Casey they were always "my amazin' Mets."

However, for the Old Perfesser, 1964 proved an unhappy year. He attended an Old-timers Day at Shea Stadium, and despite the low standing of his club he received more applause than any other hero of past years. Stengel rarely missed a drink when anyone was passing them out, and he had a reputation for holding his liquor better than any man in baseball. After some postgame celebrating, however, he was a bit tottery, and when he got into a friend's car to drive home he stumbled and fractured a hip.

Catcher Wes Westrum was appointed temporary manager, and when Casey's recovery still left him with a decided limp in 1965, Westrum was made full-time manager. In effect, the fall following the Old-timers Game marked the end of Casey's career as an active participant in big league baseball. He lasted longer than any one but the venerable Connie Mack. In sharp contrast to his treatment by the Yankees, Stengel remained on the Mets' payroll as vice-president in charge of Cali-

Casey Stengel and Leo Durocher meet before the opening of the 1951 Yankees-
Giants World Series.   Acme Telephoto

fornia. When the amazin' Mets won their first pennant and World Series in 1969, Casey was as proud of them as if he were still team manager. "After all, they still are my boys," he insisted.

Naturally Casey was elected to the Hall of Fame. I was appointed in
1964 to the Veterans Committee for the election of old-timers into the
shrine and I am proud that the first man I voted for was Ol' Case. Casey
and his faithful wife Edna gloried in the honor. He and Edna appeared
at every Hall of Fame installation from 1965 until 1974, with Casey an-
nually delivering the funniest and most popular talk at the private dinner for Hall of Famers the night before the newly elected men are in-
stalled.

In 1974 Casey made the transcontinental trip alone. Edna was sick in California. As Mary's death left me alone too, Casey invited me to eat with him. "We're both alone now," he said, "and you talk my language."

We talked over a host of things that summer—Casey's early squabbles with Brooklyn's Squire Ebbets, his rollicking days with the Pirates and Phillies, his two home runs in the 1923 Giants–Yankees World Series. He reminded me that earlier in 1974, when Hank Aaron's pursuit of Babe Ruth's record was the top baseball subject, I had made a short talk at the Governor's Dinner in St. Petersburg and said, "Everyone is wondering whether or when Hank will wipe out Ruth's record, but there is a man here, Casey Stengel, who may have an even more endurable record than Ruth, as the winning manager of five successive world championships." Casey later pulled me aside and said, "You seem to understand what that record really means. I doubt if anyone can beat it under the present play-off system."

In 1975 we all missed Casey, and the annual dinner just for Hall of Famers wasn't the same without the Perfesser's annual discourse. Our news then from Glendale, California, wasn't good: Edna was failing and Casey was little better. Then shortly before the 1975 World Series, we learned that Casey never again would say, "You can look it up in the record."

Ah, what a record! And what a guy!

22

BASEBALL: THEN, NOW AND TOMORROW

> The Ball once struck off,
> Away flied the Boy,
> To the next desir'd Post,
> And then Home with Joy.

This bit of verse was probably the first ever written about baseball. American? Wrong—British. It appeared in the *Little Pretty Pocket Book* of 1744 under the one-word title "Baseball." Nearly one hundred years later, the American game of baseball was allegedly devised in Cooperstown, New York, in 1839. Our national game had already come a long way as an organized professional sport when I saw my first big league game as a boy in 1904.

In 1904 the two major leagues (the American League was created in 1901) were landlocked by rules and tradition in a territory that embraced only a small portion of the nation—the so-called Northeast Corridor from Boston to Washington and a strip across the industrial Midwest, north of the Mason-Dixon line, to St. Louis. Only ten cities had teams: New York had three, including Brooklyn; Chicago, Philadelphia, Boston, and St. Louis had two each; Washington, Pittsburgh, Cleveland, Cincinnati, and Detroit each had one. (In those days St. Louis and Boston ranked as the fourth- and fifth-largest cities in the na-

253

tion; today they are eighteenth and sixteenth respectively, though Boston's metropolitan area provides its one team with a vast market for the game.)

Until the 1950s the conservative baseball establishment frowned on any thought of changing its setup. But well before Bill Veeck of the St. Louis Browns and Lou Perini of the Boston Braves wished to move their teams, Ed Barrow, then president of the International League, had nominated Toronto for "the Bigs." Now, sixty years later, Toronto has been embraced by the American League.

The Federal League made its appearance in 1914, bucking the monopoly of the big leagues by building ball parks and fielding teams in Brooklyn, Pittsburgh, Chicago, and St. Louis (big league cities), as well as Baltimore, Buffalo, Indianapolis, and Kansas City. This league called itself "the third major league," and it did attract some big league players by waving more liberal contracts under their noses. But the venture proved to be ill-fated, for the market could not stand twenty-four teams, especially additional teams in those cities where big league ball was already available. At the end of the 1915 season a hefty settlement by big league owners brought down the curtain on the Federal League operation.

The next attempt to shatter established patterns came in the late autumn of 1941, when plans were readied to move the old St. Louis Browns to Los Angeles. But the Japanese struck at Pearl Harbor on December 7 and scuttled not only most of our Pacific Fleet but also plans for opening the Pacific Coast to major league baseball.

Then in 1953, within a month of the opening of the big league season, the Boston Braves—one of the remaining charter National League clubs—were suddenly whisked out of Boston and dropped into enthusiastic Milwaukee, where they attracted 1,826,397 fans. The Braves' move started an unstoppable trend. After the 1953 season ended, the St. Louis Browns were moved to Baltimore. In 1954 the Philadelphia Athletics were purchased from Connie Mack and his family; they opened the 1955 season in Kansas City. Going back before the Civil War, Philadelphia had had teams named "Athletics," first in the early rival of the National League called the American Association, and finally in the American League from 1901 onwards. The departure of the Athletics caused many a heartache in Philadelphia.

The move of the A's was as nothing compared to the news, after the 1957 season, that the Brooklyn Dodgers—loved and scolded by the Flatbush Faithful—were to be yanked out of Ebbets Field and transplanted in the greener and commercially richer fields of Los Angeles. Only a year before, Brooklyn had won its eleventh National League pennant. Some Dodger fans remain in a permanent state of shock brought on by the departure of their team.

As if this were not enough tragedy for New York, Horace Stoneham soon afterward announced the transfer of the New York Giants to San Francisco. To New York fans this seemed even more incredible, for the Giants had often been the most profitable of National League teams as well as the most successful in terms of pennants won. The franchise enjoyed almost as much prestige as the flagship of a fleet of U.S. Navy warships.

In 1961 the American League, finding eight clubs too limiting in the face of demands for new franchises, and enjoying even larger television income, expanded to ten teams. The National League followed suit in 1962. Recognizing the mistake of leaving New York without a team, the National League awarded a franchise to Mrs. Joan W. Payson and a few small stockholders. They fielded the Metropolitans, who immediately became the Mets—the "amazing Mets." The other new additions to the big leagues were the Houston Astros, first called the "Colt 45's," a second Los Angeles team for the American League, and the Minnesota Twins, which were actually the transplanted Washington Senators of Calvin Griffith, Washington regaining a franchise under a different ownership.

The two leagues were now pointed firmly in the direction of expansion and enlargement. In 1969 they each split into Eastern and Western Conferences, each conference consisting of six clubs. The new clubs in the National League were Montreal and San Diego; in the American, Kansas City and Seattle. The Kansas City team of 1955–67 had been moved to Oakland in 1968. Seattle, after a bad year at the gate in 1969, moved to Milwaukee under different ownership (the Braves had left Milwaukee for Atlanta in 1966). In a postseason shuffle after the 1971 season, the Washington Senators, much to the distress of Commissioner Bowie Kuhn, who grew up in the District of Columbia, wandered off and became the Texas Rangers.

How Seattle regained a team for 1977 is largely the result of a $90,000,000 suit which the City of Seattle filed against the baseball establishment. A new syndicate with more capital than the first owners and a new 60,000–seat stadium were other factors.

What does the future hold for further expansion? There isn't much more room in the continental United States for profitable franchises. But New Orleans, with its new super-astrodome, sorely needs a tenant to play eighty-one games in it. Miami, with its baseball-loving Cuban community, and the fast-growing Memphis area are other possibilities. Perhaps before another decade we will have a club in Honolulu, Hawaii. If we do—and airplanes are flying faster all the time—Japan may get into the picture. (In 1974 the two leading Japanese teams held their own with the touring New York Mets, who had to wait for the fifth game before scoring a victory.)

If Cuba and the United States could learn to live with each other, Havana could be a real addition to one of the leagues. Before Castro, Havana fielded a strong team in the Florida International League. According to Earle Halstead, owner-editor of the official Baseball Blue Book, baseball has flourished in Cuba under the revolution. "I would say that today there are fifty players in Cuba good enough to be considered big league prospects," Earle tells me. More importantly, Cubans pay money to watch baseball, and Havana is a city of over one million inhabitants. Castro himself is a baseball buff, and still pitches on occasion. He once almost signed a Washington contract.

One of the questions most frequently asked me is, "What difference do you see between players of Ty Cobb's era and those of today?" My answer always is, "Their size." In my prime I was nearly five foot eleven. When I conversed with such early Giants and Yankees as Larry Doyle, Josh Devore, Georgie Burns, Birdie Cree, Fritzie Maisel, Bill McKechnie, Hans Lobert, Ferdie Schupp, Roger Peckinpaugh, and Aaron Ward, I was taller than any of them. There were scores of others in the big leagues who were shorter than I.

Today, when I am among the Mets players like Tom Seaver, Jerry Koosman, Jon Matlack, and Craig Swan, though I am now about 5 feet 10½ inches I am always looking up. And of course a man as tall as Dave Kingman did not exist in 1911 or 1921 or 1931. Among the first really tall star players in the big leagues was Hank Greenberg, who came up for good in 1933, at 6 feet 4 inches, weighing 210. Lefty Bob Grove of the A's and Red Sox was another big one at 6 feet 3. A man of Hank's or Lefty's size attracts no attention today in a baseball uniform.

Among the players in the World Series of 1905 (Giants vs. Athletics) you could count the six-footers on one hand. Mathewson, the Giants' pitching ace, was 6 feet 1½. Their first baseman, Dan McGann, was 6 feet 2. Connie Mack's ace right-hander, Chief Bender, was 6 feet 2, and Jack Knight, a utility infielder fresh out of Central High School in Philadelphia, was also 6 feet 2. Rube Waddell, out of the Series with a shoulder injury, was 6 feet 1 and a fraction of disputed size. That was it.

In the Series the following year (White Sox vs. Cubs), the great Mordecai ("Three-finger") Brown (won 237, lost 127) was 5 feet 10. It is hard to find a pitcher so small today, let alone a pitcher with a winning percentage of .653 who pitched 3,171 innings and gave only 2,708 hits. Figure for yourself how low an average hits-per-game Brown compiled. And his *lifetime* earned run average was 2.06. Could he possibly have done any better if he had been 6 feet 3 and 225 pounds?

These Mathewson-era players were not small men, but men who would look small on modern teams. Back around 1900 there were some genuinely little men who were heroes of the game. Today's fans might

Tom Seaver recording his 2,000th strikeout at Shea Stadium in July, 1975. The batter is Dan Driessen of the Cincinnati Reds.   UPI

find them hard to take seriously if they saw them step to the plate. As a kid fan in Philadelphia, I saw them all play, and they remain vivid in my mind's eye. For example, there was Hugh Duffy, the player who compiled the highest batting average in one hundred years of baseball, an outfielder for Boston, .438 in 1894. Hughie stood 5 feet 7 and weighed 168.

The second-best average is the remarkable .432 in 1899 by the pint-size Willie Keeler, then with the Baltimore Orioles in the National League. His nickname, "Wee Willie," tells the story—5 feet 4½. Compared to stocky Duffy, built like a fireplug, Keeler looked almost skinny. He gave a simple but complete explanation of his successful hitting when he said, "I hit 'em where they ain't." In the same season that he hit .432, Keeler also ran off baseball's then-longest consecutive hitting streak, forty-four games. This record survived until 1941, when Joe Di-Maggio, 6 feet 2, raised it to fifty-six games in a row.

Jesse Burkett, 5 feet 8, had three .400 batting years. John McGraw, 5 feet 7, was a flash afield and had a lifetime batting average of .330. Tommy Leach, who specialized in inside-the-park homers, was a scant 5 feet 6.

These heroes of the turn of the century comprise a "big little five."

How do they compare with some of today's headline makers? The surprising 1976 Phillies feature Gerry Maddox at 6 feet 3, Mike Schmidt at 6 feet 2, and Greg Luzinski at 6 feet 1. Pitcher John Candelaria, the new pitching wonder boy of the Pirates, is 6 feet 7. Dave Kingman, who threatened the Ruth-Maris homerun marks until injured in the midseason of 1976, is 6 feet 6. Carlton Fisk, whose dramatic twelfth-inning home run tied the 1975 World Series between Boston and Cincinnati at three games each, is 6 feet 2. So is Tony Perez, whose homer in the deciding game of the 1975 Series was the big blow for the Reds.

At the Red Sox 1976 spring training camp in Sarasota, thirteen of the fifteen listed pitchers were 6-footers. One of the two "shorties" was Luis Tiant, 5 feet 11, whose two victories kept Boston in the 1975 World Series.

Even though the tendency is toward bigger and bigger players, there continues to be a place for the dedicated little man. Such a man is the capable, dexterous, all-around second baseman of the Cincinnati Reds, Joe Morgan, 5 feet 7. Joe was voted the most valuable player in the National League in 1975 and 1976 and the most valuable in the 1975 World Series. He was also the one who received the most fan ballots when they chose players for the 1976 All-Star game.

Almost as noticeable as the difference in height and weight is the difference in the ethnic backgrounds of players today. At the turn of the century big leaguers were almost entirely of Irish, Anglo-Saxon, and Germanic stock, in that order. Irish names were the most numerous. The fabulous Baltimore Orioles, N.L. champions of 1893, 1894 and 1895, were led by an Irish-American manager, Ned Hanlon, and 80 percent of his team were fellow sons of Erin—John McGraw, Willie Keeler, Hugh Jennings, Joe Kelley, Sadie McMahon, Kid Gleason, Dennis (Dan) Brouthers, Joe McGinnity. They had one Dutchman on the club, Heinie Reitz, the second baseman.   Other famous Irishmen of the period were Cornelius McGillicuddy (Connie Mack), former Washington and Pittsburgh catcher and later famous manager, and Pat Moran, who managed the first pennant winners of the Phillies. There were even more Irishmen playing in the first decade of the twentieth century.

Honus Wagner was a stalwart figure to head the brigade of Germans. Others were Harry Steinfeldt, the third baseman of the Cubs along with Tinker, Evers, and Chance; Frank Schulte, crack Cub right fielder; Germany Schaefer, Detroit second baseman and clown; Otto Knabe, Phillie second baseman; Charley Schmidt, Tiger catcher, Dutch (later Casey) Stengel, pitcher Jeff Pfeffer, and catcher Otto Miller of Brooklyn. Later Babe Ruth, Frank Frisch and Lou Gehrig were to provide other famous German names.

Along with the Irish and Germans there was a large contingent of players whose ancestors had arrived so many generations earlier that they could not be regarded as ethnics but only as Americans. They were largely of English and Scottish stock—the numerous Smiths, Joneses, Browns, and Robinsons, along with such players as the ace pitchers Walter Johnson and Grover Cleveland Alexander, the dashing Ty Cobb, the roving Tris Speaker, and Sam Crawford.

In the early days of my baseball reporting, there was only one player of Italian ancestry, Ed Abbattichio. He was originally signed by the Phillies, but soon went to the Pirates as a second baseman, and for about four years played alongside the great Wagner. Sports writers quickly condensed his name to Abbey, and he appears as such in the early box scores. The next Italian was Ping Bodie, a slugging outfielder who came up with the White Sox the same year I hit New York, 1911. His real name was Francesco Pezzola, but Pacific Coast League writers changed that to Ping Bodie before Pezzola ever reached Chicago.

In the 1920s and 1930s we had a great surge of Italian-American players. Many New York fans of Italian ancestry had hardly heard of baseball until Tony Lazzeri joined the Yankees in 1926. They would come to Yankee Stadium crying, "Poosh 'em up Tony," which became Lazzeri's nickname. Actually Tony had been preceded on the big league scene by two other sons of Italy: Rinaldo Angelo Paolinelli— who became Babe Pinelli to sports writers—a third baseman 1918–27, principally with Cincinnati, and later a fine umpire; and Lou Fonseca, 1929 American League batting champion, with a .369 average, beating out Al Simmons (.365), Heinie Manush (.355), Jimmy Foxx (.354), and Tony Lazzeri (.354). In later years Lou managed the White Sox and then became a member of the American League's promotion department.

Then came the DiMaggio family; the super-DiMag named Joe, the Yankee Clipper; little Dom, youngest and smallest, who sparkled for ten active years at bat and roaming center field for the Red Sox; and strikeout-prone Vincent, who lasted a decade with five clubs in the National League on the strength of his fielding.

Who can forget the arrival of those two inhabitants of St. Louis's so-called "Dago Hill," Yogi Berra and his buddy from across the street, Joe Garagiola? Yogi batted in bushels of runs for the Yankees and starred for them in many World Series. And his managerial successes— and subsequent firings—with the Yanks and Mets are fresh in fans' memories. As our top-paid TV baseball broadcaster, Joe likes to belittle his talents at bat and behind the plate, but he hung in there for nine seasons, and no one can take away his marvelous opening year, 1946, and his .316 batting average in the World Series that autumn.

At about the time that Abbey and Bodie paved the way for the parade of Italian players, Harry Coveleski, a lefthanded Pole, came out of the Shamokin, Pennsylvania mines to pitch for the Phillies. In the last week of the 1908 season he beat the contending New York Giants three times, which forced the Giants into a play-off with the Cubs for the pennant, a game the Giants lost. Coveleski was immediately dubbed "the Giant Killer." Covey didn't last long with Philadelphia, but later became a twenty-game winner with Detroit. His younger, smaller, and right-handed brother Stanley came to Cleveland in 1916 and pitched well enough to win a plaque in the Cooperstown Hall of Fame. His greatest feat was beating the Dodgers three times in the 1920 World Series, allowing them only 2 runs and 15 hits.

For a spell the Coveleskis were the only Poles in big league ball, but in 1924 they were joined by Al Simmons, born Aloysius Syzmanski, who became a top star with the Philadelphia Athletics, twice American League batting champion and another Hall of Famer. Simmons was followed by a number of other Polish players, the most distinguished being Stan "the Man" Musial of the Cardinals and Ted Kluszewski, big-armed first baseman of the Cincinnati Reds. The most prominent Polish player of the present generation is the mighty "Yaz" of Fenway Park, Carl Yastrzemski. Carl is a third-generation American of Polish Long Island potato farmers.

Irish, German, Italian, and Polish players all have made their marks in baseball, but no players have changed the game as much as blacks. It began in 1946, when Jackie Robinson signed a Montreal contract as a farm hand of the Brooklyn Dodgers. Branch Rickey, then Brooklyn vice president-general manager, signed the Negro League star and promoted Robinson to his top team, Brooklyn, in 1947. The so-called breaking of the color line shook the nation.

For a while I thought that Hi Bithorn, a Puerto Rican who pitched for the Cubs, 1942–43 and 1946, and for the White Sox in 1947, might be entitled to be called the first black player to appear in a big league uniform.

Late in the winter of 1946–7, when I was working in St. Louis, I was invited to see a performance of Katherine Dunham's all-black dance troupe. I did not know the man who had arranged for me to sit in the wings throughout the performance. During the intermission he brought over one of the women dancers and introduced her to me. "She is a first cousin to Hi Bithorn, the pitcher," he explained to make conversation.

"Yes," the girl volunteered immediately. "My mother and Hi's mother are sisters."

Back in my hotel room I began to wonder whether the conversation was intended to tell me something. Perhaps this stranger was the public relations man for the show. It had been rumored among baseball writers and in clubhouses when Bithorn came up in 1942 that he was part black. However, I have since been assured by a Puerto Rican baseball authority that Bithorn was not black, despite my curious experience.

When the Jackie Robinson announcement was made, I talked with Sam Breadon, president of the St. Louis Cards. I recall his somewhat condescending comments: "Robinson is a good player. There may even be three or four other blacks in the country who can play well enough to get a chance in the big leagues." Sam lived long enough to see how badly he had underestimated the potential of black ballplayers.

True, it was only a trickle at first. The Browns signed two that year: Hank Thompson, a talented third baseman, and Willard Brown, an outfielder. Brown was gone by the end of 1947, but Thompson went on to be a top utility man wth the New York Giants. When Don Mueller was injured in the Dodgers-Giants National League play-off series in 1951, Thompson played right field in the Giants-Yankees World Series, with Willie Mays in center field and Monte Irvin in left field. This was the first all black outfield ever put together in the majors. Monte went on to a top post in the office of baseball Commissioner Bowie Kuhn, and into the Hall of Fame. Wondrous Willie became, in my opinion, the greatest of black players so far and a cinch for early Hall of Fame induction.

Mays had close competitors in Hank Aaron, the leader in lifetime home runs, among other records, and in Frank Robinson, great outfielder and home run hitter with Cincinnati and Baltimore, now in command of the Cleveland Indians as the first black manager. Another black superman in baseball was Puerto Rico's greatest player Roberto Clemente, the splendid Pirate slugger, base runner, thrower, and outfielder. Millions of Americans and all of Puerto Rico mourned when in 1972 the mercy plane on which he was flying plunged into the Caribbean shortly after takeoff for a flight to Nicaragua. Clemente personally was taking a planeload of food, medical supplies, blankets, and clothes to the victims of a severe earthquake in that Central American country.

Today black athletes, those from the U.S. together with those from neighboring Caribbean countries, occupy one third of the lockers in big league clubhouses and the percentage grows each year.

Today no one cares much whether a rookie is white or black. The main question is "Can he play ball?" If he can, he gets acceptance. For the last decade, Pirates general manager, Joe B. Brown, has had more blacks than whites on his team. And his policy has paid off in the standings as well as in the exchequer. Since the leagues split up to Eastern and Western Conferences in 1969, the Pirates have won the Eastern conference five times, and they won the World Championship in 1971. The Pittsburgh crowds have been the best in the club's history.

Baseball has helped to cut away at some of the separation of the races. In the 1975 World Series neither the Red Sox nor the American League rooters cared a rap whether Louis Tiant, Boston's most effective pitcher, was black, brown, blue, or white so long as he could check

Cincinnati's fearsome offense. On the other side, it mattered little whether Joe Morgan was red, green, or black, so long as he could field skillfully and drive in those runs.

Some old-timers like to believe that the old warriors of the playing days of McGraw, Jesse Burkett, and Wilbert Robinson were hardier and withstood pain better than present-day players. When they dislocated a finger they stuck it into the ground to work it back into position, shook it a few times, and went on playing. When a pitcher had a sore arm, he just kept pitching, believing it was best to exercise the soreness out. A case can be made that some modern players baby themselves more than necessary.

In the earlier days, teams had smaller squads—18 players, with 4 or 5 pitchers. As late as 1905 the Giants had a 6-man staff and one of them pitched only 38 innings. Mathewson pitched 339 innings (32–8); McGinnity, 320 innings (22–16); Ames, 263 innings (22–8). Even in the earlier American League days, President Ban Johnson would slap a severe fine on any club that tried to bypass the 18-player restriction. When I was a kid, some clubs had only one utility man for both the infield and outfield. In my native Philadelphia, the Phillies utility man in 1905 was a shorty at 5 feet 7—Otto Krueger, known as Oom Paul Krueger, the name of the president of the South African Boer republic. The Giants had Sammy Strang, who also was a good pinch-hitter; Brooklyn had John Hummel on hand for all purposes; and the Cubs had "Circus Solly" Art Hofman. He eventually succeeded Jimmy Slagle as the team's regular center fielder. If more than one injury vexed the manager, he would play the extra catcher or one of the pitchers in the vacancy.

It was much the same in the other league. When a player, especially a catcher, was injured, a team would borrow a player from another league club or employ a semi-pro. I recall how Connie Mack of the 1905 Philadelphia Athletics downgraded shortstop Monte Cross in midseason to a bench utility role and played Jack Knight, a tall youngster recently out of Philly's Central High, as his regular shortstop.

The Athletics had a good center fielder that year in Danny Hoffman, but he was badly injured in August when he was beaned by Jesse Tannehill, the Red Sox left-hander. Danny was out for the season. Connie Mack simply went to a small town nearby for a replacement. He found a stocky chap by the name of Briscoe Lord, who had starred on the Upland, Pennsylvania, semi-pro club. Mack went on to win the pennant with young Lord in center field. Lord also was his center fielder against the New York Giants in the World Series. But there the Cinderella story ends, for Lord was a setup for the Giant pitcher, hitting but 2 singles in 20 times at bat. Against the great Mathewson, Bris was lucky to get a foul, and went 0 for 12. However, he did hang around the big league for nine seasons.

Fred Lieb and Manager Joe Cronin of the Boston Red Sox—all business just before the opening of the 1946 Boston-St. Louis World Series.   George Dorrill

Fred Lieb and Joe Cronin reminiscing in Cooperstown, New York, in August 1976.

While I worshipped that 1905 "A's" team—and it did have a fine pitching staff in Rube Waddell, Eddie Plank, Chief Bender and Andy Coakley—I am sure it could not have won a pennant in today's American or National leagues without help.

Present-day teams start in the early spring with squads of 40: they are later cut to 30, and when they play their regular schedule they are down to 25. However, if a player sustains an injury, his team can immediately put him on a ten-day injury list and call up another player from one of the parent club's farm teams. So the manager always has 25 players on hand, including some 10 pitchers. There are usually 4 regulars, 4 middle relievers and spot pitchers, and 2 short-relief men for the crucial last one or two innings. No manager makes better use of the 10 pitchers at his disposal than Sparky Anderson, manager of the 1975 and 1976 World Champion Reds. The 1975 Reds staff had only 15 complete games, 8 going to Don Gullett. Compare that with early twentieth-century baseball, when Jack Chesbro completed 48 for the New York Highlanders in 1904; Vic Willis completed 45 for Boston (N.L.) in 1902; and Joe McGinnity had 44 for the Giants in 1903.

Present-day ballplayers seem far more prone to injury than those who manned the big leagues earlier in the century. Big league managers now can rarely play their regular lineup for a full week at a time. Often a club has four or five of its players in the hospital tent, even though the present-day men are better protected, carry bigger gloves, and wear batting helmets at bat. (Early in the century, Roger Bresnahan of the Giants was the first catcher to wear a breast protector.)

In the early years of the National League there were no training rooms. Connie Mack used to reminisce with me about his years in Washington in the late 1880s. He had caught in the minors for Hartford, Connecticut, where his leading pitcher was a tall, skinny guy like himself, Frank Gilmore. In Hartford, Gilmore and Mack were known as the "Shadow Battery." After they graduated to the old Washington National League Club in September 1886, Washington fans changed their name to the "Bones Battery."

"Anyhow, they put Frank and me up in a boarding house, where we shared a double bed," related Mack. "Frank developed a sore arm and I had a charley horse. Wintergreen was the only remedy for our aches, so we would spend half the night rubbing each other with wintergreen. I worked on his arm and he on my legs. Gosh, you could smell our room a block away."

Training conditions were little changed by the time I reached New York in 1911. The Giants had the luxury of a trainer—more properly a rubber—a black man by the name of Ed Mackall. At night Eddie issued a laxative to all the players and sports writers. "Take one of these," he told me. "Special orders from Mr. McGraw." Mac apparently wanted neither constipated ballplayers nor constipated writers.

In Brooklyn the clubhouse man who took care of the players' uniforms, balls, and bats, also doubled as the trainer.

About this time ball clubs began to have dressing rooms for visiting players. Until then they had dressed in their hotel rooms and were toted to the ball park in horse-drawn buses. In the spring of 1906 the Giants were being driven to the old Phillie park at Broad and Lehigh, later known as Baker Bowl, in open barouches. The carriages were drawn by black horses wearing black blankets with white lettering: NEW YORK GIANTS-WORLD CHAMPIONS, 1905. Heckled by Philadelphia fans, Roger Bresnahan kicked out of his carriage at the jeering fans. He lost his balance, fell to the street, and with his fists and spikes fought his way to a corner grocery store where he was rescued by police. He later was fined $5 for disorderly conduct!

Today, all clubs have fine quarters for visiting players. The training rooms are fitted with whirlpool and sitz baths and electric devices for stimulating circulation in any part of the body. The trainers and assistant trainers no longer are rubbers; they are skilled physical therapists. Some are chiropractic physicians; others have academic credentials in physical education.

The earlier players were notoriously poor tippers, especially since on the road they lived beyond their means. The general tip for services of any kind was a dime. Today, with the big salaries, tips are lavish. Drinking was usually at the corner saloon, where beer was five cents a glass—it was ten cents at their hotel. The clubs picked up most of the checks for meals on the road, with the understanding they would not go over $6 a day. If the club secretary paid out $6 in cash, an advance for a day's meals, most of the players would go to a cheap beanery, eat for three or four dollars, and pocket the rest.

The average salary for a ball player in 1911 was $4,000, and some of the less opulent clubs paid from $2,800 to $3,800. Salaries for the stars today are so high—and still going higher—that it is difficult to strike an average. UPI judged the pay of an average player of 1977 as $95,149— an amount close to the entire payroll of any two combined clubs (the Phillies, Brooklyn Dodgers, Browns, Senators, or Cardinals) of sixty-five years ago. Of course $3,500 bought far more than it does now; and such a salary, even though rarely augmented in the off-season, was a lot better than making a dollar a day in some unskilled job or $15 a week as a trained artisan.

While the present-day players still drink beer, especially right after a game, now they also go for drinks with higher alcoholic content— scotch, bourbon, gin and, more recently, vodka. They say if you indulge freely, vodka doesn't give you the same headache and bad breath when you get up in the morning as gin.

The earlier players spent most of their social evenings in the red-light districts of the major league cities, or "Down the Line" in such training cities as Macon, Savannah, Jacksonville, and San Antonio. The bordellos were patronized largely by the team's bachelors. But often the married men went along to drink beer, play pranks, and to kid the madam and her girls. Sometimes, it's true, the married went along for business. The present-day player goes in more for "the free stuff" that is floating around. Players exchange telephone numbers to contact sports-minded girls—not prostitutes, but girls employed in offices, often in good positions, widows, divorcees, swingers, and girls looking for fun and excitement with men and boys in the headlines.

Of course, night ball has made tremendous changes in all aspects of the big league picture. It has doubled, tripled, even quadrupled attendances in several parts of the big league belt. "It will make every day a Sunday," predicted Sam Breadon when night ball first was advocated. Televised night games have brought a fresh new income to the club owners; and Marvin Miller, head of the Ball Players Association, has seen to it that a goodly share of this new income trickles down to the players.

Night ball has also changed the social life of most present-day players. In the era of daylight play only, players were supposed to check in to their rooms at 11 P.M., and on special occasions, midnight. Under such conditions it was easy for coaches to keep track of them. But with night ball, the players on most clubs are allowed an hour for dinner and then another hour after that. That brings checking-in time to 2 A.M. or later. And if there is any partying after that, the player, unless he has the capacity of a Babe Ruth, may not be in too good shape the next day, especially if an afternoon game is on tap.

Another difference between players of the teens, twenties and thirties, and those of today is that the modern player marries earlier and has more children. At the training camps of my early years, you never saw a small child, and there were comparatively few wives. Recently however, the Cincinnati Reds claimed thirty-five children among their players' families.

With compulsory education in force in most states, the present-day player is much better schooled and has a better knowledge of current affairs than his predecessors. Such Hall of Fame stars as Hans Wagner, Nap Lajoie, and Cy Young had achieved all of their school education by the time they were twelve. That was true of many of their teammates.

To a degree, of course, a man is bound to get some education just by traveling around the country. I know some of the players learn geography that way. On the Yankee training trips of 1916 and 1917, we had a pleasant-faced young pitcher from Tennessee, who wore a big fluffy bow tie. In 1916 we came up from the Yankee training base in Macon, Georgia, to New York via Birmingham, Memphis, Chattanooga, Nashville, and Louisville. In 1917 it was via Charleston and Columbia, South Carolina, Raleigh, North Carolina, and Norfolk, Virginia. As we were passing through a stretch of tidewater North Carolina, Sammy Ross sat in the seat next to me, and asked, "Mr. Fred, when will we be passin' through Tennessee?"

A little surprised, I replied, "We're miles east of Tennessee. In fact, we don't pass through Tennessee on this trip."

"Well, we sure passed through Tennessee last year," continued Ross. "I know 'cause I pitched a game in Nashville."

I went on trying to explain that this time we were coming up on a northeastern course. We weren't too far from the Atlantic, I explained, so we would miss Tennessee.

Sammy still was not satisfied or convinced as he said, "Maybe you're right, Mr. Fred. But I still don't believe you can come up from the Deep South without touching Tennessee. And I'd have you know that Tennessee is a mighty big state!"

I doubt one could find any rookie today so lacking in fundamental geography. At least half of the young ballplayers who come up today can boast of having gone to college, whether well known or hidden in the mountains of Tennessee or Montana.

As for their behavior, they still cuss, argue, and fight, as did the players of my early training camps. However, in both eras I have come across players with deep religious convictions. Such a player was Earle Combs, Hall of Fame center fielder of the great Yankee World Champions of 1927–28. Combs didn't drink, smoke, or swear, read his Bible daily, and didn't care who knew it. You still find a few of those Earle Combs types among the shaggy-haired rookies of 1977.

Deep down, there actually isn't much difference between the old and the new players. In my early days they were mostly good kids at heart—especially if you separated them from their partying, macho associates—the kind of kids you would feel pleased to have in your own home. I have been privileged, too, to know many of their wives. With only a few exceptions, they were splendid women who stood for decency and respectability in their homes and in their personal conduct. The love, sweetness, and inherent decency of these ladies helped make their husbands the heroes that so many of them became.

Some things never change and one example is the club owners. I often hear, "The old club owners loved the game—they were in it for the glory that comes from winning; these modern guys think only of the money angle." This may seem so, but the old club owners, many of whom Judge Landis personally despised, were no angels. The big difference is that so much more money is now involved. Charley Ebbets, the Brooklyn squire, was a contributor to baseball, and many nice things can be said about him. He was a bookkeeper when he first went to work for the Brooklyn club in the 1890s. As president of the club, he had a high bookkeeper's chair on which he sat, and from which he argued with his critical fans. One day, I heard him shout, "You call me cheap! I am the only club owner who doesn't have an automobile. I come to the ball park in a streetcar!"

But Charley was cheap. One day when Al Cutair, who covered Brooklyn for the New York *Press*, was in Ebbets' office, Charley was in a strident argument with the woman who washed the Dodger uniforms. "You want to make a living," Cutair heard the club president say. "If I pay what *you* want for washing these uniforms, *I* can't possibly make a living!"

Colonel Jake Ruppert loved baseball, especially winning baseball, but actually he was conned into buying a half interest in the Yankees by the belief that he could change the nickname of the New York team to the Knickerbockers, the name of his best-known brand of beer. After the sale, he issued a statement that henceforth the New York American League club would be called the Knickerbockers. The managing editors of the thirteen New York newspapers in 1915 held a meeting and voted: "Nix. No 'Knickerbockers.' " Frustrated and annoyed, Ruppert nevertheless went through with his agreement with Til Huston, his partner, and Frank Farrell, the former owner, for the sale of the franchise.

Another who thought he could advertise his product through a baseball connection was Robert Ward, head of Ward Brothers, whose best-known product was Tiptop Bread. James Gilmore, president of the independent Federal League, duped Robert Ward into thinking he could get national promotion of his bread if he put a second team in Brooklyn. The Wards built a new park and stocked it with players obtained in raids on the major and stronger minor league clubs. The name of the new team was to be the Tiptops. As in the case of the New York Knickerbockers, the associated Greater New York managing editors said, "No! No Tiptops." For want of a better name, the team became best known as the Brookfeds.

William F. Baker, a former New York City police commissioner who was once owner of the Philadelphia Phillies, had a reputation for squeezing a nickel even tighter than Squire Ebbets. When Chuck Klein, Baker's young outfield slugger, began hitting home runs at a Ruthian pace in 1929, Baker ordered an additional screen of twenty feet added to the screen which already stood atop the right field fence at Baker Bowl. Baker professed his abhorrence for "cheap home runs" and said if Chuck Klein wanted to enter the wholesale hume runs market he should *earn* his homers. Klein suggested the cheapness was on the other side, that Baker didn't want a 50-home-run player on his team because of the salary he would have to be paid. Even with the higher screen, Klein hit 43 home runs in 1929 and 40 in 1930.

When the Pirates began slipping badly in 1914, owner Barney Dreyfuss would go into the clubhouse and berate the players. He was particularly severe on big Ed Konetchy, the Bohemian first baseman. Dreyfuss told me, "Clarke ordered me to get out of the clubhouse and to stay out. One day I opened the clubhouse door, stuck my head inside, and yelled, 'Konetchy, you have it up to here,' putting my fingers up to my throat. Then I slammed the door, but I am sure that Koney and the other players got the point." That was ownership in the pre-World War I style.

In the other league, Charles Comiskey, the Chicago White Sox owner and a former star first baseman, had a reputation for the niggardly sums he wrote into his players' contract. Many blame the Black Sox scandal of 1919 on the poor salaries Comiskey paid his players.

Harry Frazee, owner of the Boston Red Sox in Ruth's early days, was also a theatrical promoter. Frazee, in his contract differences with Babe, held that he couldn't pay a ballplayer more than he paid his top actor. He bought the Red Sox when they were high—World Champions of 1915–16—and sold them when they were low—in the A. L. cellar in 1923. What happened in between those years is known in Boston as "the rape of the Red Sox," and old-time Boston fans still hold Frazee guilty of the crime. As he needed money to pay installments on his purchase price, or to make up for losses at the gate, or to find cash to back another musical, Frazee sold his players, over a period of a few years "down the river" to New York. Players who were disposed of one at a time or in bunches, were Babe Ruth, Carl Mays, Herb Pennock, Waite Hoyt, Joe Bush, Sam Jones, Everett Scott, Mike McNally, Duffy Lewis, Joe Dugan, Elmer Smith and Wallie Schang. Had Frazee solved his financial problems another way and kept Ruth and those superb pitchers, he just might have established the kind of dynasty with his Red Sox that the Yankees built under Ed Barrow's general managership—Barrow being another import from Frazee's club.

Today club owners are wealthier, and while a goodly number are in baseball for capital gains and tax shelters, there are among them some true fan-owners who really enjoy the game and the improvement they have made in their respective clubs. Such a man is Ray A. Kroc, the McDonald hamburger king. He and his son, treasurer John Kroc, have taken a personal interest in the San Diego club and have been thrilled at the Padres' general improvement, especially the work of the once-well-nigh-unbeatable pitcher Randy Jones.

Another newcomer who shows a lot of fan interest is Theodore Turner, the new owner of the Atlanta Braves. Ted gets so excited during rallies that he personally goes out on the field to lead Atlanta's cheering sections. He already has been called before the National League president to be advised that a system of bonuses for the team is not permissible in big league ball. Feeney also had to lecture Ted that he can't put the number 17 on the back of pitcher Andy Messersmith, an expensive free agent that Turner had picked up for a substantial sum. It just happens that Miami Television Station 17 is the main source of Ted Turner's wealth; and it was with money made through Station 17's advertisers that Ted was able to buy and refurbish the Atlanta ball club.

Charley Finley has been the bad boy of baseball ever since he purchased the Kansas City Royals. He has been rebuked by American League presidents Joe Cronin and Lee MacPhail, and frequently has been on the carpet of Commissioner Kuhn. He precipitated the open breach between himself and his ace pitcher, Catfish Hunter, by withholding $50,000 of Catfish's salary in 1974. Charley paid the amount in his own way, from a special fund. Instead he lost a million-dollar pitcher and saw the reserve clause, hitherto considered the bastion of baseball, shot full of holes. The Catfish took his differences with Finley to a panel of arbitration, which declared Hunter a free agent. Hunter subsequently negotiated a neat contract with the Yankees for an estimated $2,850,000.

However, one must credit the turbulent Finley with a fair measure of baseball acumen. With no general manager and the thinnest office staff in baseball, he built up a club good enough to win successive world championships in 1972, 1973, and 1974. His club won its fifth straight Western Division title in 1975 and barely lost out to Kansas City in 1976. And Charley himself has his good points. I got to know him quite well during Finley's suit against Commissioner Kuhn in January of 1977. Though I was a pro-Kuhn witness, Charlie twice complimented me on my testimony.

Early in the 1976 season Finley started to break up his great team, bringing on more trouble for himself. After trading to Baltimore his strongest hitter, Reggie Jackson, and his star left-handed pitcher, Ken Holtzman, Charley tried to sell outfielder Joe Rudi and crack relief pitcher Rollie Fingers to the Red Sox for $1,000,000 each, and southpaw pitcher Vida Blue to the Yankees for $1,250,000. Commissioner Kuhn disallowed these sales, and ordered Rudi, Fingers, and Blue to return to Oakland. Admitting that the sale of players for cash had long been a practice in pro baseball, Kuhn felt that selling three ballplayers for $3,250,000 was carrying it too far. He saw such sales killing baseball's close races, with pennants sure to go consistently to a few select clubs.

Since I had watched Connie Mack unload the stars of two great clubs for financial reasons, and Harry Frazee's destruction of the Red Sox, I was in sympathy with Kuhn's position. I also noted the domination of the Yankees from 1921 to 1964, when they won 29 American League championships and 20 World Series in 43 years. I thrilled to the successes of these great baseball machines, but I also saw what overpowering Yankee strength did to the rest of the league. The American League fell from being top dog to the position of subordinate. It fell behind in attendance and slipped from getting most positions on annual All-Star teams to getting two or three men. Only in World Series did the junior league manage to hold its own. In one year, 1955, the rest of the league was so poor that on July 4 the Yankees were the only club with a percentage over .500. I feel Kuhn was trying to prevent the recurrence of such a condition.

Despite the fact that there was one-sided competition in the divisional races of 1976, the major league attendance that year climbed to new heights. The attendance at Vets' Stadium in Philadelphia—with only two National League flags in ninety-three years up to 1976—and at Riverfront Stadium in Cincinnati were fantastic. Each ran to around 2,500,000.

There has recently been a lot of adverse or downright bad publicity for baseball. We have seen the feud between Marvin Miller's Players Association and the owners in the spring of 1976 culminate in the closing of training fields and clubhouses; then Finley's sale of his stars; the Andy Messersmith case; the two pro-players decisions in the courts and the long squabble over the new players' contract, with a four-year contract, partially satisfactory to both sides, finally agreed upon. The amazing thing is that baseball took it all in stride, and despite the growth of other sports, baseball got as full coverage in the nation's sports pages as when it was the one big summer sport.

In recent years, we have seen some astonishing records set. Hank Aaron, the Milwaukee designated hitter, finally has laid down his bat with the end of the 1976 season. I once believed that Babe Ruth's 714 homers would last forever. Now I see no one exceeding Hank's new record of 745. In addition to Aaron's new home run standard, he has a collection of other records that formerly belonged to Ty Cobb and Stan Musial. Cardinal Lou Brock's stolen base record of 118 in 1974 is safe from himself—he now is thirty-seven years old—or any other current base runner. Nolan Ryan of the California Angels, who had two no-hit games in 1973, a third in 1974, and a fourth in 1975, was bothered with a sore arm for most of the 1976 season. It prevented him from trying for a fifth to break his tie with Sandy Koufax. But he thinks his arm is again healthy in 1977, and he will try for that fifth no-hitter. I think he will make it. He has had a string of three successive 300 strike-out years, with a record top of 383 in 1973. If he makes it a fourth time in 1977 it will establish another new record. There is an old saying in baseball: "Records are made to be broken."

And the fans are still coming. With an expensive new training park in

Hank Aaron caught by a telephoto lens in the act of smashing home run number 715 to break the record held by Babe Ruth.   UPI

St. Petersburg, where the $3.40 fans get the full glare of the hot Florida sun, they set new attendance records in the Florida Grapefruit League as well as in the Cactus League of Arizona-California. On top of that, the major league had well over a million fans for its 26 opening games in April.

Early losses by the Yankees, Reds, Red Sox and Phillies indicate there will be no runaways, as there were in 1975, and we may have four races right down to the wire. The entire nation is interested to see whether George Steinbrenner III can succeed in his effort to buy a pennant, or a world championship. The late Col. Jacob Ruppert of New York showed that it could be done. And one of the most beloved men in sport, Tom

Johnny Bench has just put a tag on a base runner trying to score.

Yawkey, late owner of the Red Sox—also termed the Gold Sox—tried it for four decades, but his club won only two league flags, no World Series.

The baseball world is topsy-turvy, with the players in the driver's seat. Sixteen players played out their options in 1976, including the remaining stars of the Oakland A's: Joe Rudi, Rollie Fingers, Sal Bando, Gene Tenace, Don Baylor and Campy Campaneris. They sold themselves for sums their former club owner, Charley Finley, placed at $10,000,000. Reggie Jackson, crown jewel of the lot, went for $2,900,000 to the Yanks. Don Gullett of the Reds landed with the Yankees for $2,000,000 for six years. Other prize pickups were Bobby Grich, Dave Cash, Gary Mathews, and Bill Campbell. All signed contracts for five or six years. Pitcher Wayne Garland of Cleveland signed a million-dollar contract for ten years.

Most everyone agrees that such huge salaries are unhealthy for the game of baseball. Other players, who already had been under contract—Pete Rose and Johnny Bench of the Reds, Jim Palmer of the Orioles, Luis Tiant of the Red Sox and Steve Garvey of the Dodgers—had their signed contracts fattened until they were within reach of Jackson and Morgan. A club owner such as Ebbets, Baker or Dreyfuss would die of fright if he saw the combined payrolls for the National and American Leagues for 1977.

Salaries will continue to rise in 1977, but I see a general meeting of all baseball—the major leagues, the commissioner's office, the players' association—to discuss means of bringing new sanity to the game.

The great game must continue to grow and prosper. I see no decline in baseball interest, with the possible exceptions of badly riddled Oakland, Minnesota and maybe Atlanta, despite Ted Turner's antics. For 1977, I see more record big-league attendances, a more interesting World Series than in 1976, and the addition of Washington and New Orleans to the National League and possibly Memphis to the American League.

Before I lay down my scorecards, I would like to see another master shortstop who is the equal of Honus Wagner for all-around play, hitting, fielding and base running. I have seen a half dozen players who could play second base on anybody's All-Star team—Nap Lajoie, Eddie Collins, Rogers Hornsby, Charley Gehringer, Frankie Frisch, and Joe Gordon. At first base, you could take your pick between Lou Gehrig, George Sisler, and Bill Terry; and at third base a manager would consider himself blessed if he had his choice of Pie Traynor, Jimmy Collins, or Brooks Robinson to defend the "hot corner." Only at shortstop does one player, Honus Wagner, stand all alone, supreme. The nearest to him are Joe Cronin, former American League president; Arkie Vaughan; Phil Rizzutto; and Peewee Reese—all great, but no Wagners. Grand and marvelous will be the day when his equal arrives.

MY ALL-TIME ALL-STAR TEAMS

I have from time to time in the past responded to many requests—from editors of baseball yearbooks, guides, monthly magazines, and from writers looking for material for an off-season column—for my choices for this or that all-star team.

Here I have the opportunity to pay my tribute to the men I believe are the all-time greats. Here my choices do not go into a pot, to be tallied with the choices appearing on ballots sent in by other writers. Here no editor or columnist can veto one of my choices or replace one of my pitchers with his own boyhood favorite. These teams are mine, and on them I stand.

With my own eyes I have seen all but six of these players perform.

The only way an all-time, all-star aggregation can be selected justly today is by slicing up baseball's history into twenty-five-year segments. In 1977, as I write this, such a division is rather neat, as the following lists show. The chief problem is that some players might just as well have been placed in an earlier or later twenty-five-year period than in the period I assigned them. Some fans may argue, for example, that Bobby Wallace belongs in the 1901–1925 period rather than in 1875–1900, or Dazzy Vance and Waite Hoyt in 1901–1925 instead of in 1926–1950. Perhaps such fans have a point; on such niceties of judgment has many a hot-stove argument been waged.

In general I regard the pitchers at or near the top of each list as superior to those near the bottom, but I am not prepared to defend the exact order in which these names appear. Why did I pick eight in each period? Simply because that is the minimum number of men who deserve all-time, all-star rating.

I select two catchers for each period, again to avoid doing injustices. I would hate to have to pick between Bill Dickey and Mickey Cochrane (1926–1950), but if pressed to the wall I would give the nod to

Sweet William. So, too, I give Yogi a very slim edge over Campy (1951–1975).

As for Lou Gehrig and Bill Terry at first base (1926–1950), I refuse to declare anything other than a tie. Lou had a clear edge in every batting statistic except lifetime average, where Memphis Bill edged him, .341 to .340. But Bill Terry was the greatest fielding first baseman I ever saw, with the possible exceptions of George Sisler and Hal Chase when Hal was giving it his all.

I add a utility infielder and outfielder just to include one more worthy. Tom Seaver, Catfish Hunter, and Johnny Bench, it could be argued, belong on the 1951–1975 team. They look like certainties for the Hall of Fame—if each can have two or three more good years—and great prospects for selection on some later writer's all-star team for 1976–2000.

Here they are—and let the arguments begin!

	1876–1900	1901–1925	1926–1950	1951–1975
Infielders:				
First base	Fred Tenney	George Sisler	Lou Gehrig, Bill Terry	Gil Hodges
Second base	Nap Lajoie	Eddie Collins	Charley Gehringer	Jackie Robinson
Shortstop	Bobby Wallace	Hans Wagner	Joe Cronin	Pee Wee Reese
Third base	Jimmy Collins	Frank Baker	Pie Traynor	Brooks Robinson
Utility	John McGraw	Rogers Hornsby	Frank Frisch	Joe Morgan
Outfielders:				
Left field	Jesse Burkett	Ty Cobb	Ted Williams	Hank Aaron
Center field	Hugh Duffy	Tris Speaker	Joe DiMaggio	Willie Mays
Right field	Willie Keeler	Babe Ruth	Stan Musial	Roberto Clemente
Utility	Billy Hamilton	Harry Heilmann	Paul Waner	Mickey Mantle
Catchers:	Buck Ewing	Roger Bresnahan	Bill Dickey	Yogi Berra
	Mike Kelly	Johnny Kling	Mickey Cochrane	Roy Campanella
Pitchers:	Cy Young	Walter Johnson	Bob Feller	Sandy Koufax
	Charles Radbourn	Christy Mathewson	Bob Grove	Warren Spahn
	John Clarkson	Grover Alexander	Carl Hubbell	Bob Lemon
	Tim Keefe	Eddie Plank	Ted Lyons	Early Wynn
	John Galvin	Jack Chesbro	Dizzy Dean	Whitey Ford
	Mickey Welch	Mordecai Brown	Red Ruffing	Robin Roberts
	Amos Rusie	Ed Walsh	Dazzy Vance	Bob Gibson
	Bob Caruthers	Rube Waddell	Waite Hoyt	Juan Marichal

POSTSCRIPT

I cannot close without thanking some of the people who moved me to write this book and then helped out along the way. In no particular order, these are: Dave Scott, a longtime friend and now a free-lance editor who prodded me and then used his blue pencil to my benefit; Catherine Rossbach, managing editor of Coward, McCann & Geoghegan, whose enthusiasm for the project never faltered and whose advice as a new-generation baseball fan and as an editor I have come to trust; Ken Smith, director of publicity for the Hall of Fame in Cooperstown; my former fellow worker at *The Sporting News*, Clifford Kachline, Hall of Fame historian, who gave invaluable help in checking my facts and figures and in tracking down desired photographs; John F. Redding, Hall of Fame librarian, who offered unstinting cooperation in providing photographs from the picture library files: Johnson Spink, editor-publisher of *The Sporting News*, who offered me inspiration and cooperation; and Joe Durso of the New York *Times*; Jack Lang formerly of the Long Island *Press*; Bob Broeg of the St. Louis *Post-Dispatch*; and Jerry Holtzman of the Chicago *Sun Times* for getting me needed information. Finally, I thank Larry Ritter, baseball-minded professor of economics at New York University, author of the marvelously nostalgic *The Glory of Their Times*, for his words of encouragement at the start of my labors and for his foreword at the end of my labors. Without any of these, this book of memories would have been very much harder to bring off.

At eighty-nine years of age as I write this final page, the chances are that I am the oldest professional baseball writer ever to do a book on the subject. Which reminds me:

Last winter, walking through Williams Park in St. Petersburg, I was stopped by a friend who introduced me to two elderly men. One of them said to me, "You've brought a lot of joy into my life with your years of baseball writing. I never miss your columns in the St. Petersburg *Times* at this time of year. Gosh, when I was a boy and young man in New York, I used to enjoy your father's baseball writing in the *Press* and later in the *Morning Sun*. He used to write under the name of Frederick G. Lieb."

I chuckled. Perhaps thinking he had said something ungracious, my new acquaintance added immediately, "I tell you truthfully, you're a better writer than your father was!"

April, 1977

—FRED LIEB
St. Petersburg, Florida

INDEX

Figures in italics refer to captions.

Aaron, Henry, 16, 59, 150, 164–5, 233, 252, 271, *272*, 277
Abbey, Ed, 259
Adams, Babe, 58
Alden, Ezra Hyde, 23, 24
Alexander, Grover Cleveland, 155, 185–90, *187, 189,* 277
Allen, Johnny, 29, 232
Allen, Mel, *235*
Ames, Leon "Red," 34, 82, 84, 142
Armour, Bill, 56, 57
Associated Press, box scores of, 36, 37, 68
Atlanta Braves, 255, 270
Attell, Abe, 112
Austin, Jimmy, *60*
Averill, Earl, 9

Baer, Bugs, 18, 123
Baker, Frank "Home Run," 11, 60, 68, 77–80, 88; his career record assessed, 84–5
Baker, William F., 59, 122, 244, 268
Ball Players Assn., 266, 271
Baltimore Orioles, N.L., 13, 58; A.L., 254
Bancroft, Dave, 245
Barron, Clarence W., 23–4
Barrow, Ed, 25, 45, 64, 106, 156, 254, 269
Barry, Jack, 82, *88*
Baseball, changes in game seen by Lieb, 253–71
Baseball Magazine, 21, 74
Baseball Writers Assn., 117, 118, 271; New York chapter of, 18; discussion of Cobb's disputed 1922 "hit" by, 70–1
Bates, Johnny, 34
Bauer, Hank, 235
Bedient, Hugh, 87, 89, 93
Beebe, Fred, 34
Bench, Johnny, 140, *273,* 276
Bender, Albert "Chief," *15,* 19, 78, 83, 84, 264; duels with Mathewson, 78, 81–2
Bennet, Eddie, 156
Benswanger, Bill, 48, 49
Berra, Yogi, 238, 259, 276, 277
Bishop, Max, 192, 193
Bithorn, Hiram, 260
Black Sox scandal, 102, 115–6
Blake, Sheriff, 193
Blue, Vida, 270
Bodie, Ping, 259
Boley, Joe, 191, 192
Borton, Babe, 98
Boston Braves, 10, 13, 139, 254
Boston Red Sox, 236, 269, 270; blunder over Royal Rooters' tickets, 90–93; World Series vs. Giants in 1912, 86–95
Bowerman, Frank, 142
Boyd (of *Evening World*), 73
Breadon, Sam, 122, 188, 190, 261, 266
Brennan, Al, 228
Bresnahan, Roger, 38, 277
Brock, Lou, 59, 271
Broeg, Bob, 221
Brooklyn Dodgers, 10, 13, 26, 49, 171, 260; vs. Yankees: in 1949, 236–7; in 1952, 237–8; in 1953, 239–40; in 1955, 240
Broun, Heywood, 32, 98, 103, 142, 212–14, 218
Broun, Heywood Hale "Woody," 214
Brown, Joe B., 261
Brown, Joe E., 66
Brown, Mordecai "Three-finger," 58, 256, 277
Brown, Warren, 18
Brown, Willard, 261
Brush, John T., 35, 37, 41, 84
Bulger, Boze, *40*
Burkett, Jesse, 59, 257, 277
Burns, Bill, 112
Burns, George Henry, 192
Burns, George Joseph, 129, 142

Bush, Joe, 132, 230, 245, 269

Cady, Forrest, 87
Caldwell, Ray, 68, 155
California Angels, 255
Campanella, Roy, 236, 238, 276, 277
Carey, Max, 219, 220, 246
Carrigan, Bill, 136
Caruthers, Bob, 277
Chance, Frank, 38, 52, 98, 103, 188
Chandler, Albert "Happy," 116, *231*
Chandler, Spud, 232
Chapman, Ray, 134–36, *137*
Chase, Hal, 52, 97–103, 105, 129, 248, 276
Chesbro, Jack, 277
Chicago Cubs, 10, 38, 58, 191–5
Chicago White Sox, 63, 105–113
Chipman, Bill, 215
Cicotte, Eddie, 56, 106, *107*, 109, 110, 111, 112
Cimoli, Gino, 240
Cincinnati Reds, 10, 101–2, 122, 133, 182; attendance in 1976, 271; World Series of 1919, 106–13
Clarke, Fred, 21, 45
Clarkson, John, 277
Clemente, Roberto, 261, 277
Cleveland Indians, 62–63, 133, 134, 136, 238, 240
Coakley, Andy, 170, 172, 264
Cobb, Ty, 11, 12, 21, 43, 45, 46–7, *54, 60, 65,* 71–2, 80, 85, 151, 198, 233, 277; acquisition by Detroit, 56; batting and base-stealing records, 59; boyhood of, 53–4; disputed "hit" in 1922 of, 68–71; fights, 57, 59–61; as minor leaguer, 55–6; prejudices, 57–8; rated vs. Ruth, 150–1; shooting of father, 64; wealth, 62
Cochrane, Mickey, 166, 193, *194*, 197, *199*, 201, 205–6, 275, 277
Coleman, Bob, 246
Collins, Eddie, 12, 21, *22*, 23, 52, 62, 78, 79, 80, 86, *88, 107*, 111, 273, 277
Collins, Jimmy, 52, 91, 273, 277
Collins, Joe, 236, 238

Collins, Ray, 87, 90
Combs, Earle, *173*, 267
Comiskey, Charles, 100, 108, 110–1, 269
Connolly, Tom, 74, 80
Considine, Bob, 154, 164, 167
Coombs, Jack, 79, 82, 83
Coveleski, Harry, 259–60
Coveleski, Stan, 134, 260
Cox, Billy, 238, 239
Crandell, Otey, 82, 83
Crane, Sam, 32, *209*
Cravath, Gavvy, 85
Crawford, Sam, 47, 57, 64, 74, *75*
Cronin, Joe, *263*, 277
Crosetti, Frank, 173
Cross, Harry, 33, 34, 50
Cross, Lave, 19
Cross, Monte, 19, 262
Cuba, prospective big league location, 256
Cunningham, Bill (writer), 185
Cunningham, Billy, 245
Cunningham, Bruce, 197, *199*
Cutair, Al, 268
Cutshaw, George, 244
Cuyler, Kiki, 43

Daley, George Herbert, 83, 123, 125
Daley, George W., *40, 69,* 156
Daniel, Dan, 106, *217*
Daubert, Jake, 110
Davis, Harry, 19, 21, 41, 80
Dawson, Jim, *217*
Dean, Dizzy, 9, 277
Delahanty, Ed, 14, 16–17, 47
Detroit Tigers, 56–62, 71, 122
Devens, Charley, 152
Devlin, Art, 142
Devore, Josh, 82, 83, 86, 87, 93, 95
Dickey, Bill, 29, 179, 182, 275, 277
DiMaggio, Dom, 259
DiMaggio, Joe, 145, 197, 233, 235, 257, 259, 277
DiMaggio, Vince, 259
Dineen, Bill, 47
Ditmar, Art, 241

Donlin, Mike, 142
Donovan, Wild Bill, 47, 122
Dooin, Red, 20
Douglas, Phil, 129
Dover Hall (hunting lodge), 66, 131
Doyle, Larry, 29, 38, 74, 83, 89, 93, 142, 146
Dreyfuss, Barney, 48, 49, 122, 269
Dreyfuss, Sammy, 48
Dryden, Charley, 20, 98
Duffy, Hugh, 257, 277
Dugan, Joe, 167, 168, 176, 269
Duncan, Pat, 109, 110
Durocher, Leo, 161, 162, 166–7, 251
Dykes, Jimmy, 156, 191, 192, 193, 195

Ebbets, Charley, 39, 77, 243, 267–8
Eckert, William D., 116
Edgren, Bob, 38
Edwards, Bruce, 236
Ehmke, Howard, Lieb's scoring decision against, 72–74
Eller, Hod, 109
Ely, Fred, 45
Engle, Clyde, 56, 93
English, Woody, 192
Evans, Billy, 59
Ewing, Buck, 277

Faber, Urban "Red," 107
Farnsworth, Bill, 67
Farrell, Frank, 35, 67, 98
Federal League, 100, 140, 213, 254, 268
Feeney, Chub, 270
Feller, Bob, 9, 87, 134, 143, 277
Felsch, Oscar "Happy," 106, 107, 112
Fenway Park, embankment and wall, 87–88
Ferrell, Wes, 232
Fingers, Rollie, 270
Finley, Charley, 224, 270–1
Fitzgerald, John "Honey," 91, 92
Fletcher, Art, 10, 80, 82, 86, 87
Flick, Elmer, 47
Fonseca, Lou, 259
Ford, Whitey, 150, 237, 241, 277

Foster, John, 32, 37, 209
Foxx, Jimmy, 16, 191, 193, 194, 195, 232
Frazee, Harry, 130, 118, 269
French, Larry, 197, 199, 203
Frick, Ford, 116, 152, 174, 216
Frisch, Frank, 52, 162, 197, 199, 273, 277
Fuchs, Judge Emil, 143, 166
Fullerton, Hugh, 81, 98, 106, 107
Furillo, Carl, 238

Galvin, John, 277
Gandil, Arnold "Chic," 106, 107
Garagiola, Joe, 259
Gardner, Larry, 86, 95
Gedeon, Joe, 105, 129
Gehrig, Lou, 12, 16, 52, 153, 162, 171, 173, 175, 183, 197, 199, 200, 202, 203, 273, 276, 277; at Columbia, 169–70; at Hartford, 169, 170, 171, 172; becomes superstar in 1927, 174; consecutive game streak, 172–3; marries Eleanor Twitchell, 178–9; relations with Ruth, 176; MVP prizes, 184; physical deterioration, 180–1; his "day" at Yankee Stadium, 182
Gehrig, Mom, 153, 169, 170, 174, 176, 177, 178–9, 180, 182, 184
Gehringer, Charley, 52, 273, 277
Gibson, Bob, 277
Gibson, George, 47
Gilbert, Billy, 141
Gilliam, Junior, 239
Gilmore, James, 268
Gleason, Kid, 107, 108
Gomez, Vernon "Lefty," 181
Gordon, Joe, 181, 273
Gowdy, Curt, 36, 235
Gowdy, Hank, 144
Graham, Frank, 11, 210, 217
Grant, Eddie, 34
Grant, George Washington, 142
Gray, William, 37, 38, 39, 41
Grayson, Frank, 131
Griffith, Clark, 48

Grimes, Burleigh, 9, 244
Grimm, Charlie, 178
Groh, Heinie, 110, *111*, 232
Grove, Robert Moses "Lefty," 87, 143, 195, 197, *199*, 202, 203, 277
Gumpert, Bert, *217*

Haas, Mule, 192, *194*
Hall, Charlie, 87
Hall of Fame, *see* National Baseball Hall of Fame
Hamilton, Billy, 219, 220, 277
Hanna, Bill, 26, 28, 32, 67, 68
Harding, Warren G., 151
Harris, Bucky, 9, 144, 234
Harrison, Jim, *40, 216*
Hartsel, Topsy, 19
Hassett, Buddy, *249*
Hays, Will, 151
Heilmann, Harry, 18, 277
Hendrix, Claude, 105, 129
Hennigan, Willie, *216*, 218
Henrick, Tommy, 236
Henrickson, Olaf, 93
Herman, Billy, 9
Herrmann, Garry, 41, 81, 100, 103, 133, 139–40
Herzog, Charlie "Buck," 59, 80, 82, 105
Heydler, John, 48, 101, 102, 105, 108, 162, 198, 230; proposes use of designated hitter, 232
Hildebrand, George, 119–20
Hilltop Park, *see* New York Highlanders
Hirth, Charles, *231*
Hodges, Gil, 238, 277
Hoffman, Danny, 262
Hofman, Art, 262
Holtzman, Ken, 270
Hooper, Harry, 89, *91*, 93
Hornsby, Rogers, 43, 52, 57, 59, 233, 273, 277
Houk, Ralph, 238, 250
Houston Astros, 255
Howe, Irwin, 68, 69, 70
Hoyt, Waite, 127, 132, 137, 151, 162, 167, 168, 198, 269, 275, 277

Hubbell, Carl, 143, 277
Huggins, Miller, 120, 129, 131–3, *133*, 134, 135, 151, 154, 171–2, 234, 229–30; suspension of Ruth in 1925 by, 157–8
Huggins, Myrtle, 154, 229–30
Hughson, Tex, 236
Hummel, John, 262
Humphries, Joe, 31
Hunt, Marsh, 174
Hunter, Catfish, 77, 127, 140, 270, 276
Hunter, Herb, 197, 198, *199*
Huntington Street Park, Philadelphia, 17, 20
Huston, Col. Tillinghast, 112, *118*, 119, 123, 129–30, 131, 151, 158, 218
Hutchinson, Fred, 232

Irvin, Monte, 261
Isaminger, Jimmy, 20

Jackson, Joe, 106, *107*, 109, 110, 111, 112
Jackson, Reggie, 270
Japan, status of baseball in 1931 in, 200
Jennings, Hugh, 21, 58, 59, *61*
Johnson, Ban, 41, 61, 62, 63, 70, 92, 95, 108, 112, 220, 262; dislike of Landis, 122
Johnson, Billy, 236
Johnson, Ruby, 9
Johnson, Walter, 12, 43, 87, *121*, 134, 143, 150, 185, 190, 229, 233, 277
Johnston, Jimmy, 242
Jones, Davey, 57
Jones, Randy, 269
Jones, Sad Sam, 132, 245, 269

Kahan, Oscar, 223
Kamm, Willie, 197, *199*
Kansas City Royals, 254, 255
Keefe, Tim, 277
Keeler, Willie, 47, 58, 257, 277
Keener, Sid, 222
Keio University, 200
Kelly, George, 197, *199*, 202

Kelly, Mike, 277
Kerr, Dickie, *107*, 109, 110
Kieran, John, 68, 70, 71
Kinder, Ellis, 236
Kiner, Ralph, 9, *231*
Klein, Chuck, 268–9
Klem, Bill, 83, 119
Kling, Johnny, 277
Kluszewski, Ted, 260
Knight, Jack, 67, 262
Knolls, Doc (trainer), *199*
Konetchy, Ed, 39, 269
Kopf, Larry, 108, 109
Koufax, Sandy, 271, 277
Krapp, Eugene, 20
Kritchell, Paul, 170
Kroc, John, 269
Kroc, Ray A., 269
Krueger, Otto, 262
Kryhoski, Dick, 236
Kubek, Tony, 240
Kuhn, Bowie, 10, 43, 116, 224, 255, 270–1
Ku Klux Klan, player-members of, 57
Kuzava, Bob, 238

Labine, Clem, *235*
LaGuardia, Mayor Fiorello, 182
Lajoie, Napoleon, 11, 14, *15*–16, 47, 51, 52, 266, 273, 277
Landis, Kenesaw Mountain, 97, 102, *117*, *118*, *124*, 129, 130, 134, 171–2, 245; action against Black Sox, 112–3; disagreement with J.G.T. Spink, 220; dislike of Ban Johnson, 122, of Rickey, 122; as golfer, 123–5; names Lieb head of expedition to Japan, 198; suspends Ruth, 118–9; toasts the 18th Amendment, 123
Landis, Mrs. K.M., 120
Lang, Al, *217*, *231*
Lanigan, Ernest J., 25, 26, 28, 31, 37, 81
Lannin, Joe, 95
Lapp, Jack, 83–4
Larson, Don, *235*
Lasker, Albert D., 151, 152

Lavagetto, Cookie, *51*
Law, Vernon, 43
Lazzeri, Tony, 176, 186, 259
Leach, Tommy, 45, 232, 257
Leidy, Bill, 55
Lemon, Bob, 277
Lenz, Jack, 71
Leonard, Hubert "Dutch," 62, 63, 136
Lewis, Duffy, 86, 87, 88, *91*, 95, 269
Lieb, Fred, assesses Ruth vs. Cobb, 150–1; assumes role as official scorer, 36; chief scorer, World Series of 1922–4; column on Wagner, 47–8; conducts expedition to Japan, 197–206; conversation with Alexander in 1950, 185–6; employed by New York *Press*, 25–28, by *Sporting News*, 221; friendship with Gehrig, 174; and Gehrig's ailment, 180–2; involvement in Mathewson Day, 140–3, in suspicions about Mays, 129–30; marriage, 28; relationship with Landis, 117–8, 119–21, 123–5; scoring decisions, 67–75; writes for *Baseball Magazine*, 21–2; working schedule as baseball writer, 215–7
Lieb, Marie Theresa (Mrs. R. Leslie Pearsall), 225–6, *227*
Lieb, Mary, 28, 174, 203, 204, 212, 214, 225, 226–8, *227*, 232; Gehrig confides in, 176–7
Lindell, Johnny, 235, 236
Linderman, Fred, 179
Lindstrom, Fred, 144
Lobert, Hans, 34
Loes, Billy, 237
Lopat, Eddie, 238
Lopez, Al, 232, 240
Lord, Bris, 77, 262
Los Angeles Dodgers, 254
Los Angeles *Times-Mirror* purchase of *Sporting News* by, 224
Luderus, Fred, 85
Lynch, Tom, 39, 41, 73–4
Lynn, Fred, 233
Lyons, Red, 277

McAleer, Jim, 90, 93, 95

McCarthy, Joe, 154, 191, *192*, 234, 236, 237, 241

McCready, Joe, 85, 118

McDougald, Gil, 238, 239

McGarigle, Bob, 136

McGinnity, Joe, 29, 142

McGraw, John, 18, 29–31, *33*, 34, 35, 45, 47, 58, 78, 80, 84, 93, 95, 101, 102, 105, 140, *141*, 145, 146, 237, 241, 243, 245, 257, 277; and Gehrig, 169–70, 172; and reporters, 215

McInnis, Stuffy, 62, *88*, 98

McIntyre, Matty, 57

Mack, Connie, 12, *14*, 19–20, 61, 78, 80, 82, 83–4, 167, 191, 193, 195, 201, 228–9, 241, 250, 254, 262, 270

McKechnie, Bill, 166, 186, 188–90, *189*

McMullin, Fred, 106, *107*

McNally, Mike, 269

MacPhail, Larry, 166

McQuade, Judge, 127

McQuillan, George, 34

McRoy, Bob, 90, 92, 93, 95

Magee, Lee, 102, 105

Magee, Sherry, 85

Maglie, Sal, *235*

Malone, Pat, 193

Mann, Arthur, 174

Mantle, Mickey, *235*, 237, 239, 277

Mapes, Cliff, 235

Maranville, Rabbit, 155, 176, 197, *199*, 200, 201–2; birthday party for, 203–4

Marichal, Juan, 277

Marnaux, Al, 226, 244

Marquard, Rube, 11, 38–9, 78–9, 80, 81, 82, 84, 86, 88, 90

Martin, Billy, 238, *239*, 240

Masterson, Bat, 38

Mathewson, Christy (Matty), 11, 34, 38, 43, 47, 77, *78*, 79, 80, 87, 89, 93, 94, 95, 101, 103, 134, 139–46, *146*, 150, 185, 186, 233, 248, 277; assessment of, 143–4; death, 145; income, 140; poison-gas lung injury, 139; testimonial game for, 139–43; vs. Bender in 1911 Series, 78, 81–2

Mays, Carl, 119, 127–37, *128*, 269; beaning of Chapman by, 134–6; cleared by Landis, 130, 134; pitching record, 136–7

Mays, Mrs. Carl, 129, 134

Mays, Willie, 230, 233, 261, 277

Mazeroski, Bill, 43, 240

Meany, Tom, 230

Menke, Frank, 81

Mercer, Sid, 18, 26, 28, 29, 34, 73, 95, *209*, 218

Merkle, Fred, 73, 83, 84, 93, 94, 95, 232

Messersmith, Andy, 270, 271

Metkovich, George, "Cat," 246

Meusel, Bob, 118, *173*, 176, 229, 230, 245

Meusel, Emil "Irish," 129

Meyers, Chief, 41, 79, 80, 82, 95, 142

Miller, Bing, 191, 192, *194*, 195

Miller, Marvin, 266, 271

Milwaukee Braves, 238, 240, 254

Milwaukee Brewers, 255

Minnesota Twins, 255

Mitchell, Clarence, 226–27

Mize, Johnny, 160, 236

Mole, Fenton, 236

Montreal Expos, 255

Moore, Earl, 34

Moran, Pat, 34, 101, 140, 185

Moreland, George, 21, 25

Moren, Lew, 34

Morgan, Joe, 258, 277

Moriarty, George, 198

Morley, Christopher, 142

Mueller, Don, 261

Mullaney, Teddy, 17

Mullin, George, 47

Munsey, Frank, 28, 207

Murphy, Danny, 19, 83

Murphy, Irish John, 29

Murray, Red Jack, 29, 86, 93

Musial, Stan, 9, 43, 260, 277

National Baseball Hall of Fame, 9, 10, 16, 186; candidacy of Carl Mays for, 136

National Commission (baseball governing body), 39, 41, 103

Navin, Frank, 166

Neale, Greasy, 109
Nee, Johnny, 29
Nehf, Arthur, 192, 193, 245
New York *Daily News,* 218
New York Giants, 10, 26–7, 34–5, 37–41, 139, 141, 144, 240, 255, 260; in 1911 Series, 77–84; 1912 Series, 86–95; in 1916 season, 10; in 1919 season, 101–2; in 1921 Series, 127–9; in 1951 season, 237; ticket sales figures in 1911, 39–41
New York Highlanders, 26, *27,* 97; name changed to Yankees, 35
New York Mets, 201, 248–50
New York *Press,* 17, 25–8, 85; box scores, 37
New York Press Club, 18
New York Yankees, 26–27, 132, 182, 270–1; greatness of 1927, 175; hire Stengel, 234; season of 1928, 64; Series of 1921, 127–9; sign Gehrig, 170; Series record under Stengel, 236–41

Oakland A's, 255, 270
O'Brien, Bucky, 86, 90
O'Day, Hank, 74–5
O'Doul, Frank "Lefty," 176, 178, 197, *199,* 204–5
Oldring, Rube, 82
Oliver, Tom, 197, *199,* 203
Olmo, Luis, 236
O'Loughlin, Silk, 61
O'Malley, Walter, 237, 238
O'Neill, Frank "Buck," *69, 217*
Orr, John, 123, 125
Ott, Mel, 16
Overall, Orville, 58

Pafko, Andy, 238
Page, Joe, 236
Parnell, Mel, 236
Paskert, Dode, 34, 35
Paulette, Gene, 105, 129
Payson, Mrs. Joan W., 255
Pennock, Herb, 132, 137, 198, 245, 269
Perini, Lou, 254
Perry, George, 129, 130

Phelon, Bill, 80–1
Philadelphia Athletics, 19–20, 64, 254; Series of 1911, 77–84; batting outburst vs. Cubs in 1929 Series, 191–5
Philadelphia News Bureau, 23, 24, 25
Philadelphia Phillies, 10, 13, 34, 72, 122, 185, 186, 237, 244; 1976 attendance figures, 271
Phillips, John, 236
Pinelli, Babe, *239,* 259
Pipp, Wally, 171, 172
Pittsburgh Pirates, 10, 43, 45–6, 48–50, 58, 244; defeat Yankees in 1960, 240
Plank, Eddie, 17, 19, 78, 83, 264, 277
platooning, 235, 243
Player's Fraternity, 62
Polo Grounds, 29, *30,* 38, 83, 139, 142; fire at, 35; plans for new structure at, 37–8
Price, James R., 25, 28, 32, 97, 98
Pride of the Yankees, 174

Quinn, Bob, 246
Quinn, Jack, 191

Radbourne, Charles "Old Hoss," 277
Raschi, Vic, 236, 237, 238
Rath, Morris, 110
Reardon, Beans, *249*
Reese, Peewee, 238, 273, 277
Reidenbaugh, Lowell, 223
Rennie, Rud, 195, *216, 217*
Reynolds, Allie, 237, 238
Rice, Grantland, 31–2, 55, 56, 207–10, *209,* 218
Rickey, Branch, 122, 260
Ring, Jimmy, 109
Ripley, Bob "Believe It or Not," 18, *40*
Risberg, Charles "Swede," 106, *107,* 110
Rizzuto, Phil, *239,* 273
Roberts, Robin, 277
Robinson, Brooks, 52, 273, 277
Robinson, Frank, 261
Robinson, Jackie, 238, *239,* 260, 261, 277

Robinson, Wilbert, 95, 131, 242
Roe, Preacher, 238
Rogers, Will, 120
Rolfe, Red, 237
Rommel, Ed, 191
Root, Charley, 178, 191, 192
Rose, Pete, 59
Ross, Sammy, 267
Roth, Mark, 136, 216
Rothstein, Arnold, 112
Roush, Eddie, 9, 108, 109, 110, 232
Rowan, Jack, 34,
Rucker, Nap, 56
Rudi, Joe, 270
Ruel, Harold "Muddy," 197, *199*
Ruelbach, Ed, 58
Ruether, Walter "Dutch," 107
Ruffing, Red, 277
Rules Committee (of organized base-ball), 74–75
Runyon, Damon, 28, 31, 32, 36, 84, 207, *209*, 210–2, 218
Ruppert, Col. Jacob, 35, 118, 123, 171, 218, 245, 268; palm reading of by Mary Lieb, 227–8
Rusil, Amos, 87, 277
Ruth, Babe, 11, 12, 16, 18, 43, 45, 64, 75, 115, 116, 118, 120, 129, 146, 147–68, *153, 157, 163, 165,* 172, 174, 201, 230, 233, 252, 277; and Aaron, 164–6; appetites, 154–5, 156–61; assessed by Lieb, vs. Cobb, 150–1; *Babe Ruth Story, The,* 154; boyhood, 154; and boys, 161–2; German background, 153–4; as pitcher, 150, 229; relations with Gehrig, 176; suspension by Huggins, 157–8; testing of reactions, 152
Ruth, Claire, 160, 164, 167
Ruth, Helen, 160
Ryan, Nolan, 143, 271

St. Louis Browns, 132, 157, 254
St. Louis Cardinals, 10, 121, 186
St. Mary's Industrial School, 154
Sallee, Slim, 108
Salsinger, Harry, 150

San Diego Padres, 255
San Francisco Giants, 255
Schaek, Ray, 107, 108, 110
Schang, Wallie, 119, 269
Schauer, Rube, 213
Schmidt, Charlie, 57
Schoendienst, Red, 144
Schreckengost, Ossie, 19
Schulte, John "Wildfire," 85
Schumacher, Harry, *217*
Schupp, Ferdie, 213
scoring decisions, 67–75; Lynch's advice on, 73–74
Scott, Everett, 68, 70, 172, 269
Seaver, Tom, 77, 140, 145, 276
Segar, Charley, *167, 216, 217*
Sewell, Joe, 171
Sewell, Luke, 198
Sewell, Rip, 232
Seybold, Socks, 19
Shanks, Howard, 72
Shawkey, Bob, 68, 127, 132
Sheehan, Tom, 118
Shibe Park, 59, 78, 80, 81, 191, 195
Shinners, Ralph, 197, *199*
Shotton, Burt, 186, 236
Simmons, Al, 191, 193, *194,* 195, 197, *199,* 260
Sinclair, Harry, 100
Sinnott, Jimmy, 160
Sisler, George, 52, 100, 173, 233, 273, 276, 277
Slagle, Jimmy, 262
Slocum, Bill, 159, 162, 174, *216, 217*
Smith, Elmer, 269
Smith, Hal, 240
Smith, Red, 210, 220
Snider, Duke, *235,* 238
Snodgrass, Fred, 11, 56, 80, 83, 93, *94*
Southworth, Billy, 245
Spahn, Warren, 134, 277
Sparrow, Harry, 95
Speaker, Tris, 12, 57, 59, 62, 63, 64, 84, 85, 89, *91,* 92, 94, 95, 134, 136, *137,* 197, 243, 277
Speed, Keats, 17, 18
Spink, Alfred H., 25
Spink, C.C. Johnson, 222–24

Spink, Charles, 25
Spink, J.G. Taylor, 81, 150, 219–22, *223*, 246
Sporting Goods Dealer, The, 224
Sporting News, The, 25, 81, 111, 219–24; purchase by Los Angeles *Times-Mirror*, 224
Stahl, Jake, 87, 90, 93
Stallings, George, 97, 103, 243
Stengel, Casey, 198, 233–252, *235, 247, 249, 251;* acquires nickname, 234; appointed manager of Mets, 248; as Brooklyn outfielder, 242–4; dropped by Yankees, 241; elected to Hall of Fame, 251, as Giant outfielder, 244–6; hired by Yankees in 1948, 234; managerial record, 234, 241; World Series record, 236–41
Stephenson, Riggs, 195
Stevens, Harry, 140, 142, *209*, 210
Stoneham, Charles, 102
Stoneham, Horace, 255
Strang, Sammy, 262
Street, Gabby, 57, 101
Strunk, Amos, 62, 83
Suzuki, Sotaro, 201
Swope, Tom, 222

Tenney, Fred, 277
Terry, Bill, 9, 52, 100, 173, 273, 276, 277
Terry, Ralph, 240
Tesreau, Jeff, 73, 87, 89
Texas Rangers, 255
Thomas, Ira, 82, 83
Thompson, Hank, 261
Thomson, Bobby, 83, 237
Throneberry, Marv, 250
Tiant, Luis, 59
Tidden, George, 32
Toney, Fred, 127
Topping, Dan, 240–1
Torre, Joe, 201
Traband, Harvey, 131
Trautman, George, *231*
Travers, Albert Joseph, 61, 62
Traynor, Pie, 43, 52, 273, 277
Trumbull, Walter, 33, *209*

Turner, Ted, 270–1
Twitchell, Eleanor, 178–79, 180–82, 184

Uhle, George, 133
Underwood, George, 242

Vance, Dazzy, 232, 275, 277
Vander Meer, Johnny, 72, 232
Vaughan, Arky, 273
Vaughan, Irving, 222
Veeck, Bill, Jr., 254
Veeck, Bill, Sr., 151, 152
Veteran's Committee of Hall of Fame, 219
Vick, Sammy, 135
Vila, Joe, 32
Virdon, Bill, 240
Vitt, Ossie, 74

Waddell, Rube, *15*, 17, 19, 20, 87, 143, 264, 277
Wagner, Hans "Honus," 11, 14, 15–16, 20, 21, 43–52, *46, 51*, 64, 207, 210, 248, 266, 271–2, 277; assessment by McGraw and Barrow, 45; Lieb's 1933 column on, 47–8; nickname, 49–50; return as coach, 48–50
Wagner, Heinie, 87
Wakatauki, Reijiro, 204
Walberg, Rube, 191
Wallace, Bobby, 275, 277
Walsh, Christy, 118, 147, 161, 162, 166, 176
Wambsganss, Bill, 20, 68
Waner, Lloyd, 43
Waner, Paul, 43, 155, 277
Wanninger, Peewee, 172
Ward, Chuck, 244
Ward, John Montgomery, 219
Ward, Robert, 268
Warren, Gov. Fuller, *231*
Waseda University, 200, 201–2, 205
Washington Senators, 120–21, 144, 255
Wattenberg, Fred, 228
Weaver, Buck, 106, *107*, 113

Webb, Del, 234, 241, 248
Wedge, Will, 18, 174
Weiss, George, 122, 123, 234, 235, 241, 248
Welch, Mickey, 277
Westrum, Wes, 250
Whalen, John, 37
Wheeler, Jack, 32, 79, 81, 140, *209*
Wilkinson, Roy, *107*, 110
Williams, Claude "Lefty," 106, *107*, 108, 109, 110
Williams, Ted, 233, 277
Wills, Maury, 59
Wilson, Hack, 155, 166, 192, *194*
Wilson, Jimmy, 189
Wiltse, George "Hooks," 84, 142
Witt, Whitey, 72, 167
Wolf, Bob, 164
Wolfe, Ed (Jim Nasium, *pseud.*), 20
Wood, Paul, 90
Wood, Smokey Joe, 62, 63, 87, *89*, 90, 92

Woodling, Gene, 235, 239
Wynn, Early, 277

Yaeger, Abe, 37
Yankee Stadium, 147, *148–9*, 182
Yarborough, Rev. John, 53–54, 57
Yastrzemski, Carl, 260
Yeager, Margaret Leach, 232
Yeager, Tommy Leach, 232
Yerkes, Steve, 89, 94, 95
Yomouiri Shimbun (Tokyo newspaper—sponsor of expedition to Japan), 176, 201
Young, Cy, 47, 266, 277
Youngman, Heinie, 56

Zeider, Rollie, 20, 98
Zimmerman, Heinie, 12, 102, 105, 129

1924 GIANT-WASHINGTON SERIES
Fred Lieb—chief scorer, Nick Altrock, Ty Cobb, Babe Ruth,